QUEEN
VICTORIA'S
GENE

QUEEN VICTORIA'S GENE

D.M. Potts and W.T.W. Potts

ALAN SUTTON PUBLISHING LIMITED

First published in the United Kingdom in 1995
Alan Sutton Publishing Limited
Phoenix Mill · Far Thrupp · Stroud · Gloucestershire

British Library Cataloguing in Publication Data

Potts, W.T.W.
  Queen Victoria's Gene
  I. Title II. Potts, D.M.
  929.72

ISBN 0-7509-0868-8

Typeset in 10/13 New Baskerville.
Typesetting and origination by
Alan Sutton Publishing Limited.
Printed in Great Britain by
Butler & Tanner, Frome, Somerset.

Contents

List of Illustrations

Preface

Our interest in this subject began over ten years ago with the discovery of two hand-written scrolls in the Royal Society of Medicine, London, that demonstrated that Queen Victoria could not have inherited the gene for haemophilia which afflicted some of her family and many of her descendants. Logically, she had to have been a mutation or illegitimate. As we pursued the historical and scientific evidence we began to explore the possibility of using a genetically determined marker to test the identity of 'Anna Anderson', who claimed to be Anastasia, daughter of the last Tsar of Russia. Since then the recently developed technique of DNA fingerprinting, together with the discovery of some preserved gut fragments, has been used to exclude the possibility of any relationship between Anna Anderson and the Romanovs. At the same time DNA fingerprinting has confirmed the identity of the bones of the last Russian tsar, the tsarina and three of their daughters. New information has come in so rapidly and frequently that at times we doubted if this book would ever be completed.

Beginning with the problem of the possible identity of Anna Anderson as the tsar's daughter Anastasia we have extended our investigation into the vastly greater sphere of the influence of the gene for haemophilia on the history of the last century. It has led us into many aspects of history which we hope our readers will find as fascinating as we have.

During the course of this work we have been assisted by many and obstructed by a few. We are particularly grateful to Dr John Graham of North Carolina and Dr Peter Howie of Edinburgh for advice and encouragement. Dr Mahir Mahran of Cairo was kind enough to draw to our attention medical data on the death of Princess Charlotte. In addition, we have been assisted by Dr H. Magallón of Madrid, the late Lady May Abel Smith, Hugo Vickers and Marlene Eilers. We would also like to thank Mrs Margaret Gibson for her patience in preparing and frequently revising the manuscript, Miss Andrea Clarke who prepared the tables and figures and Dr I. Nelson for help with the index.

Introduction

'Dost thou not know, my son, with what little wisdom the world is governed', the sage Count Oxenstierna observed in the seventeenth century. Few could claim that it is better today.

The facts of history are infinitely complex but the desire to see a pattern is great. Some historians believe that the interaction of a multitude of players must smooth and average the effects of individuals to produce recognizable trends and forces which may be identified and used to generalize, explain and even predict the future course of events – though usually with little success.

The themes chosen by historians reflect their own times. When the church was the patron of historians the theme of Bede's great history was the conversion of the English people. When the historian was dependent on private patronage history was usually written in terms of the lives of great men, even though they were often ruthless rogues. Contemporary Marxist historians believe that human affairs are driven primarily by economic forces. Biologists, from the social Darwinists of the nineteenth century to the sociobiologists of today, emphasize the importance of biological concepts.

The human brain perceives patterns in order to simplify and make sense of the endless information with which it is bombarded. Even where no pattern exists the brain will often create one, hence the astronomer Lowell saw canals on Mars and eighteenth-century microscopists saw little men hunched up inside the head of a sperm. We are all liable to false conclusions at times.

This book is about a single molecular error in one gene in one individual – the gene for haemophilia that Queen Victoria carried. It not only had an immediate and profound effect on Victoria and her family but, ultimately, on millions of others in Europe and around the world. In tracing the history of this genetic mistake, we hasten to add that we do not believe human genetics is the key to history – indeed, we do not believe that there is any key. Genetics is merely one of the pieces of the jigsaw that is worthy of recognition and study. However, because it involves such an intimate part of human nature it can often be more fascinating than the economic forces which so attract contemporary historians.

Genetic differences may affect human affairs through the individual, as with Victoria's gene, or through the population as a whole. The influence of human genetics on history has attracted the attention of several scientists, such as C.D. Darlington and J.B.S. Haldane. On many occasions the genetic differences between races have had a decisive influence on the course of history, although these influences are often not obvious. The genetic susceptibility of the more isolated human populations to the infectious diseases common in the Old World, such as influenza, diphtheria, tuberculosis or smallpox, was largely responsible for the collapse of the Amerindian, Australian aboriginal, Hawaiian and Maori populations in the face of European settlement. These diseases had originated in the Old World, where the populations had developed a high degree of resistance, at the price of countless deaths over many millennia. European settlement was far less successful in Africa, where the native population shared the same diseases but were in turn themselves partially immune to yellow fever, to which the Europeans had little resistance. The resistance of the Africans to yellow fever allowed the Africans to multiply in central America and the West Indies, where the European perished. Similar differences have no doubt played a vital but now unrecognized role in the distribution of races in the Old World. Each resistance originated in a single, or in a few, fortunate mutations, affecting only a handful of atoms in the immensely long molecular chains that make up the DNA (deoxyribonucleic acid) which codes the genetic information in each cell in our bodies.

Although the influence of the individual on history is now at a discount with many historians, the story of Queen Victoria and the gene responsible for haemophilia illustrates the effect of the change of a single molecule in the DNA on both individuals and on the nations of Europe. It is pertinent that recent developments in mathematics, rather misleadingly referred to as the 'catastrophe theory', show that under certain circumstances an infinitesimal change in conditions can dramatically alter the fate of a whole system, and at the critical points the interactions become so complex that the effects of small changes cannot be calculated.

This catastrophic defect appeared in the British royal family when Britain's industrial revolution and its victory over Napoleon had combined to make it the dominant nation in the world, a position it held for the rest of the nineteenth century. Many of Victoria's descendants inevitably held positions of power which magnified the effect disproportionately. When the First World War broke out the British king, the German emperor, the Queen of Spain and the Tsarina of Russia were all grandchildren of Queen Victoria, and both the Queen of Spain and the tsarina carried the defective gene. The tsarist system in Russia might have survived had the tsarevitch not inherited one important abnormal gene from Victoria. While the lack of resistance to certain epidemic diseases has destroyed whole peoples, a single mutation in Queen Victoria, or one of her ancestors, destroyed a dynasty and drove history along a new course.

In a later chapter we explain the reasons for the various modes of inheritance of the gene for haemophilia. It is sufficient here to note that it only affects males but can be transmitted through a female carrier, like Queen Victoria, who showed no symptoms. On average, half the sons of a female carrier will be haemophiliacs and half her daughters will be carriers in their turn. Even odder, a haemophiliac man cannot pass the defect on to his sons, or to their descendants, but all his daughters will be carriers. The fact that the Duke of Coburg, the son of Prince Leopold, Queen Victoria's haemophiliac son, was a fit man, played a significant part in the rise to power of Adolf Hitler.

The affairs of royalty fascinate many, even dedicated republicans, partly because human society is primitively hierarchical and the majority seem to have a need to idolize the few or the one, whether prince or pop star, and partly because hereditary rulers and their families are subject to fewer constraints than average citizens and often display bizarre and fascinating extremes of human behaviour.

So discrete and significant has been the impact of haemophilia on history since Victoria that on two occasions our quest turns into an historical detective story. Was Queen Victoria really the daughter of the Duke of Kent? Could Anna Anderson, the eccentric lady who lived in Charlottesville, Virginia, have been Anastasia, the daughter of last Tsar of Russia? The answers to these latter questions are not of great historical significance but they continue to intrigue.

CHAPTER ONE

God Save You! Where's the Princesse?

The story of Queen Victoria's gene alternates between a series of intensely intimate events and a series of geopolitical movements that still affect our world. Even the domestic happenings of the monarchy come under public scrutiny and are frequently documented in considerable detail.

On the evening of Wednesday 5 November 1817 eleven officers of state, including the Archbishop of Canterbury and the Chancellor of the Exchequer, were gathered in the chilly, candlelit chambers of Claremont House, near Esher in Surrey, to observe the young Princess Charlotte deliver her first baby. Naturally, everyone hoped for a son – a son who would one day be crowned King of England.

Princess Charlotte Augusta's place in history derives almost solely from the tragedies surrounding her short life. She was the only daughter of Prince George, the eldest son of George III, who was to become Prince Regent in 1811. The circumstances of her conception had been gross, even by Regency standards. Concerned at the failure of any of the king's fifteen children to produce even one legitimate heir, though they had nearly a dozen recorded illegitimate ones, parliament offered to meet the Prince Regent's debts if he were to marry. The prince had already contracted a morganatic marriage with a Mrs Fitzherbert. His debts by this time exceeded £200,000, and he reluctantly agreed to marry but unwisely delegated the task of finding a suitable bride to his current mistress, the Countess of Jersey. The countess astutely calculated that if the bride were sufficiently unattractive *she* would be able to retain the prince's affection. The prince was a close friend of Beau Brummell, who had revolutionized personal habits of cleanliness and was himself unusually fastidious; the prince set fashion and determined taste. The countess therefore chose Caroline of Brunswick, a first cousin of her lover, who was short, gauche and not noted for bathing. In a further attempt to sabotage the match she appointed herself the bride's dresser; she then covered Caroline's hair in a foul-smelling concoction and added

1

a beaver hat and bright red cheeks to the bridal array. Her final touch was to lace the bride's supper with a large dose of Epsom salts. How many of these tricks were noticed by the prince is uncertain because he came to the wedding ceremony drunk and by nightfall he was so intoxicated that he fell over the fender in the bedroom and spent the night in the hearth. However, he had recovered sufficiently by the morning to justify the taxpayers' investment of £200,000; it was the only time the husband and wife ever had intercourse. Years later in 1820, when the Prince Regent had become George IV, he attempted to divorce Caroline on the grounds of adultery. During the notorious trial of Caroline, Lady Cooper recorded: 'She says it is true she did commit adultery once but it was with the husband of Mrs Fitzherbert. She is a drôle woman.' Luckily for the Prince Regent the bride conceived and nine months later Caroline delivered a large baby, following a twelve-hour labour. The infant was named after her paternal grandmother, Queen Charlotte.

The Prince Regent had been thirteen when the American colonies declared their Independence, twenty-three when he married Mrs Fitzherbert and thirty-three when he married Princess Caroline. His first marriage had been without the consent or knowledge of his father King George III; it had also been illegal because Mrs Fitzherbert was Roman Catholic. She was somewhat older than George, and he certainly loved her, although this did not prevent him accumulating additional mistresses such as the Countess of Jersey. Three days after Charlotte's birth the Prince Regent willed his now solvent estate to Mrs Fitzherbert while to Princess Caroline he left a derogatory 'one shilling'. In his will he described Mrs Fitzherbert as, 'my wife in the eyes of God and who is and ever will be such in mine', and from the moment of her birth, it was apparent to the Court and to the nation that Charlotte would be his only legitimate heir.

When Charlotte was growing up her father took little interest in her and forbade her mother to see her. As an adolescent she suffered from recurrent bouts of abdominal pain, insomnia and alternating excitement and depression. It is likely that she suffered from the hereditary disease porphyria, which was the probable cause of her grandfather, George III's, episodes of excitability. Porphyria is due to a defect in a single enzyme. The victim is unusually sensitive to sunlight and has episodes of abdominal pain and of excreting very dark urine. The condition causes partial paralysis of the autonomic nervous system which controls the guts and womb. It may therefore cause indigestion, flatulence and difficulties in labour.

In 1814, when she was eighteen, Charlotte was courted by and fell in love with a handsome European aristocrat, Leopold of Coburg, a junior member of a minor German ducal family. The Prince Regent disapproved of the match and it was only with the assistance of Charlotte's uncle, the Duke of Kent, that the young couple managed to keep up a secret correspondence. Unlike her mother's courtship, Charlotte's relationship with Leopold seems to have been genuinely loving and romantic and after two years the Prince Regent relented. The country was delighted and Mr Wilberforce described the union to the House of Commons as 'a marriage of the heart', and her marriage to Leopold, who was created Prince of Great Britain for the occasion, appears to have been very happy. The couple were married in May 1816. Charlotte was twenty-one years old, a well-nourished woman with a long, slightly bent nose and golden-brown hair which she wore in ringlets. Fanny Burney the novelist described her as 'quite beautiful', adding that it 'was impossible not to be struck with her personal attraction, her youth and splendour'.

Charlotte conceived in the month of her marriage but miscarried in July. She may have had a second spontaneous abortion but became pregnant again early in 1817. At 7 p.m. on Monday 3 November, after forty-two weeks of pregnancy, her waters broke and Princess Charlotte had 'sharp, acute and distressing' labour pains. Sir Richard Croft, the 55-year-old royal accoucheur, had moved into Claremont three weeks earlier. He occupied Prince Leopold's dressing room which connected with Princess Charlotte's bedroom in one corner of the house. Mrs Griffiths, who had been wet-nurse to Charlotte's uncle Edward Duke of Kent, had also moved in as the royal midwife. At 11 p.m., Croft conducted a vaginal examination and found the neck of the womb dilated to the size of a halfpenny. The examination was of course carried out without any asepsis or washing of hands and with Sir Richard wearing the cravat and high collar of Regency London. Labour was proceeding slowly but in a not untoward way. Charlotte remained in strong labour and at 3 a.m. vomited. Throughout history obstetricians have watched and waited, and in the early years of the nineteenth century their options for intervention were few. Croft did the only positive thing he could and summoned the officers of state.

The tradition of senior officials attending at the birth of an heir to the throne was intended to prevent anyone substituting another infant. It was not very effective. In 1688 when James II's Catholic wife Mary gave birth to a son she was accused by Mary, her Protestant stepdaughter and wife of William of Orange, of smuggling another infant into the birth chamber. It was said the royal midwife brought the substitute infant concealed in a warming-pan. The baby was indeed Mary's and his birth had been witnessed by sixty-seven people, including the Lord Chancellor, Lord Privy Seal, numerous male members of the aristocracy and many ladies-in-waiting.[1]

During Charlotte's labour the officers of state crowded into the breakfast room which, like Leopold's dressing room, also opened directly into Charlotte's chamber. By 8 a.m. on the Tuesday morning quite a crowd was assembled, including the two archbishops, Mr Vansittart, the Chancellor of the Exchequer, the Earl Bathurst, Minister of War and the Colonies, and other aristocrats and political leaders. Naturally, the midwife, Mrs Griffiths, and several ladies of the court were also in attendance. By Tuesday morning Charlotte's pains had begun to get weaker and Sir Richard sent for a second obstetrician, Dr Baillie, who was his brother-in-law. Charlotte herself was stoical, keeping a promise to Mrs Griffiths not to 'bawl or shriek'.

A second vaginal examination was performed at 11 a.m., but the cervix had only dilated slightly, in readiness for the expulsion of the baby. Sir Richard Croft drafted a letter to be carried by hand to a third royal physician, Dr John Simms, a 69-year-old botanist with an uncertain interest in obstetrics. Then vacillating, Croft held the letter back. The officers of state and the bystanders continued their wait. Finally at 9 p.m. on the Tuesday, another examination showed the neck of the womb to be fully open, but by this time Charlotte had been in labour for twenty-six hours and she was almost too weak to push out the baby.

To add to Charlotte's problems she was probably also very anaemic. The diet recommended for aristocratic women who were pregnant had little meat and was especially light in vegetables, the two best sources of iron available. In addition she had been bled several times. Three months earlier Charlotte had written to Croft, 'I am certainly feeling much better for the bleeding'. One month before delivery a press statement announced that, 'Her Royal Highness submitted to four incisions in the arm without effect in consequence of the veins being deeply buried . . . [therefore] blood was ordered to be drawn from the back of the hand where the operation has been several times successfully performed . . . with great relief to her Royal Highness.'

The practice of 'therapeutic' bleeding was virtually universal until well into the nineteenth century. If, for example, a woman's periods were too heavy or too light or didn't come at all, she was bled. Blood was removed either by leeches or by opening a vein. European obstetricians recommended a woman 'be bled at least three times, in the fifth, the seventh and last month in order to avoid haemorrhage and to prevent the child from growing too large'. If a woman haemorrhaged at delivery more blood was taken from her veins.[2]

The labour pains during the second night of Charlotte's ordeal were irregular and weak. Croft and Baillie had attended enough labours to know that things were going wrong, but it may have been their very familiarity with the dangers of childbirth that made Croft dither. Eventually, Croft sent the letter he had written earlier to Simms, who arrived well after midnight. The doctors consulted in Leopold's dressing room but Simms still did not see Charlotte directly.

Obstetric forceps had been in use for well over one hundred years and consisted of two separate blades, much like modern forceps, and a pair had been taken to Claremont in case of a difficult delivery. Each blade could be passed around the baby's head and then slotted into each other like a pair of tongs. The blades applied traction to the head while protecting it.[3] Medicine, however, is a cautious profession, and those who advise royalty are usually particularly conservative. Predictably, Croft did not use the forceps he had brought along. At noon on 5 November some meconium from the baby dribbled from the vagina. Meconium is the greenish-yellowish contents of an infant's gut and it is an important sign that the foetus is distressed.

Fifty hours after her ill-fated labour began, at 9 p.m. on Wednesday 5 November Charlotte delivered a stillborn child. The distress after so harrowing an experience must have been doubly painful when it was realized that the baby was the boy every princess yearns for. For one hour, heroic efforts were made to resuscitate the child. Its lungs were inflated and everything possible attempted, from 'rubbing salt and mustard' and 'putting brandy in its mouth'. In retrospect, it seems likely the child had been dead for some hours, perhaps since the middle of the day.

Although the stillbirth was a great tragedy, Charlotte was young and there was no reason why she should not conceive many more times. Mrs Griffiths, the midwife, wept bitterly and it was the bereaved Charlotte who comforted her, saying it was the 'will of God'. The officers of state, having been shown the dead body, retired after their long sad vigil.

Uterine contractions were now too weak to expel the placenta and once again the three obstetricians consulted. It was agreed that Sir Richard Croft should remove the placenta by hand. He wrote afterwards, 'In passing my hand I met some blood in the uterus but no difficulty, until got to the contracted part [of the uterus]. . . . I afterwards peeled off nearly two thirds of the adhering placenta with considerable facility.'

The operation, no doubt, added to Charlotte's already considerable distress. When it was completed, she felt a final labour pain. Croft speaks of the loss of 'very little fluid blood or coagulum'. As was the contemporary practice, a broad bandage was then placed round Charlotte's abdomen, probably by Mrs Griffiths. The princess's pulse was steady after the removal of the placenta and she showed great courage and stamina; 'talked cheerfully and took frequently of mild nourishment' – chicken broth, hot wine, toast and brandy. At one point Charlotte joked that her attendants were trying to make her tipsy. The obstetricians retired to bed but around midnight the princess began to show signs of blood loss, complaining of ringing in her ears. She vomited once and showed 'extreme restlessness and great difficulty breathing'. Almost certainly Charlotte was bleeding into her uterus but the bandage would have made it difficult to detect any enlargement. If, as we have seen, she was already anaemic due to an inadequate diet and two or more episodes of blood-letting during pregnancy, then her extreme state is easy to understand. Croft was called and noted her pulse had passed the hundred mark and was feeble and irregular.

Other likely diagnoses have been suggested, including a pulmonary embolus or an attack of porphyria. In the case of an embolus a clot of blood forms in the veins of the pelvis or legs and then breaks off to lodge in the lungs and bring about death. We have noted that Charlotte may have shown symptoms of porphyria earlier in her life and a fatal attack can develop after an otherwise normal delivery. The record of excitement and difficulty in breathing would fit with such a diagnosis. A later writer claimed Charlotte put her hands over her abdomen and cried, 'Oh, what a pain!', but this may well be an embellishment to already dramatic events.

Whatever the correct diagnosis, at 2.30 a.m. on the morning of Thursday 6 November 1817 Princess Charlotte died. Her husband, Leopold, was by her side. Her father the Prince Regent received news of his daughter's labour and travelled to London from Suffolk, but did not arrive until after her death. Her mother was in Italy and even by December did not really know what had happened. Queen Charlotte was in Bath and heard of her granddaughter's death late the same day. The old king, George III, now senile and confined to Windsor Castle, never knew of the death of both direct heirs to his throne.

In keeping with the British royal tradition the corpses were embalmed the next day. Already there was controversy over the cause of death and Sir Everard Home, the king's sergeant-surgeon, turned the embalmings into post-mortems. 'The child was well formed and weighed nine pounds. Every part of its internal structure was quite sound.' The brain and lungs of the mother were normal but, 'The uterus contained a considerable quantity of coagulated blood and extended as high as the navel and the hour glass contraction was still apparent.' The stomach and intestines were dilated.[4]

The princess and her child were buried at Windsor on 19 November, amid widespread and sincere national mourning. The harvest had been bad, and the victory at Waterloo two years earlier seemed less glorious against rising unemployment and depression. On the day after

Charlotte's death, *The Times* reported, 'we never recollect as strong and general an expression and indication of sorrow'. Later it was said, 'It was really as if every household throughout Great Britain had lost a favourite child'. The Duke of Wellington called the tragedy, 'one of the most serious misfortunes the country has ever met with'. Lord Byron heard about the death while he was in Venice and wrote, 'The death of the Princess Charlotte has been a shock even here and must have been an earthquake at home'. Even Napoleon, exiled to the remote island of St Helena after his defeat at Waterloo, commented, 'What has happened to the English that they have not stoned her accoucheurs?'

In fact, Prince Leopold, the Prince Regent, and Baron Stockmar, the prince's personal physician from Coburg, all wrote to Sir Richard Croft commending his 'zealous care and indefatigable attention'. Looking back with today's knowledge, then if Charlotte died from blood loss, her life might have been saved on two occasions; first, by forceps delivery some time earlier on the Wednesday, and second, by more careful management after the manual removal of the placenta. The risk of intra-uterine bleeding following delivery, with few or no external signs, was understood at the time. Unfortunately, the habit of binding the abdomen after delivery interfered with Croft's ability to follow what was happening.[5]

Sir Richard was deeply burdened by a sense of total failure and inadequacy. The press and the coffee gossips of London were less kind than Prince Leopold and the Prince Regent, and Croft remained depressed, sleeping poorly. However, he was still sought after as an obstetrician and in February 1818 attended the wife of one of the king's chaplains, Revd Dr Thackeray. In a reversal of roles, Thackeray noticed the physician's depression and entreated him to rest. 'What is your agitation compared to mine?' snapped back Croft. A few days earlier, a fellow surgeon said Sir Richard was 'so melancholy, that it was quite distressing', adding, 'his mind was so absorbed that he would not give answers to questions'.

On the night of 13 February 1818 Croft retired to his rooms in Wimpole Street. The Revd Thackeray and his wife were also sleeping overnight in his house. At about 2 a.m. they heard a noise, like someone falling off a chair, but took no notice of it. A little later a servant girl found Sir Richard 'on his back, with a pistol in each hand; the muzzles of both were at either side of his head. He was quite dead.' A post-mortem was held the same day and the jury returned a verdict of 'Died by his own act, being, at the time he committed it, in a state of mental derangement'. They commented on the fact that just prior to his death he had been reading Shakespeare's *Love's Labours Lost* and had reached the page with the words, 'God save you! Where's the Princesse?' The twentieth-century obstetrician, Sir Eardley Holland, who wrote at length about Charlotte's death, aptly described the whole sad episode as a 'triple obstetric tragedy'.

With the death of Princess Charlotte there was once again no British heir to the throne. The old demented George III was still alive but senile and he died three years later. His son, the Prince Regent, was fifty-eight years old and the death of Charlotte and her stillborn son had eliminated his only legitimate grandchild. His numerous sisters and sisters-in-law were all past child-bearing age. George III and his wife Queen Charlotte had had fifteen live born children – the largest brood born to any British monarch – and thirteen of them survived to be adults. The next generation had produced eleven illegitimate children; even one of the royal princesses, Sophia, contributed her quota, but there were now no legitimate grandchildren. With Charlotte's unexpected death, the succession stakes were in disarray.

CHAPTER TWO

Dynastic Climbers

Leopold married Princess Charlotte in 1816. His family dukedom took its name from Coburg in what is now northern Bavaria in Germany. Its ancient and picturesque buildings survived the Second World War and it is still dominated by the Veste Coburg castle, with steep pitched roofs and battlements, on the hill above the town and the later Ehrenburg Palace below. Leopold's ancestors had a long history in this small picture-postcard town, and thanks to his ambitions and abilities, his descendants and collaterals were to rule, for a while, half the world.

Like the Habsburgs, the family of Coburg gained more by mating and parenthood than Napoleon or Charlemagne ever did by the sword. In medieval times the lands that are now Germany were divided into numerous small principalities loosely joined together as the Holy Roman Empire, which historians hasten to point out was not in any way an Empire, could hardly claim to be Roman and certainly wasn't Holy. Coburg was one of the smaller fragments of the Holy Roman Empire – a freckle on the map was one description – and was ruled by the House of Wettin. As the Reformation spread among the patchwork of states, some remained Catholic and others became Protestant. One of the Wettin heirs, John the Constant, gave sanctuary to Martin Luther. Protestant loyalties led to Coburg's defeat but the family remained staunchly anti-Catholic. In one seventeenth-century siege, they offered to hang anyone thinking of converting to Catholicism over the castle battlements in chains. It was the staunch Protestant tradition of the Coburgs that made them suitable marriage partners for the British monarchy.

The family suffered alternately from over-fertility and extravagance. In the seventeenth century, Ernst the Pious saw the Coburg lands divided between seven sons. In the eighteenth, the Duke Ernst Francis married Sophia Antoinette, whose high-spending ways contributed to his bankruptcy. Their eldest son, Francis Duke of Saxe-Coburg-Saalfeld[1] (1750–1806), married twenty-year-old Augusta of Reuss-Ebersdorf in 1777 and proceeded to have nine children. Augusta, like other aristocratic women, used wet-nurses and often became pregnant within a few months of delivery.

It was this large brood which began the Coburg climb up the European dynastic ladder. The first step was relatively unexpected. In 1795 the Tsarina Catherine of Russia, herself a German, summoned Duke Francis and his family to St Petersburg so she could select a bride for her second grandson, the Grand Duke Constantine. Although it seemed unlikely a Coburg bride would ever sit on the throne of Russia, it was an honour for the small impecunious German family and the household promptly set out on an overland trek and voyage of well over one thousand miles to St Petersburg.

Like a good fairy tale, the grand duke had to choose between three young sisters, Sophia, seventeen, Antoinette (named after their overspending grandmother) sixteen, and Juliana, aged fourteen. All were considered marriageable by eighteenth-century aristocratic standards but none was consulted as to whether they wished to wed a man they had never seen and whose language they could not understand. However, the actual mate selection turned out to be more of a pantomime than a fairy tale. As the princesses alighted from their coach, watched by the tsarina from a window, the eldest princess tripped over her train and fell out of the coach flat on her face. The second princess got down on her hands and knees to help her sister. Fourteen-year-old Juliana, however, had the regal good sense to gather up her long dress and get down from the coach gracefully. She had sufficient poise to impress the tsarina and was chosen as the bride. The grand duke, in a show of hostility that was to characterize the marriage, commented, 'If it must be so, I will marry the little ape. It dances very prettily.' Constantine was even more sadistic than most in the Russian royal family and was known to knock out the teeth – and even the eyes – of his soldiers, and to test their discipline by marching them into the river up to their chins before ordering the about-turn.

Juliana, like many of the Coburgs, was strong willed but after six years of domination by the grand duke, she left and returned to Coburg – still childless. It is unlikely Juliana suffered from primary sterility, that is the inability to bear children due to hormonal or anatomical defects, but it is possible that as a fourteen-year-old she was not fully mature sexually. There is evidence that the age of first menstruation has fallen in western countries from about seventeen to twelve since the early nineteenth century. It is also known that the first few menstrual cycles after puberty may not be associated with ovulation. Perhaps by the time Juliana was ovulating, the marriage relationship had deteriorated and Constantine was already enjoying the many alternative sexual outlets available to a Russian grand duke. Constantine's brother, who was then the reigning Tsar Alexander I, allowed Juliana a divorce and Constantine a morganatic marriage with a second wife – a marriage which was legal but which required the grand duke to renounce his claim to the Russian throne.

Had Constantine and Juliana remained married a Coburg would have reigned as tsarina when Alexander I died without an heir in 1825, but the House of Coburg had to wait another hundred years before one of their members sat on the Russian throne. Nevertheless, Juliana's marriage did help her siblings on their dynastic climb. Her two sisters, who had fallen from their carriage in St Petersburg, both married minor European noblemen, and Juliana's marriage gave her brothers Ernst and Leopold access to the Russian Court. They became instant generals in the Russian army, Leopold at the tender age of fifteen. Summoned to fight in the war against Napoleon, they arrived a few days too late to be present at the Russian defeat at Austerlitz (1805).

The House of Coburg was usually on the losing side in battle and the winning side in bed. In 1806 the town of Coburg was overrun by Napoleon's army. Depressed by defeat, Duke Francis died of pneumonia, leaving his nine children to recover the family fortunes in marriage. Tsar Alexander took up the cause of his ex-sister-in-law's family and talked Napoleon into restoring their lands.

Ernst, who was now duke and ever ready to marry up among the royal families of Europe, became engaged to the tsar's sister, the Grand Duchess Anna. Unfortunately he also established a sexual liaison with a

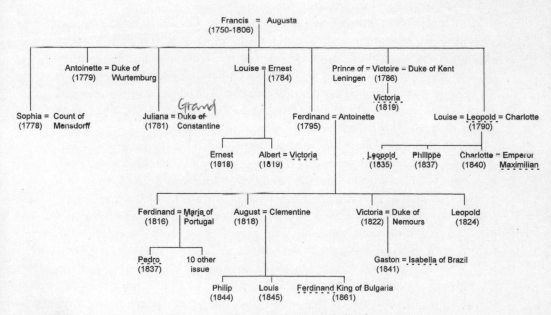

The House of Coburg. Monarchs and heirs apparent underlined.

young and beautiful Greek woman, named Pauline Panam. Pauline, disguised as a boy, followed Ernst back to Coburg and shortly afterwards announced she was carrying his child. The kings and aristocracy of Europe fathered many bastard children, and sometimes they were abandoned, sometimes their mothers were paid off and occasionally they were given titles, as were the children of William IV. Pauline, however, was doubly problematical, now that Ernst was officially engaged to the duchess. Pauline proved to be a spirited lady unwilling to be discreetly put away. As the pregnancy became more visible, Ernst lodged her with his twenty-year-old sister, Victoire, but from her chambers she complained loudly to both Ernst and his mother, the widow Augusta. In one exchange of letters, Augusta chided, 'No, Pauline, neither you nor your child will ever become objects of hatred or persecution: . . . unless you seek to act the part of a mistress. In such case you would experience my utmost severity.' And, Augusta added, cognizant of the sufferings of childbirth in the early nineteenth century, 'Adieu, Pauline, I pray God that he may enable you to meet with fortitude the painful moments that await you'. Pauline called her son Ernst after his father, and sensibly retired to Frankfurt on a small pension from her former lover. Eventually news of the scandal she caused reached the Court at St Petersburg and Ernst's betrothal to Grand Duchess Anna was broken. Later Pauline wrote some profitable memoirs and married a wealthy husband.

Ernst settled for a less distinguished bride, Louise, the sixteen-year-old heiress of the Saxe-Gotha estates. She was described as 'a dear sweet little person, not exactly pretty but very attractive in her extreme youth and vivacity'. The honeymoon was stormy but fertile and in less than a year a son was born, also called Ernst. He was put to a wet-nurse and his mother conceived again rapidly. Her second son, Albert, was later to be Queen Victoria's consort. He was born on 27 August 1819, three months after his cousin, Princess Victoria of Kent, had been born in England. They were both delivered by the same midwife, Madame Siebold.

A few years after Albert's birth Duke Ernst divorced Louise and she was sent into exile. She was never to talk to or to hug her two children again, although unbeknown to them she would occasionally disguise herself as a peasant woman and creep into the market square of Coburg to watch them from afar. She remarried but did not live to see her sons by her first marriage reach maturity; she is said to have died of uterine cancer at the early age of thirty. It was probably a cancer of the cervix. Cervical cancer behaves in many ways like a sexually transmitted disease and may be caused by a sexually acquired virus. It is a disease associated with the early initiation of sexual intercourse and multiple sexual partners or with marriage to a man who has had many sexual partners. Duke Ernst also remarried after the death of Louise, this time to his 33-year-old niece, a rather solid woman who remained childless.

Leopold grew to maturity during the turbulent years of the Napoleonic wars. Ernst and Leopold mingled with the many aristocrats who peopled Napoleon's court in Paris. In 1807 he met the empress, who to his youthful eyes was merely 'Old Josephine'. Allied by marriage to the Russian royal family and a youthful general in the Russian Army, Leopold found himself on the winning side in 1815 and soon travelled to London with the extraordinary ambition of capturing the heart of the heiress to the British throne. After 1815, and for the next half century, Britain was the world's greatest power. It had defeated France, the old rival, it had started the Industrial Revolution, it was the world's most powerful economy and was the possessor of a vast and rapidly expanding empire. Whoever was fortunate enough to marry Charlotte would have unparalleled power and influence. Although he had little seniority among the many visitors in the celebrating capital, he actively pursued Princess Charlotte – then aged nineteen. Once again, the Russian connection may have been helpful. Leopold's first days in London, however, gave his matrimonial ambitions little encouragement. Princess Charlotte was already engaged to Prince William of Orange but had confided to the tsar's sister that she did not want to marry such an ugly and drunken man. Although Charlotte did indeed leave her Dutch prince, she did so only to fall in love with a Prussian one. Stubbornly, the 25-year-old Leopold stayed on in London dogging the princess' footsteps. He wrote not of love but of diplomacy to brother Ernst! 'I only decide to do so [remain in London] after much hesitation and after certain very singular events made me glimpse the possibility, even the probability, of realising the project we spoke of in Paris.'

Although Leopold had to return to Coburg when the husband of his youngest sister Victoire died, he had already made some sort of an impression on Charlotte. Her father, the Prince Regent, was strongly opposed to the Prussian marriage and ordered his daughter to Cranborne Lodge in Windsor, forbidding her visitors. Her Prussian Prince Charming did not ride over to rescue her but returned to Prussia and some months later broke off the engagement. In her disillusionment, Charlotte's thoughts turned to Leopold. She wrote to a friend, like her suitor more in a practical than romantic frame of mind: 'At all event, I know that the worse off, more unhappy and wretched I cannot be than I am now, and all in all if I end by marrying Prince L., I marry the best of all those I have seen, and that is some satisfaction.'

Nationally and in the eyes of the Prince Regent, the match was certainly preferable to the Prussian and the Dutch affairs. Leopold was invited back to London in February 1816 and, on 2 May, married Princess Charlotte. The marriage, which had begun as a step in Leopold's dynastic ambition and as an acknowledged second best for Charlotte, soon developed into one of genuine love. Leopold had self-confidence won on the battlefields of the Napoleonic wars and sophistication gained at the French court. He was sexually experienced and according to rumour had been seduced by the Empress Josephine's daughter Hortense, who was seven years older than Leopold and herself pregnant with her first son at the time of the affair. The boy in question later reigned as Napoleon III. Leopold's brother's mistress Pauline Panam claimed Leopold entered her room at Coburg one night and made sexual advances to her when she was pregnant with Ernst's child, and there is evidence that he had an affair with his sister-in-law Louise, the mother of Prince Albert. But, whatever the details of Leopold's earlier life, his personality complemented Charlotte's disposition and the happiness of the royal couple was very apparent to the British citizens, who had suffered two generations of an unlovable royal family. Leopold and Charlotte were a handsome couple and each had something to give to the other, making the loss, first of their son and second of Charlotte, all the more tragic.

Leopold was only twenty-seven at the time of Charlotte's death and had been created Prince of Great Britain on his marriage. The British parliament had voted him £50,000 a year – a truly princely sum at the time – and the income continued after Charlotte's untimely death. Some of it he sent to Coburg to support his widowed sister Victoire, while he himself travelled widely and enjoyed a number of mistresses. In Vienna, he had the Countess Ficquelmont and in London, Lady Ellenborough, but it was in Germany that he was eventually swept off his feet by an actress, Caroline Bauer, who in age and looks reminded him of Charlotte. At first she was not impressed with Leopold who was now thirty-seven, wore a wig and was cautious to the point of dullness, but a morganatic marriage was arranged and consummated in London in 1829. Leopold was unwilling to give Caroline his family name and make her his heir in case the opportunity should arise to make a more advantageous marriage, and the marriage, in fact, soon ended in divorce. Like his brother's mistress, Pauline Panam, some years earlier, Caroline also wrote her memoirs and died prematurely, in Caroline's case by committing suicide.

Leopold was indeed offered the throne of Greece but overplayed his hand by demanding a vast loan and a French princess to go with it. Many years later he commented that 'Greece would have satisfied better my imagination and poetic tastes'. In 1830 the Belgians revolted against Protestant Dutch rule. It was perhaps the only revolution that literally began with an impassioned audience in an opera house. The British prime minister, Palmerston, saw political capital in nominating Leopold as king of the new country and he received backing from Russia and Prussia. Leopold, although nominally a Protestant himself, was elastic where religion was concerned and he was formally elected king by the Belgians themselves in 1831. The Dutch, furious with the settlement, invaded and were led by the same Prince of Orange that Leopold's dead wife Charlotte had rejected as a bridegroom. Once again Leopold had to take to the battlefield and once again he was on the losing side. However, the French armies came to his rescue and defeated the Dutch.

As usual, the Coburgs turned defeat on the battlefield into victory by marriage and Leopold became betrothed to Princess Louise, the daughter of his rescuer. Leopold was by now forty-two and his bride, as Charlotte had been sixteen years earlier, was only twenty. Nevertheless, Louise invested the politically motivated marriage with a certain youthful romanticism, saying it was impossible to find a husband 'more delicate, more normal, more religious, more healthy or of such a sweet and equal humour'. She was to bear him four children, although above the royal bed Leopold kept a large painting of his first wife Charlotte and their dead child, ascending into a cloudy sky. His first daughter, later to become the tragic wife of the Emperor Maximilian of Mexico, was also called Charlotte.

Leopold had one or two more extra-marital relationships but in the main devoted himself to ruling and to orchestrating the marriage of other Coburgs into the royal families of Europe. It was 'Uncle Leopold' who introduced Victoria, the future Queen of England and the daughter of his sister Victoire, to his nephew Albert, the future Prince Consort. Leopold died in 1865 and 'Charlotte' was the last word to pass his lips.

CHAPTER THREE

Victoire and Victoria

Twelve of Queen Charlotte's fifteen children were still alive when Princess Charlotte died in 1817, but once again there was no direct heir to the British throne. The daughters and daughters-in-law were past the menopause but three sons remained unmarried, the Duke of Clarence (later William IV), the Duke of Kent and the Duke of Cambridge. Her granddaughter's obstetric catastrophe had been the very opposite of the old Queen's obstetric performance. Queen Charlotte's labours had been brief and her second son was said to have been delivered after only three labour pains. The queen employed wet-nurses for all her children, so she did not enjoy the contraceptive protective effect lactation offers: for seven consecutive years she had a baby every year. Yet among her descendants only her eldest child, the Prince of Wales, had produced a legitimate heir – and she had just died.

In what contemporary gossips had called the 'Hymen's War Terrific', the king's offspring who were able set about trying to father an heir to the throne. The Duke of Wellington called the king's brothers, 'the damn'est millstones about the neck of any government that can be imagined' and the poet Shelley called them 'the dross of their dull race'. These were exaggerated phrases but not entirely misleading. Most of the royal brothers were middle aged, in debt and several were more in love with their mistresses than with their wives.

The Prince Regent eventually succeeded to the throne on the death of George III in 1820 and reigned for ten years. His coronation as George IV was a famous pantomime. Prize-fighters were employed to control the guests and to exclude his wife, the hated Queen Caroline, and her supporters. It was an unpopular reign and George IV was abused by parliament, cartoonists and the press. As had been predicted, he never made up the quarrel with his queen. On his death, the obituary in *The Times* observed, 'There never was a creature less regretted by his fellow creatures than the deceased King. What eye has wept for him? What heart has heaved one throb of unmercenary sorrow?'

Frederick Duke of York and Albany, the second son of George III, died of heart failure in 1826 while his brother was still on the throne. He had been married for twenty-five years to Frederica, daughter of the King of

16

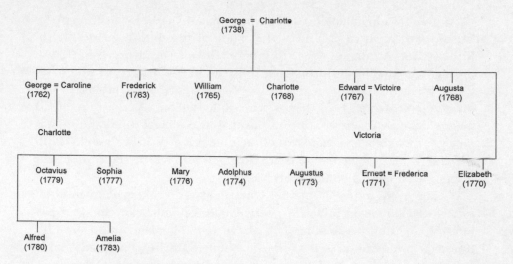

The family of George III, with dates of birth.

Prussia, but his real love was his mistress Mary Ann Clark and he had been accused of abusing his post as Commander-in-Chief of the Army by selling commissions on her behalf. Neglected Frederica was childless and led a separate, eccentric existence surrounded by pet parrots and monkeys. She died shortly after her husband and Frederick's line played no part in the succession stakes.

King George's third son, William, Duke of Clarence, was the one least deserving of Shelley's description. He had served as a midshipman in the navy when only thirteen years old and had seen action at Gibraltar in 1780. He visited North America and was the only member of the British royal family ever to see the Union Jack fly over New York. Washington and his rebel soldiers made plans to capture the young prince, but he did not fall into their trap. William also travelled in Europe and served under Lord Nelson in the West Indies. He was best man at Nelson's wedding and remained a personal friend until the Admiral's death at Trafalgar.

For twenty years William lived with a sparkling and beautiful actress, Dorothea Jordan, by whom he had ten children. She was dubbed as a 'child of nature whose voice was cordial to the heart . . . whose singing was like the twang of Cupid's bow'. The children were named Fitz Clarence by William and 'les bastards' by his detractors. In most things William was amiable and solid, if occasionally eccentric and, prior to Princess Charlotte's death, he saw no need to interrupt his happy liaison with Mrs Jordan.

The one shadow in William's life was that his father had forced the British parliament to pass a law that none of his children could marry without his permission. Realizing his children could not inherit the throne he parted from Dorothea in 18ll. 'Could you believe, or would the world believe that we never had for twenty years the semblance of a quarrel', she wrote of her happy years with William. At the time of his niece's death, William was fifty-two, his hair was almost white and he was portly, although by the standards of the time not grossly overweight. With the end of the Napoleonic wars, a whole new set of Protestant princesses became accessible as potential brides.

William wrote to his old mother Queen Charlotte, 'I have ten children totally dependent on myself, I owe £40,000 for which, of course, I pay interest, and I have a floating debt of £16,000'. Marriage would solve his financial problems as well as the inheritance, as he could reasonably expect parliament to vote him an increased royal pension. However, in the midst of hunting for an acceptable bride he fell in love again, this time with Miss Wykeham, who was wealthy but had no royal blood in her veins and was therefore unacceptable as a potential queen.

William courted Miss Wykeham by announcing that he hadn't a single farthing but he could make her a duchess and possibly Queen of England. She accepted, but the engagement was vetoed by the Prince Regent, acting head of the family while his father George III was senile. Disappointed in love he laid aside his marriage plans until the death of Charlotte, in 1817, spurred him into action once again. In the spring of 1818, he wrote to his oldest illegitimate son, 'I have delayed till the last moment writing in hopes of being able to inform you who is to be [my wife]. I can now with truth tho' not with satisfaction my heart being with Miss Wykeham. It is to be the Duchess of Saxe-Meiningen, whose beauty and character are universally acknowledged. She is deemed poor, dear innocent young woman created to be my wife. I cannot, I will not, I must not ill use her.' And, added William, 'What time may produce in my heart I cannot tell, but at present I think and exist only for Miss Wykeham. But enough of your father's misery.'

The marriage to Princess Adelaide of Saxe-Meiningen took place in the summer of 1818 and the following March she delivered a daughter, but the infant lived for only a few hours. The next conception ended in a miscarriage and the next in a daughter[1] who died as an infant in March 1821. There were rumours of later pregnancies including still-born twins, but no legitimate heir of William was to survive: Miss Wykeham had been deserted in vain.

On the death of George IV in 1830, William, then aged sixty-five, inherited the throne. 'In the evening', wrote the Russian ambassador's wife of the Court, 'we all sit at the round table. The King snoozes and the Queen does needle-work.' William died of pneumonia in 1837.

The Duke of Kent, the fourth son of George III, had been Queen Charlotte's largest infant. Born on 2 November 1767, he was christened Edward Augustus, after an uncle who had died a few days previously. He was a precocious child and grew into a pedantic adult. His mother, ever busy with new pregnancies, denied him even the remote, circumscribed contact most aristocrats gave their children. True to the British tradition of the eighteenth and early nineteenth century, he was educated in Spartan and sometimes cruel ways. His sister Augusta recalled seeing Edward's older brothers pinioned by their arms and thrashed with a long whip. It is not clear whether Edward received this treatment as a child, but he certainly grew into a complex adult, his personality embracing both sadism and tender concern.

At seventeen, Edward was sent to Hanover, Germany. 'Every morning in the week', he wrote back to London, 'I study 4 hours, 1 in German, 1 in law, 1 in artillery and 1 in history; and also 1 hour every evening, 3 times a week upon religious subjects, and 3 times a week the classics.' Throughout his life he was an energetic man, who liked to rise early and work hard, yet he was cast in the intrinsically frustrating role of the fourth son of the monarch, a prince frequently in the public eye but never required to do any real job.

As a young man he lived above his means and ran up debts. He was unusually tall and dressed foppishly. In 1790 he came home to England, but was hastily despatched to join the king's garrison in Gibraltar. Life on the Rock was hot and tedious and the Duke of Kent's surroundings were sparse. Although in debt, he had prestige and power and found little difficulty discovering women to share his bed. 'What follies do we see, every day, committed by youth', wrote his conscientious Colonel, Richard Symes.

In seeking a long-term relationship, Edward was meticulous and unemotional. He engaged a Mr Fontiny to travel to southern Europe and find him a suitable concubine. An appropriate young lady, Thérèse Bernardine, was recruited from Marseilles and brought by Mr Fontiny to live, along with her maid, in an apartment outside the garrison quarters. This was not what the prince intended:

As the commission with which I charged you to find for me a young lady to be my companion and mistress of my house was very detailed, and the talent for music which I wanted her to have was not at all the chief object which I asked you to watch for . . . I confess to you quite plainly that I do not know to what to attribute this way of acting [lodging the woman in another house] on your part, when you have heard from my own lips more than twenty times before you left for Marseilles that under no circumstances would I ever consent to lodge under another roof than mine the person who is to be my companion and friend.

Edward wrote to the lady:

I dare flatter myself that in signing your contract you felt it was only a simple form you had to observe purely out of delicacy for Fontiny's sake: I hope also that from the moment you receive this you will be convinced that your arrival will be welcome with all the respect of which a young man is capable who is consumed with happiness at making your charming acquaintance . . . come as quickly as you can, with just your maid and my confidential servant, who will have the honour of being your guide: it will bring me the happiness of seeing you very soon, and in taking [you] immediately [to] the place I have planned for you, you will give me the best proof of your affection. . . . I will keep the cottage warm and expect from the moment of your arrival our life will begin to be happy and content.

There was little doubt where she was to give 'the best proof of her affection' and when it came to telling her, in the same letter, about his worldly possessions the first thing he mentioned was his bed! Colonel Symes was equally direct in writing to General Grenville in England: 'With the promise I obtained from the Prince of his ceasing any further importation from England, I now wish France had been included, from whence, a Lady is just arrived whose company here at present would have been very well dispensed with.'

Edward's French mistress was to play a key role in his life and her reproductive history is an important piece of circumstantial evidence in our chronicle of Victoria's gene. We will return to her early life in Chapter 6. In Gibraltar, Thérèse was known as Madame de St Laurent. Apparently, she fulfilled her contract, kept the duke happy in bed, was discreet and accepted his martial ways. When the garrison was transferred to Quebec, *The Times* of London described the retinue who boarded the ship for Canada as 'rather domestic than princely; a French Lady, his own man, and a Swiss valet'.

Even by the harsh standards of the time, Edward was a martinet who collected tall men for his marching troops as other men might collect stamps. He fussed over the details of their uniforms, filled their unhappy days with inspections and marches and treated them more cruelly than

1 *Princess Charlotte and Prince Leopold at the opera. The Royal Collection © Her Majesty the Queen.*

2 *Claremont House, three miles from Windsor, was built for Clive of India by Capability Brown, better known for his gardens, and his partner Henry Holland. Princess Charlotte died here. It was used by Victoria before her coronation and after her marriage. During the revolutions of 1848 Victoria wished to retreat to Claremont but was dissuaded by Albert. It was later the home of Prince Leopold, Victoria's haemophiliac son. During the Second World War it was used by the Hawker Aircraft Company and parts of the Hurricane fighter, which helped to win the Battle of Britain, were designed here. It is now a school.*

3 Duchess Louise with
her sons Ernst and Albert.
Albert later married Queen
Victoria. Original in the
Schloss Ehrenburg in
Coburg.

4 Sir John Conroy, Master of
Victoria's household after the death
of the Duke of Kent. From a painting
by A. Tidey in the National Portrait
Gallery.

5 *The Duchess of Kent with Princess Victoria in 1834 when Victoria was fourteen. From a painting by Sir George Hayter. The Royal Collection © Her Majesty the Queen.*

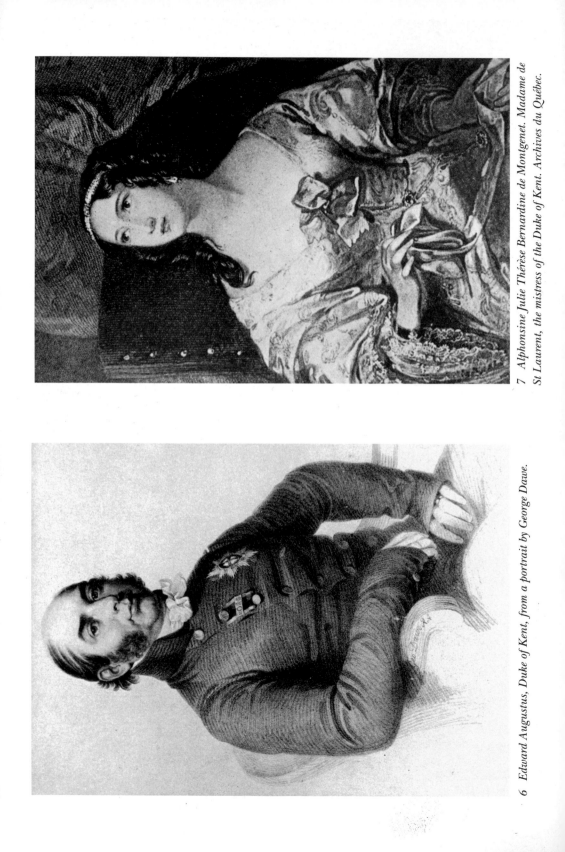

7 Alphonsine Julie Thérèse Bernardine de Montgenet. Madame de St Laurent, the mistress of the Duke of Kent. Archives du Québec.

6 Edward Augustus, Duke of Kent, from a portrait by George Dawe.

8　*Duke Ernst of Saxe-Coburg-Gotha. Portrait by George Dawe. Schloss Ehrenburg, Coburg.*

9 *Prince Albert I during his last illness, 1861. Albert is holding the* Trent *papers (p. 38)
in his hand. From a posthumous painting by E.H. Corbould, based on a photograph taken
in 1859 by Miss Day. The Royal Archives © Her Majesty the Queen.*

10   *Queen Victoria and Prince Albert with their children, 27 May 1857. Left to right, Prince Alfred, Prince Albert, Princess Helena, Prince Arthur, Princess Alice, Queen Victoria with Princess Beatrice, the Princess Royal, Princess Louise, Prince Leopold and the Prince of Wales. The Royal Archives © Her Majesty the Queen.*

11 *Prince Leopold with Sir William Jenner at Balmoral in 1877. Leopold is confined to a wheelchair following an episode of bleeding. Hulton Deutsch Collection Limited.*

12 *Three generations. Left to right, Prince Leopold of Battenberg, Marie Louise, Princess Aribert of Anhalt with Prince Edward of York, Victoria Mary, Duchess of York, with Princess Mary of York, Prince Alexander of Battenberg (on ground), George Duke of York with Prince Albert of York, Queen Victoria, Prince Arthur of Connaught, Louise Margaret, Duchess of Connaught, Beatrice, Princess Henry of Battenberg, Princess Patricia of Connaught (on ground), Princess Victoria Eugénie of Battenberg, Princess Helena Victoria of Schleswig-Holstein, Prince Maurice of Battenberg. The Royal Archives © Her Majesty the Queen.*

cattle. The Governor of Halifax wrote, 'The Prince cannot resist the temptation of taking a fine man into his Regt., nor a fine horse into his stable at any rate whatsoever.' His devotion to military affairs was total to the point of obsession. 'He is wrapped up in his profession, while he studies night and day', wrote one naval observer, 'and his maxim is, that nothing is well when it can be done better.'

Edward was not in Quebec very long before he had a mutiny on his hands. The soldiers were ill-organized and often drunk, and their pathetic plot was easily uncovered. One man was sentenced to death and three were flogged, receiving between 300 and 700 lashes each. The prince was in charge of the execution parade. The condemned man, dressed in grave clothes, was forced to march behind his own coffin before 'a vast concourse of spectators', while the band played dirges. At the foot of the gallows Edward addressed the condemned man: 'Draper – you have now reached the awful moment when a few moments would carry you into the presence of the Supreme Being. As the son of your sovereign whose greatest prerogative is the dispensation of mercy, I feel myself fortunately able to do that which, as your colonel, the indispensable laws of military discipline renders it impossible for me even to think of.'[2] The mutineer was pardoned!

Oddly, this same sadistic man fell into more homely, almost tender ways, with Madame de St Laurent. Unlike his brother, the Prince Regent, Edward drank little, neither gambled nor womanized; and once with Madame de St Laurent, he remained faithful to her. The lovers were separated in 1793 when she visited Britain briefly and he travelled to the Caribbean to fight at the capture of St Lucia from the French. The two were reunited and lived a somewhat drab life for another five years in Quebec and Halifax, before returning closer to the pomp and splendour of the royal Court in London. When he left Canada, Edward left behind eleven more soldiers condemned to death for various acts of perceived indiscipline, at least three of whom are known to have been executed. The Province of Prince Edward Island in the Gulf of St Lawrence commemorates his stay in Canada.

Tiring of his exile, Edward wrote to his brother, the Duke of York:

I would take a house for [Madame de St Laurent] in the Country at some little distance off, where her menage would be totally separate from mine. She would, of course, not appear at my house on the days I give public dinners, and when I went to hers, I should consider myself as her guest, and I should avoid being seen with her at any place of public entertainment. . . . I understand it is the intention to make my separation from Madame de St Laurent a term without which I am not to be employed on the other side of the Atlantic, which, however, it is repugnant to my feelings to credit, I must at once declare that it is one which I will not admit to be dictated to me, and to which, were I to subscribe, I should consider myself as meriting every contemptible and opprobrious Epithet to which those expose themselves who commit mean and despicable actions.[3]

The prince and his lady were allowed to return to England, and then in 1802 he was transferred back to Gibraltar, this time in full command of the garrison. Again, he made the lives of his men a hell, closing down the taverns, extending parade hours, and fussing over uniforms. Within twenty months of arriving he faced the second mutiny of his career, the men attempting to storm his home. This time eleven men were sentenced to be shot and two received a thousand lashes each. Not all the sentences were carried out as the duke was ordered back to England.

Here the couple lived quietly, but not cheaply, at Castle Hill Lodge, Ealing. 'Madame did not rise very early,' wrote the young son of a long-standing Canadian friend, 'she is almost always embroidering, writing her book, drawing or reading.' Driven by debts, they moved to Brussels in 1814, but a legal marriage to a woman acceptable to his brother, who had now become Regent, and to the British parliament, was the only effective way Edward could increase his income. In 1816 he attempted to sell his comfortable residence, Castle Hill Lodge in Ealing, on which he had lavished vast funds and much care. At the same time he paid a brief visit to Leopold's widowed sister, Victoire, Duchess of Leiningen, at Amorbach and another to the Princess of Baden at Carlsruhe, but was evidently unimpressed with either as he rejoined his mistress in a rented home in Brussels, which he so transformed that its owner could hardly recognize it. He also extended and redesigned the gardens and remodelled the stables. It is said that the Emperor of Russia contributed £2,000 towards the cost of a proposed wedding of Edward and the Princess of Baden. If he did, it proved to be a bad investment, for when the Duke of Kent finally did marry it was to a woman from another court.

Fearing that his mistress might hear of his visits to prospective brides Edward arranged for the publication of a denial that he had any marriage plans. His letters show that he was deeply concerned that Madame should not be upset and clearly hoped that he would not be required to choose between his loving mistress and a strange aristocratic bride.

One of Edward's unexpected virtues seems to have been an easy manner with young people of his own class. He was relatively close to his niece, Princess Charlotte, and from Brussels he handled the 'delicate correspondence' she was having with Prince Leopold of Coburg. The duke was 'the chief promoter of [our] marriage', claimed Leopold, writing to Queen Victoria thirty years later. After Charlotte finally married, she began a lively exchange of letters with her husband's widowed sister Victoire. Charlotte and Edward now switched roles and she began encouraging Edward to marry. Charlotte's sudden and untimely death in November 1817, together with the stillbirth of her son, was a double blow to Edward who wrote, 'Indeed, I recollect no event in my life that has so completely overwhelmed me as the catastrophe at Claremont and I feel it will take time before I regain my usual spirits and composure.'[4]

Even as late as 18 December he was hoping that his brother would solve the dynastic problem and remove any need for him to marry. He wrote to his friend Wetherall, 'I ought to be first sure that the Divorce (of the Prince Regent) and that the Admiral of the Fleet (the Duke of Clarence) is not thinking of marrying'. The newly bereaved Leopold, having just lost his wife and son, saw an opportunity to keep the British crown within his family and wrote to his sister urging the match. Spurred by a sense of duty to the nation and the prospect of an additional £25,000 per annum and the payment of all his outstanding debts, Edward changed his mind. Early in January 1818 Edward wrote to Victoire asking for a decision but seemingly still hoping for a negative answer as he wrote again to Wetherall that in that case 'the matter would be at an end'. However, Victoire agreed to the marriage on condition that she could spend part of the year at Amorbach to preserve the constitutional position of her son, who as heir was required to reside at Amorbach. Edward never saw Madame de St Laurent again. She read about the courtship of Victoire in her paper over breakfast and was broken hearted. For Edward it was also a painful break and he wrote, 'As for the payment of my debts, I don't call them great, the nation, on the contrary, is greatly my debtor'. To a friend he mused before his wedding, 'I hope I shall have the strength to do my duty'.[5]

Victoire, the Dowager Duchess of Leiningen, did not share her brother's dynastic vision and drive. She lived in an isolated palace at Amorbach, given to her former husband by Napoleon. There, forty miles of rutted roads from the nearest large town, Mannheim, Victoire kept a modest court, acting as regent for her fifteen-year-old son Charles. At the same time she cannot have been blind to the duke's invitation to join the premier royal family in Europe, especially when combined with the reasonable possibility of bearing an heir to the British throne. She was restrained both by a genuine concern for young Charles and her thirteen-year-old daughter, Feodora. There were several illegitimate pretenders to the Leiningen throne and German law did not allow women to succeed as monarchs, so Charles was under the authority of the Court of Wards. The

duke promised she could spend part of the year in Germany and the
Prince Regent stepped in and persuaded the Court of Wards to let Charles
come to England for the rest of the time. Victoire and Edward were finally
betrothed at Coburg on 27 May 1818 and married two days later. After a
short honeymoon, the Duke of Kent brought his bride back to London by
leisurely stages for a second marriage ceremony, according to the rites of
the Church of England, on 11 July. The service was bilingual and the
duchess's official speech in English was written phonetically in German. At
the same ceremony the duke's elder brother William married Princess
Adelaide of Saxe-Meiningen and the Prince Regent gave both brides away:
Hymen's War Terrific had begun.

   A month later, in order to save money, the duke and his new duchess
left for Amorbach, but when the duchess found that she was pregnant
they hastily returned to Kensington Palace. The duke felt that an heir
to the throne should be British born, and a British birth might
strengthen the claim, if, as was likely, there were competitors. As at
Charlotte's labour, many distinguished guests assembled, including the
Duke of Wellington and the Chancellor of the Exchequer, no doubt
apprehensive with memories of Charlotte's confinement. Happily the
labour was a short one and a healthy baby girl was delivered at 4.15 a.m.
on 24 May 1819. She was christened Victoria. Victoire had promised
Edward a son, but the duke philosophically decided that 'the decrees of
providence are not all times wisest and best'. The duke's personal
physician, Dr Wilson, was considered to have managed the pregnancy
'to perfection', probably because he did little to interfere with the
midwife, Madame Siebold.[6]

   The war was won by a very short margin. In March 1819 Kent's younger
brother's wife, the Duchess of Cambridge, had given birth to a son and his
elder brother, William, had had a daughter, although she only survived
seven hours, and the Duchess of Cumberland, the wife of another younger
brother, had a son only three days after Victoria was born. Victoria's
christening took place one month later in Kensington Palace in the
presence of the Prince Regent. The Cupola Room was decorated with
draperies borrowed from St James' Palace and a font was brought over from
the Tower of London. The Archbishop of Canterbury held the child ready
for baptism. 'Name this child?', he asked. 'Alexandrina', replied the duke,
naming his daughter after the Emperor Alexander of Russia, a godfather *in
absentia*. The Prince Regent curtly vetoed the choice. Charlotte was offered
and also vetoed. 'Augusta', suggested the duke, but that was equally
unacceptable. By now the duchess was in tears and the duke tentatively
suggested Elizabeth but it was also refused. Eventually the Prince Regent
said, 'Give her the mother's name also, then, but it cannot precede that of

the Emperor.' So the infant was finally christened Alexandrina Victoria. As a child she called herself Drina.

Unlike every other queen, princess and duchess in Europe, Victoire breast-fed the new baby: 'Everybody is most astonished', she wrote to her mother. If she had not made this unexpected break with precedent, then Victoria, growing up in the draughty rooms of Kensington Palace, where the windows 'constantly let in the rain', might well have died like Adelaide's babies. Another wise but equally unusual step occurred when the duchess agreed to have 'our dear little girl' vaccinated against smallpox, ten weeks after her birth. Victoria was weaned at six months. She was almost annoyingly fit and did not even trouble her doting parents when she began teething at seven months. For the first three years of her life she heard only German spoken. At the age of three she started to learn English but included German words and phrases in her English for the rest of her life.

After Victoria's birth, the ever impecunious Kents decided to return to Germany, but visiting the quiet Devon resort of Sidmouth they fell in love with it and settled there in a small house, Wallbrook Cottage. An incident there showed that the duke had mellowed since his ferocious army days. A youth shooting birds accidentally shattered the window of the princess's nursery and cut the sleeve of her nightdress. Such carelessness might have filled any father with righteous indignation, but the elderly duke merely released the lad with an admonition and 'a promise to desist from such culpable pursuits'.

Plagued by mounting debts in England and worried by 'unpleasant business letters from Amorbach' the duke stayed on in Sidmouth in the expectation of 'a less severe winter, some baths in warm sea water – and to save money'. The winter, unhappily, developed into a series of storms, and however much coal the maids piled on the grates it seemed impossible to heat the rented house, every room was cold, and outside the wind and rain lashed the Devon watering-place unmercifully. One by one the family caught cold. Baby Victoria was the first but recovered quickly. After the duke came in wet and cold on Friday 7 January 1820 after looking at the horses, he rapidly developed a sore throat.

The good sense surrounding Victoria's early months is all the more remarkable in the light of the medical treatment meted out to her father. He had probably caught the common cold virus, with some secondary bacterial infection of the throat. Although he felt dreadful he kept up his social engagements and Victoire fussed over her husband with quinine and affection and, with good sense, moved the duke's bed into the largest warm room in the house.

Dr Wilson may have held back at the duchess's delivery, but he began to treat the duke's illness with the same aggressiveness he had shown as a brutal surgeon in the navy, earlier in his career. On Monday 10 January, he began applying leeches to the duke's chest and by Wednesday his illness had worsened and he was undoubtedly developing pneumonia with the pain of pleurisy, high fever and episodes of delirium. Yet the duke was only fifty-two and usually enjoyed robust health. He would probably have fought the infection well if Dr Wilson had not embarked on an increasingly desperate course of bleeding, combined with inappropriate nursing. He bled him again on Wednesday and Thursday and, a week after the illness began, he changed from leeches to cupping – incising the skin and placing a vessel filled with hot air over it so that it draws off blood. Blood was drawn from every part of the duke's body, including the head, to the great distress of the ladies of the household. 'For hours they tormented him', commented Victoire's German companion, Polyxene von Tubeuf. The duchess was suspicious of the treatments, saying, 'even if he should become weaker, the only remedy for relieving the inflammation was bleeding'. 'It is too dreadful,' she wrote, 'there is hardly a spot on his dear body which has not been touched by cupping, blisters, or bleeding.' The duke's father, George III, was also seriously ill 200 miles away in London, but one royal physician, Dr William Manton, was despatched down to Devon when news of the duke's worsening illness reached London. His brother-in-law, Leopold, set off to Sidmouth and even the Prince Regent, who had snubbed him since the christening, sent his best wishes.

Prior to Dr Manton's arrival, the duke had had a total of six pints of blood removed. The normal blood volume is eight pints, but the leeches and blisters had been applied repeatedly, removing a relatively small quantity of blood each time. Therefore, Edward's body would have rapidly replaced the fluid lost, but the red cells, packed with the haemoglobin needed to carry oxygen, take 120 days to grow in the bone marrow and at the end of twenty such episodes his haemoglobin would have been between 40 and 50 per cent of normal. Such anaemia is compatible with life, although it would have greatly exacerbated the infection and embarrassed the circulation to the heart and lungs. In addition the antibodies and white cells needed to fight the pneumonia were continually being drained into leeches and cups, and Dr Manton's unhappy therapy rapidly turned a common cold into a mortal infection. Finally, as we will see later, the duke may have also suffered from porphyria, and if this was the case his position would have been even more precarious.

When Prince Leopold and his secretary and physician, Dr Stockmar, reached Sidmouth they were taken into the duke's sickroom. Stockmar felt the anaemic, ailing man's pulse and told the duchess in German,

'Human help can no longer avail'. Edward was roused sufficiently to sign his will, which he did painfully slowly, letter by letter, with the same meticulousness that had characterized his life.

He died at 10 a.m. on Sunday 23 January, two weeks after the illness began. In a way it was remarkable he had lived so long. Years after the death Dr Manton continued to mutter, 'He would have borne more depletion', meaning more blood should have been removed. In life the Duke of Kent had been an appalling general, flogging and hanging men for military irrelevancies; he died in the care of a naval surgeon dispensing irrelevant and painful therapies.

After Edward's death, the duchess and her three children returned to London where they lived very modestly on £3,000 a year allowed by their wealthy relative, Prince Leopold. Leopold, determined that Victoria should have the best possible chance of inheriting the throne, insisted that his niece be brought up in England. They were given a set of rooms in Kensington Palace, a heavy, asymmetrical building which had grown to a semblance of grandeur in easy steps, beginning as a private house and becoming a royal residence under William III. Drina, bright-eyed and fair-haired, played with her collection of dolls with porcelain faces and a handmade musical box with an animated lady playing the pianoforte.

Immediately after Victoria's birth, Mrs Siebold the midwife had hurried back to attend the confinement of the teenage wife of Ernst, Duke of Saxe-Coburg and Saalfeld, elder brother of Leopold and of Victoire, whom we met in Chapter 2. On 26 August 1819 she delivered her second son and called him Albert. Madame Siebold remarked he would make a fine husband for his cousin Victoria.

CHAPTER FOUR

The Ugly Duckling

Between 1841 and 1857 Queen Victoria delivered nine children. One son was a haemophiliac and two daughters carried the gene. From her birth until her marriage Victoria's future reproductive capacity was subject to manipulation by an older generation. Later, when queen, she planned, worried over and attempted to control the mating patterns of her own children and grandchildren. Unfortunately, she never understood the inheritance, importance or consequences of the gene for haemophilia, which she spread throughout the royal houses of Europe.

During Victoria's early years her succession to the British throne was sometimes in doubt, but this did not hinder the political machinations of Prince Leopold, the prime dynastic climber. He later wrote ingratiatingly to Victoria about the events immediately after her father's death: 'I do not know what would have become of you and your Mama, if I had not then existed. You poor soul about 9 months old!! the state of affairs of your poor Father so bad that there was no means for the journey back to Kensington, [and] on the highest quarter, the greatest animosity and the wish to drive the Duchess to the continent.'

Leopold did help the family, although he avoided bringing his sister and her child back to his home at Claremont because a measles epidemic was raging in the area. Baby Drina (Victoria) was not only a painful reminder to him of the heir he had lost but also an opportunity to manipulate affairs in new directions. Victoria's claim to the throne, however, was not immediately secure. In December 1820 the hopes of Leopold and his sister were dashed when the Duchess of Clarence, later Queen Adelaide, wife of William IV, gave birth to a girl. She was six weeks premature but survived and was christened Elizabeth Georgina Adelaide. As the child of an older brother of the late Duke of Kent, she took precedence over Victoria. Elizabeth died in March 1821 of 'an entanglement of the bowels', or volvulus, but in August of the same year yet another threat to Victoria's succession arose. Queen Caroline, who had been estranged from her husband since her wedding night, died unexpectedly. King George IV was fifty-nine and free to marry and perhaps replace the dead Charlotte with a new half-brother or sister. Those around the monarch expected 'he will pick something up' [namely, one fertile European princess] on a trip he

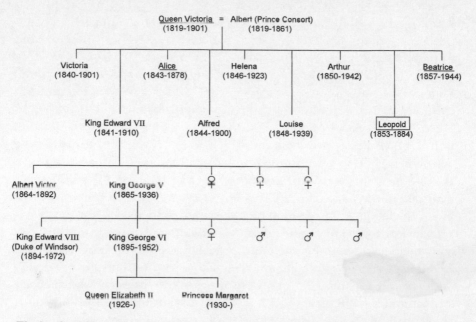

The family of Queen Victoria. Carriers of haemophilia underlined, haemophiliacs boxed.

planned to Hanover and Austria before Christmas 1821. However, he remained a bachelor, perhaps because he was becoming increasingly ill. There is very good evidence that he had inherited porphyria from his father.[1] He began to experience severe bladder pain and to take stupefyingly heavy doses of laudanum. He died in June 1830 and his brother William came to the throne. William, as we have seen, had no surviving legitimate heir.

As soon as Victoria's place in the succession stakes was restored Leopold began solidifying his plans. For Victoria trips to visit her uncle in Claremont became the 'brightest epoch in my otherwise rather melancholy childhood'.[2] Even while she was a child Leopold pressed the advantages of a marriage to Victoria of his nephew Albert. Victoria's mother, however, was coming more and more under the influence of an Irish army officer called John Conroy. Captain Conroy had been a friend of the Duke of Kent and after Edward's death he manoeuvred himself to be master of Victoire's household. While Leopold planned little Victoria's future marriage, Conroy planned to dominate her utterly through his increasing influence on her widowed mother. A remarkable picture of the relationship between Captain Conroy and Victoire Duchess of Kent can be found in the Greville diaries. Charles Cavendish Fulke Greville is an unimpeachable source. Grandson of the Duke of Portland, who had been prime minister on two occasions, and great-grandson of the Earl of

Warwick, his social standing and his occupation both placed him in a position to know and interpret the affairs of state and of men and women. As clerk to the Privy Council for many years he was in close personal contact with King George IV, King William and with the young Victoria. He was also a close friend of the Duke of Wellington and was intimate with the leaders of British society from the aristocracy to MacAuley and Sidney Smith. His diaries are comparable with those of Pepys in content and frankness. They were written for his own amusement, and as an informed, intelligent observer he had few peers. He did his best to sift fact from fiction, noting that 'Half the things one hears are untrue' and 'it is the business of every man who keeps a journal to contradict on one page what he has written in the preceding'.

It is clear from the Greville diaries that Victoria's mother was arrogant and ambitious, attempting to dominate Victoria and to keep her isolated at Kensington when she should have been taking part in Court life in London as the heiress apparent. Sir John Conroy was in his forties and the same age as Victoire, a balding man with sideburns, tight-lipped, with a slightly arrogant tilt of his head. He would cross his arms as if to hold his personality secret. Yet he was not without character and was the man whom the duchess saw most frequently and most intimately. Their extraordinary behaviour suggests that the Duchess of Kent hoped to become the power behind the throne after Victoria's accession and Regent if William IV died before Victoria was eighteen, while Sir John planned to become the power behind the power behind the throne. How far the characteristics of the mature woman reflected those of the young widow who had married the Duke of Kent fifteen years earlier must remain uncertain.

In 1801 Conroy had married the seventeen-year-old daughter of Major General Fisher, a lifelong friend of the Duke of Kent, and later his aide-de-camp. At Major General Fisher's death Conroy slipped himself into the duke's household staff. At first he regarded the appointment with some disappointment, but when the Duke of Kent died and he saw himself as the most important member of the household of the likely future Queen of England, his attitude changed. He had four sons and two daughters by his wife, but by the time he had become the dominant individual in the life of the Duchess of Kent, his marriage was taking second place to his personal ambitions. The Duchess of Kent was completely dominated by him, forgiving his mistakes and pleading for his advancement, even in the face of manifest political opposition. Conroy played the leading role in marrying the duchess's eldest and exceedingly attractive daughter, Princess Feodora, to a minor German prince, Ernst of Hohenlohe Langenburg. It seems his prime motive was to isolate Victoria, who was very fond of her half-sister.

The duchess's arrogance infuriated many who had dealings with her. When she borrowed the royal yacht she insisted on so many royal salutes from passing ships that even the amiable King William IV intervened, but Conroy, as her confidential adviser, persuaded her not to give way. In the end, the king had to make an order in Council that the yacht should only be saluted by His Majesty's ships when the king or queen themselves were on board. In her attempts to isolate Victoria the duchess even prevented her from attending the coronation of her uncle William IV. Conroy encouraged the duchess to believe that the Duke of Cumberland, next in line, had designs on Victoria's life.[3] King William generously gave Victoria £10,000 p.a., but this did little to improve relations. In 1836 the duchess refused to visit Windsor on the queen's birthday. She did condescend to go on the king's birthday but her visit coincided with the discovery that she had appropriated a suite of seventeen rooms in Kensington Palace, contrary to the king's specific instructions. This led to an explosion from the king at his birthday dinner, which was attended by about a hundred guests. After the king's health had been drunk, he made a long speech which throws a flood of light on Victoria's mother.

I trust in God that my life may be spared for nine months longer, after which period, in the event of my death, no regency would take place. I should then have the satisfaction of leaving the royal authority to the personal exercise of that young lady (pointing to the Princess Victoria), the heiress presumptive of the Crown, and not in the hands of a person now near me, who is surrounded by evil advisers, and who is herself incompetent to act with propriety in the station in which she would be placed. I have no hesitation in saying that I have been insulted – grossly, and continually insulted – by that person, but I am determined to endure no longer a course of behaviour so disrespectful to me. Amongst many other things I have particularly to complain of the manner in which that young lady has been kept away from my Court; she had been repeatedly kept from my drawing rooms, at which she ought always to have been present, but I am fully resolved that this shall not happen again. I would have her know that I am King, and I am determined to make my authority respected, and for the future I shall insist and command that the Princess do upon all occasions appear at my Court, as it is her duty to do.

'He terminated his speech by an allusion to the Princess and her future reign in a tone of paternal interest and affection, which was excellent in its way.'[4]

The Duke of Wellington's opinions of the duchess are also recorded by Greville. 'What he (Wellington) told me then throws some light on her ill humour and wrong-headedness. In the first place, the late King (George III) disliked her, the Duke of Cumberland was her enemy and George IV was always talking of taking the child (Victoria) from her.'[5] While those around Victoria fought to manipulate her, she herself was maturing into a short, slightly plump, dark-haired, intelligent and increasingly independent young woman. We do not know when she first menstruated, but it may have been as late as age fourteen or fifteen.[6] When Victoria was seventeen, and despite Conroy's influence, Leopold persuaded his sister to invite cousins Albert and Ernst to London. King William was furious, as he favoured an alliance with the Dutch royal house. Leopold's response was typical. He wrote to Victoria: 'I am really astonished at the behaviour of your elder uncle. The invitation to the Prince of Orange, the forcing him upon others is extraordinary. Now when slavery has been abolished in England, I cannot understand why you alone are to be treated as a white slave girl.'

Albert was seasick crossing the North Sea and tended to fall asleep at 10 p.m., even at important social gatherings. Victoria called Albert and his brother her 'dearest and most beloved cousins' but she was to tell Leopold later, 'I may not have the feeling for him which is requisite to ensure happiness'.

King William's wish that he would live until Victoria reached the age of eighteen, so that a regency would be avoided, was granted and she became queen on 20 June 1837, less than one month after her eighteenth birthday. On Victoria's accession to the throne a remarkable metamorphosis occurred. She demonstrated great poise and good sense. Conroy was ignored and she symbolized her independence from her mother by moving into her own bedroom. She received Lord Melbourne, her prime minister, 'of COURSE quite Alone as I shall always do all my ministers'.[7] For some time after Victoria became queen, Leopold attempted to manipulate her by letter, but eventually he overplayed his hand and Victoria established her independence. She noted, 'I have received a disagreeable letter from Uncle Leopold. My poor uncle seems to be out of humour because I have not asked his advice, but it is dear uncle's foible to imagine that his mission is to rule everywhere. I myself see no need for that.' However, he was sufficiently tactful to maintain good relations with his niece. He continued to visit Victoria every year until his death in 1865, which was caused in part by a cold caught in the freezing rooms of Buckingham Palace. The young Victoria confided in her journal that Leopold was her '"solo padre!" for he is indeed like my real father'. Yet she was getting tired of being badgered over Albert. 'I am not guilty of any breach of promise, for I never gave any', she wrote to Leopold. When it came to dynastic opportunities, however, Leopold never gave up. Two years after Victoria's coronation he once again contrived that Albert should visit England, although by this time Albert was also getting fed up with the family pressure and he decided to use the visit to end the affair 'with quiet but firm resolution'.

When the two young people met something different happened. Albert had matured from a bilious youth into a striking young man and within hours of the reunion he had swept Victoria off her feet. 'Albert really is quite charming and so excessively handsome.' Within three days she told him she would be only 'too happy if he would consent to what I wished' – namely, marriage. Albert forgot about Victoria's 'incredible stubbornness', and love triumphed. On 10 February 1840 they were married. 'Oh to feel I was, and am, loved by such an Angel as Albert was too great a delight to describe', wrote Victoria in her journal. Victoria had a 'sick headache' on her wedding night, but it does not seem to have dulled Albert's ardour and she took up her diary to write, 'ill or not, I never, never spent such an evening!! . . . He clasped me in his arms and we kissed each other again and again.' Nevertheless, the young lovers were up at 8.30 a.m., stimulating Greville to observe this 'is not the way to provide us with a Prince of Wales'. Family problems marred their early months together. The Duchess of Kent proved particularly tiresome. She suggested that she should move into Buckingham Palace with the newly weds, and when this was refused she complained to Albert that her own daughter had thrown her out of the house. At the same time Albert's father, the Duke of Coburg, repeatedly attempted to persuade his daughter-in-law to pay off his numerous creditors.

Victoria wanted to wait before having children, but neither she nor Albert had the slightest idea how to avoid pregnancy. She menstruated once after the marriage and then conceived, delivering a girl on 21 November 1840, three weeks premature and after a twelve-hour labour. During the pregnancy Victoria ate heartily and there was none of the blood-letting that had characterized the royal delivery a generation earlier. The pregnancy was marred, however, by an attempted assassination by a mentally defective youth of eighteen.[8]

The baby was christened Victoria Adelaide Mary Louisa – although her parents called her Pussy and later Vicky. On the whole, Victoria disliked little babies, talking of their 'terrible frog-like action', but both parents found great joy in their first-born. Vicky was not a carrier of haemophilia.

Queen Victoria, unlike her mother, did not breast-feed her babies. A wet-nurse had been identified in the Isle of Wight and as the birth was premature she had to be sent for unexpectedly, crossing the sea in an open boat. If a mother breast-feeds, and particularly if she breast-feeds on demand and does not give supplementary food too soon, then ovulation will be suppressed for many months, sometimes for a year or longer. Victoria and her doctors never understood that breast-feeding is nature's contraceptive. Indeed, one of her many strong opinions was an unusual disgust with the process of lactation. Later in life, when her own daughter Alice nursed her children, the queen said she was making a cow out of herself and a beast in the royal dairy was duly called Alice. Further, when Vicky, Victoria's eldest daughter, acted as wet-nurse to Alice's fifth child, Frittie (Frederick William), she dared not tell her mother in case of ridicule. The first child, the Princess Royal, had been healthy at birth but was soon thin, fretful and sick.

As Victoria was not lactating, her periods returned quickly and she conceived her second child when the Princess Royal was only three months old. At the beginning of the year she had written to Leopold, 'I think dearest Uncle you cannot really wish me to be the 'Mamma d'une nombreuse famille' . . . men never think, at least seldom think, what a hard task it is for us women to go through this very often.' Edward (later King Edward VII) was born on 9 November 1841. Again a wet-nurse was brought in and again Victoria fell pregnant quickly, delivering her second daughter Alice seventeen months after Edward's birth. Later in her life, Victoria was to write to Vicky, 'what made me so miserable was – to have the first two years of married life utterly spoilt by this occupation [pregnancy]. I c[ou]ld enjoy nothing, not travel about or go about with dear Papa. If I had waited a year – as I hope you will, it w[ou]ld have been very different.' When grandchildren began to arrive Victoria said it was 'a very uninteresting thing – for it seems to me to go on like rabbits in Windsor Park'.

The birth of their first son brought great joy and Victoria felt that he looked especially like Prince Albert. 'I hope and pray he may be like his dearest papa', she wrote to uncle Leopold. Sadly for both mother and son the prayer went unanswered. The royal nursery distanced the infant Edward from the affection he needed and his parents doted on his elder sister. Edward was soon perceived as dull and 'anti-studious', and began to stammer and to have temper tantrums. Albert and Victoria responded by setting up a strict, detailed, obsessive plan of control and education. Even Princess Alice, who was born eighteen months after the Prince of Wales, received 'a real punishment by whipping' when she was only four. To make matters worse for Edward, his sisters at least managed to keep up with their tedious and inappropriate tutoring. When he was six the queen's obsession with making the future king into 'the most perfect man' found expression in taking him 'entirely away from the women' and handing him over to a personal tutor with the threateningly appropriate name of Mr Birch.

A succession of children followed Edward at eighteen to thirty-six month intervals: Alfred in 1844, Helena in 1846, Louise in 1848, Arthur in 1850, Leopold in 1853 and the ninth and last, Beatrice in 1857. The numerous pregnancies were uncomfortable and the deliveries painful. As the children matured Victoria and Albert set about marrying them off to fulfil their own dynastic agenda. Her eldest daughter was married to the German Crown Prince Frederick William (Fritz). In a repetition of her mother's life, Vicky was introduced to her future husband when she was ten, betrothed when she was seventeen and had two children by the time she was twenty. Three other daughters, Alice, Helena and Louise were all married in their late teens, but the youngest, Beatrice, was kept at home as a companion to Mama, and only broke loose at the age of twenty-eight. 'I hope and pray there may be no results!' wrote Victoria icily, 'that would aggravate everything and besides make me terribly anxious.'

But there were to be 'results' and Beatrice, along with Alice, was one of the two daughters who were to carry the gene for haemophilia. The only one of Victoria's four boys to suffer from the disease, and therefore the first in the family to display the symptoms, was Leopold, born on 7 April 1853. His birth was remarkable because the queen was given chloroform by Dr John Snow.[9] Until that moment, relief of pain in childbirth had been highly controversial, 'a decoy of Satan', in the words of one clergyman, 'apparently offering to bless women; but in the end it will harden society and rob God of the deep earnest cries which arise in time of trouble for help.' Victoria, however, found anaesthesia in childbirth, 'soothing, quieting and delightful beyond measure'.

At first, 'little Leo' seemed a 'jolly fat little fellow, but no beauty'. The birth was followed by a worse than usual depression. Trifling disputes sometimes burgeoned, in Albert's words, into 'a continuance of hysterics for more than an hour . . . traces of which remained for more than 24 hours more'. The queen went literally for months without seeing her baby and he was left to the total care of a wet-nurse from the Scottish Highlands. When he began to walk it was noticed that he bruised easily and cried a lot. Haemophilia was diagnosed. Inevitably those who believed with the Bible that 'in sorrow thou shalt bring forth children' blamed the anaesthetic.

Victoria's attitudes, particularly to members of her own family, were extreme to the point of being unbalanced. This was particularly the case with Leopold, who was treated with contempt throughout his childhood but became his mother's confidential adviser in state affairs in early manhood. This was in contrast to her attitude towards her eldest son, the

Prince of Wales, who came to be regarded as retarded and was disliked by his mother in his youth, but was positively hated by her after Albert's death.

Leopold's childhood was pariicularly unfortunate. A chronic invalid with an awkward stance, due to haemorrhages into his joints, he was, according to his mother, a bad speaker and generally unattractive, although later in life he was evidently an excellent public speaker. Perhaps the immediate separation of all the children from their mother the moment they were born produced an emotional distance. Victoria's comments on the poor child are often brutal. Vicky married soon after Leopold's birth and when he was five the queen wrote to her daughter in Berlin, 'He bruises as much as ever but unberufen[10] 1,000 times – is free from any at present; but he holds himself still as badly as ever and is very ugly, I think uglier than he ever was.'[11]

A few months later she wrote again in a similar vein, 'As for Leopold he still bruises as much as ever, but he has (unberufen) not had any accidents of late. He is tall, but holds himself worse than ever, and is a very common looking child, very pale in face, clever but an oddity – and not an engaging child though amusing.' When the Crown Princess had a baby, grandmother dreaded that it might resemble its unfortunate uncle: 'If you remember what Leopold was! I hope, dear, he won't be like the ugliest and least pleasing of the whole family. Leopold was not an ugly baby, only as he grew older he grew plainer, and so excessively quizzical; that is so vexatious.'[12]

Two months later, discussing the heights of her children, Victoria commented, 'Leopold was the smallest when born . . . and he is the tallest (certainly of the boys) of his age of any of you, and the ugliest', adding a few lines later, '. . . an ugly baby is a very nasty object.'[13] The queen was so ashamed of the unhappy invalid that she left him behind when the rest of the family went on holiday to Balmoral, explaining: 'Leopold still has such constant bad accidents that it would be very troublesome indeed to have him here. He walks shockingly – and is dreadfully awkward – holds himself badly as ever and his manners are despairing, – as well as his speech – which is quite dreadful.'[14]

However, by the time he was six even his hypercritical mother was beginning to recognize his intelligence. 'It is so provoking as he learns well and reads fluently'. The little praise that came was nearly always mixed with derogatory remarks, 'but his French is more like Chinese', and 'He is very clever and amusing but very absurd child'.

Leopold came much closer to his mother after the disgrace of his elder brother. Just as Victoria considered Leopold ugly and awkward, so she later bewailed Prince Edward's perceived stupidity. One of the odd medical fashions of the mid-nineteenth century was that of phrenology, the 'science' of predicting a person's moral and intellectual character by feeling the shape of the skull. The Prince Consort brought in Sir George Coombe who confirmed Victoria and Albert's worst fears by describing Edward's brain as 'feeble', 'the organs of ostentativeness, destructiveness, self esteem, etc. are all large, intellectual organs only moderately developed'. In fact Edward seems to have been a normal affectionate child saddled with inhuman and unachievable goals by his parents, where timetables filled their son's life with lessons from 8 a.m. to 7 p.m., six days a week. One lesson he never received was that on human reproduction. With no elder brothers, and deprived of friendship with boys of his own age, puberty must have been a particularly painful time.

When he was a student at Cambridge and aged twenty Edward was sent one summer vacation to an army training camp at the Curragh of Kildare, near Dublin. At the end of the ten-week course one of his fellow officers, a great-uncle of the present Lord Carrington, deposited a vivacious young actress, Nellie Clifden, in his bed. The prince enjoyed the experience and made sure Nellie came back with him to Windsor. The liaison became the gossip of the London clubs and eventually Stockmar, now Albert's private secretary, told his father. Albert became literally sick with concern. He may have feared that Edward would come to behave like Albert's own father or, worse, like Albert's brother Ernst. Certainly, Albert knew all about the sexual behaviour of the Duke of Kent's generation and perhaps he knew even more than we do today. Something must have sparked the hysterical letter he wrote his son, 'with a heavy heart upon a subject which has caused me the greatest pain I have yet felt in this life. . . . You must not, you dare not be lost! The consequences for this country, and for the world would be too dreadful.'[15] Suffering from inflamed gums and 'greatly out of sorts' Albert followed up his long letter with a train ride to Cambridge. While Prince Edward was a student at Trinity College he was forced to reside at Madingley Hall under the keen eye of General Bruce. Albert spent two hours remonstrating with his son while they walked in the cold and the rain. A contemporary record at Madingley Hall records, 'The P[rince] C[onsort] slept here on Monday Nov. 25 and he had a bad cold and cough and felt so tired after walking with his son to Dry Drayton and back by the St Neots rd (the Prince of Wales' invariable Sunday walk) that General Bruce found HRH lying on his bed when he went in to see him on his return.' Back at Windsor Albert grew sicker. Then, just as he was at his worst, a serious political crisis suddenly demanded his attention.

The first shots of the American Civil War had been fired at Charleston in January 1861. The Union forces had established a blockade and in

November of the same year they forcibly boarded a British ship, the *Trent*. Passions ran high and the Foreign Secretary, Lord John Russell, drafted an inflammatory despatch that might well have brought Britain to war with the northern states, had not Prince Albert diplomatically toned it down. 'I am so weak, I have hardly been able to hold the pen', he told his wife.

The illness worsened and on 14 December Albert died among his family. 'I bent over him & said to him, "Es ist Kleines Frauchen"[16] and he bowed his head; I asked him if he would give "ein Kuss" & he did', Victoria told her diary. Edward's escapade had coincided with the beginning of Albert's last illness and he was blamed for his father's death.

It is usually said that Albert died of typhoid spread by the ancient drains of Windsor Castle[17] but an alternative diagnosis is that he had stomach cancer, and he had certainly been ill for a long time prior to his death. No post-mortem was performed.

Victoria was forty-two. Had Albert not died she might have had at least one more child. Her devotion to him, despite the frequent quarrels, was total: 'I who felt, when those blessed Arms clasped and held tight in the sacred Hours of the night, the world seemed only to be ourselves, that nothing could part us. I felt so v[er]y secure.' England ran out of supplies of black drapery for mourning. The queen refused even to open parliament for five years. She forced her daughter Alice to select a black trousseau for her marriage to Prince Louis of Hesse in July 1862. Each night Victoria placed a grisly deathbed picture of Albert on the pillow next to her and slept clutching his nightshirt in her arms. In the morning she had hot shaving water brought to Albert's old room and his chamber pot had to be scoured daily for years after his death.

Victoria was stricken and blamed poor Bertie. Writing to her eldest daughter on 27 December, she wrote, 'Tell him [the Prussian Crown Prince] that Bertie (oh, that boy – much as I pity, I never can or shall look at him without a shudder, as you may imagine) does not know that I know all. Beloved Papa told him that I could not be told all the disgusting details (concerning Nellie Clifden) – that I try to employ and use him but I am not hopeful.' She never forgave him till the day she died. She never consulted the heir apparent on matters of state or gave him useful employment, although he had made an extremely successful visit to Canada and the USA before the Clifden affair. Deprived of significant work, he pursued women, horses and pleasure, thus fulfilling his mother's expectations. He turned to all things French in contrast to his mother's German interests. This was one of the factors which led to the 'Entente Cordiale' and the First World War.

When the Prince Consort died the young Prince Leopold was in the

French Riviera, having been sent there to avoid the English winter. He had been closer to his father than the other sons and was deeply upset. Confined to bed for months at a time, Leopold read widely – Sir Walter Scott and Shakespeare were his favourite authors – becoming the intellectual of the family.

Leopold was a little boy of nine when his eldest brother, the Prince of Wales, married. Victoria wore her widow's weeds to the wedding. 'Marry early Bertie must,' pleaded Vicky in a letter to her mother, 'if he married a nice wife that he likes, she will keep him straight.' The young lady chosen for Edward – before he could get into bed with any more actresses – was the beautiful nineteen-year-old Danish princess, Alexandra. She first visited London in 1862 – 'on approval', her parents complained. Leopold and Helen were sent to meet her boat at the docks. 'The children were greatly excited,' wrote the queen, 'Lenchen and Leopold went down, the only representatives of our family, and that poor little boy the only Prince of our family.' Alexandra gathered the nine-year-old boy up in her arms and kissed him. When Edward and Alexandra were married Edward's four-year-old nephew, Wilhelm, the future kaiser, was among the guests. When Wilhelm began to throw things across the stately choir of Westminster Abbey Leopold and his brother Alfred tried to restrain him. Wilhelm retaliated by biting both Alfred and Leopold on their legs. It must have been an occasion when Leopold's clotting factors were not grossly abnormal, and his clothing thick, as no haemorrhage or haematoma was reported. Like several of Victoria's children, Leopold was a prankster. He called his terrier bitch Vic and joked about his own disease. He was the favourite in-law of his brother Alfred's lonely wife Marie, grand duchess and daughter of Alexander II of Russia. One morning at breakfast, to gain Marie's sympathy, Leopold appeared with red-stained handkerchief and said he had had a tooth pulled. After being duly fussed over he revealed it was red paint. A vivid glimpse of his misery, and that of most haemophiliacs before Factor VIII became available, is revealed in his letters to his sister Louise:[18]

6 June 1870: I am mad with pain, so I must stop. I am in such agonies at this moment.

Four days later: I go on as usual suffering frightfully, at this moment I am in agonies of pain; my knee gets worse daily and I get more desperate daily. If this continues long I shall soon be driven to Bedlam or to Hanwell, where I shall be fortunately able to terminate a wretched existence by knocking out my brains (if I have any) on the walls; that is the brightest vision that I can picture to myself as a future.

But I must stop on account of the *awful* pain, which is torturing me.
Your wretched brother Leopold.

As Leopold matured he became known as the Scholar Prince, but his
mother continued to treat him as an invalid child. Even in his early
twenties, after he had come down from Oxford, she would send him to
his sparsely furnished room when dancing or other entertainments
occurred in case he injured himself. When he was twenty-five he
eventually stood up for himself and refused to travel to Mama's beloved
Highland home at Balmoral. What was once forbidden had become
obligatory. Victoria saw her son's independence as a threat to 'the whole
authority of the Sovereign and the Throne' and if he wouldn't go to
Scotland then she intended to order him to his 'room upstairs' in
Buckingham Palace. In fact, he went to Paris where he neither suffered a
haemorrhage nor succumbed to any other dangers of what his mother
called 'that sinful city'.

Leopold busied himself with good works, supporting the Royal
Institution for the Deaf and Dumb, and, ever-musical like his father,
became the friend of Arthur Sullivan of the Savoy Opera, and of Charles
Gounod. He was also a friend of the painter Millais and it was in Millais's
studio that he met Lillie Langtry, who was shortly to become the mistress
of his elder brother, the Prince of Wales. The prince hung a sketch of the
famous beauty over his bed but when he had his next episode of bleeding
and his mother visited him, she was furious to see Lillie's picture and, in
an unregal gesture, climbed on to the bed to remove the offending
portrait.[19]

When the Prince of Wales contracted typhoid and nearly died in 1871,
Victoria appreciated Leopold's sympathy: 'Dined with Leopold and
Beatrice. He behaves so well and shows so much feeling.' Sadly, Leopold
was never long without some new bleeding episode. In January 1875
Victoria writes again: '. . . and our dear Leopold ill. But God has been
merciful to him, and may continue to be so. . . . Went with Beatrice to
wish dear Leopold a happy new year and God knows a different one from
to the one that is past, nearly eight months of which he has spent unable
to walk and a great part a complete invalid.'

In fact, the new year did not bring relief. Leopold also had typhoid but
recovered quickly. 'Leopold doing so well that Dr Marshall said he had
nothing to report! Alas! unlucky words, which often precede a new
illness. After lunch much upset at hearing from Dr Marshall that Leopold
had a haemorrhage from bowels which is most distressing. He had sent
for Dr Hoffmeister and Sir William Jenner. Leopold himself was in
terrible distress about it. Went to see poor Leopold who was lying flat on

his back, very quiet, very pale, and looking very sad. It upset me very much to see him like that.'[20]

Another account of the same episode occurs in a letter to the prime minister: 'The Queen must thank Mr Gladstone for his kind letter of the 21st and for his enquiries after poor Prince Leopold, who has been a cause of great anxiety to her ever since the 21st December. But he passed through the typhoid fever most easily, and withstood one bad symptom so that the terrible attack of haemorrhage coming on just when he was considered quite convalescent was doubly distressing. Thank God, he is now going on very favourably, and has shown his usual great vitality.'[21]

This seems to have been the low point in his life and over the following years attacks were rare. In 1877 he became one of the queen's private secretaries and obtained a Foreign Office cabinet key giving access to state papers. This was the more remarkable because the queen never allowed the disgraced Prince of Wales, heir to the throne, to see state papers until the day she died. In 1879 it was suggested that Leopold should represent the queen at the Centenary Exhibition in Australia but the queen vetoed the proposal, writing to the then prime minister the Earl of Beaconsfield (Disraeli), '. . . she cannot bring herself to consent to send her very delicate son, who has been four or five times at death's door, who is never hardly a few months without being laid up, so great a distance.' For once Victoria's control of her children's affairs was justified. In 1880 he did visit Canada and the USA. Canadian opinion favoured his appointment as governor-general and he was keen to accept the post, but the boy who hadn't been allowed to go to Balmoral was now too valuable to be allowed to leave his mother's side. He was now a trusted adviser and intermediary between Victoria and leading politicians of the day, advising on the creation of new governments and on religious appointments: 'Leopold had previously seen Lord Hartington and had brought to the Queen intelligence of the impossibility of forming a Government with Mr Gladstone. . . . We are now playing into the hands of the Russians. The Queen feels particularly aggrieved as Mr Gladstone assured Prince Leopold on coming into office, that the Queen need be under no apprehension as to foreign affairs.'[22]

When the Archbishop of Canterbury was ill and not expected to recover the Dean of Windsor wrote, 'now as to the successor, Mr Gladstone was immediately in the field . . . and the proposition he made . . . coincided with the advice of Prince Leopold.'[23]

The ugly duckling had now become a swan, if a lame one. At this time he began to disseminate sensible ideas in education. His own had been erratic but as an invalid he may have read more widely than if he had had an orthodox education. Too ill for regular schooling he attended Christ

Church Oxford, leaving with an honorary Doctorate of Civil Law. He advocated the expansion of universities and technical training, as well as establishing a Royal Conservatory of Music. He became a Freemason.

In 1881 Victoria created Leopold Duke of Albany and the now mature ugly duckling began looking for a bride. He dreamed of the lively and beautiful seventeen-year-old Frances Maynard, stepdaughter of the Earl of Rosslyn, but she fell in love and married Leopold's equerry, the future Earl of Warwick. She was to succeed Lillie Langtry as a mistress of the Prince of Wales.[24] Leopold turned instead to Princess Helena of Waldeck, sister of the Dutch queen. His mother noted in her diary: '*1882 7th April*: Dear Leopold's birthday . . . How often has his poor young life hung by a thread and how many and wearisome illnesses has he not [sic] recovered from! Though the idea of his marrying makes me anxious, still, he has found a girl, so charming, ready to accept and love him in spite of his ailments. I hope he may be happy and carefully watched over.'

They married later that month. The queen gave the newly weds Claremont House, where Charlotte had died and great-uncle Leopold had lived when in England. Shortly before the wedding Leopold was incapacitated with an episode of severe bleeding after slipping on an orange peel in a French hotel and on his wedding day the queen noted in her journal, 'It is very trying to see the dear boy on the important day of his life still lame and shaking'. He was bedridden a second time at the birth of his daughter Alice in February 1883. Victoria had also injured her leg at the same time and when she visited her parturient daughter-in-law and sick son she wrote 'and I came as a third helpless creature, it had quite a ludicrous effect'.

While Helena was carrying their second child, the royal doctors sent Leopold to Cannes to escape the unusually severe winter. His anxious mother noted: '*21st Feb 1884*: Leopold started for Cannes to stay at the Villa Merada, Capt. Percival's little villa there, as he thinks he requires a little change and warmth but he is going alone as Helene's health doesn't allow her to travel just now. I think it a pity he should leave her.'

Here Leopold fell on a staircase of his hotel and died of a brain haemorrhage a few hours later. Victoria wrote, '. . . there was another cipher coming from Mr Royle, saying he had to announce that my darling Leopold had died at 3.30 this morning quite suddenly in his sleep from the breaking of a blood vessel in his head. Am utterly crushed.'

Helena's second child, Charles Edward Leopold, was born after Leopold's death in France. As the gene for haemophilia can only be carried on the X chromosome, which boys inherit from their mother, he had to be free of the disease. He lived to 1954 and had six children, all of whom, in turn, were without any risk of haemophilia or being carriers of

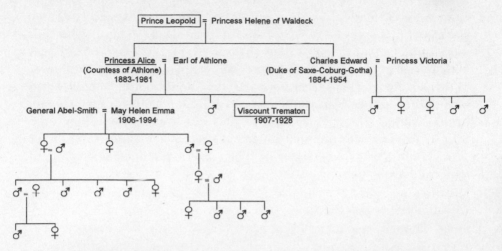

The family of Prince Leopold. Carriers of haemophilia underlined, haemophiliacs boxed.

the disease. In 1900 he inherited the old dukedom of Saxe-Coburg and Gotha from his uncle the Duke of Edinburgh and Saxe-Coburg: the Duke of Edinburgh's only son had died childless the previous year and the Duke of Connaught, the next in line, had wisely renounced his claim in order to remain British. Charles Edward enthusiastically threw in his lot in his ancestral homeland, rising to the rank of General in the German Imperial Army. When the German Empire collapsed in 1918 he was forced to abdicate his dukedom but he went on to play a key role in Hitler's rise to power, and this is a story we will return to in Chapter 10.

During her reign Queen Victoria came to rule the largest empire the world had seen or was to see; more cities were founded in her name than Alexander the Great dreamed of; her engineers undertook works more ambitious than Rameses had raised and her troops fought on frontiers the Romans and Persians never reached. She was also the carrier of a lethal gene. Just as she had been manipulated to mate with a particular man, so she in turn chose the brides and grooms for her own children. What she could not do was to control the genetics of haemophilia although, as we will see in the next chapter, the general principles of the inheritance of haemophilia were understood during Victoria's childbearing years. Unfortunately, the relevant scientific knowledge did not penetrate to royal circles and the uncontrolled spread of the gene among her grandchildren was to change the course of world history.

Would history have been different if Victoria's eldest son, Edward Prince of Wales, had been the ugly duckling and Leopold had been a healthy child? Leopold became president of the Royal Society of Letters and vice-president of the Society of Arts. The contrast with his elder brother the Prince of Wales, whose interests rarely extended beyond wine, women, gambling and song was remarkable. Or what if Vicky had been a carrier and perhaps her son, the future kaiser, a haemophiliac, while Alice's family had been normal? There might not have been world war in 1914 or a Russian revolution in 1917. Or what if the unfortunate haemophiliac Leopold had fallen on his head five months earlier, or if Charles Edward had inherited his father's lethal gene and died young? There might not have been war in 1939 and thirty million people might have lived a lot longer.

CHAPTER FIVE

The Bleeders

Haemophilia, the disease carried by Queen Victoria, which was manifest in Prince Leopold and passed on by two of her daughters, was well recognized in her day. However, the nature of the disease, both genetically and physiologically, has only been understood since her death. The medical knowledge we have today enables us both to ameliorate most of the disease's painful and life-threatening consequences and to ask some novel historical questions.

Until very recently, haemophilia was, in the words of one twentieth-century victim of the disease, 'an everlasting bloody nuisance'. In order to understand the condition it is necessary to understand why and how blood clots. Only the smallest animals can get by without a circulatory system. All other animals need a liquid carried around the body in a system of pipes to transport the products of digestion, waste materials, oxygen and carbon dioxide. In mammals like ourselves, the cardiovascular system works at relatively high pressure, carrying blood at high speed to every organ through literally miles of blood vessels and capillaries. Over a lifetime the human heart pumps the equivalent of about 300,000 tons of blood through the body and lungs – enough to fill the world's largest supertanker – yet even a slow leak is potentially disastrous as we only have about eight pints of blood at any one time.

All living animals face a profound problem in that some injury is almost inevitable, whether this is massive trauma breaking a major blood vessel or minor damage to relatively few capillaries. An automatic repair system is essential, but evolution has had to produce a mechanism that won't be triggered accidentally, blocking essential blood vessels, yet will respond quickly to localized damage. Needless to say the system is necessarily complex and it has taken a great deal of scientific time and effort to understand how human blood clots.

Throughout much of Victoria's reign the nature of haemophilia was in doubt. Some pathologists thought it was due to a defect in the blood vessels and a follower of the phrenologist Gall said it was the male equivalent of menstruation. However, in 1891 Wright showed that the blood of haemophiliacs took longer to clot, when stored in a glass tube, than that of a normal person.

Scientists had already demonstrated that blood contains a dissolved protein which they called fibrinogen. When a clot forms it is converted to a tangled network of fibrin, plugging any hole through which blood might escape. The conversion of dissolved fibrinogen into solid fibrin is rather like the action of rennet on milk, and we now know that an enzyme called thrombin is necessary for a fibrinogen to turn to fibrin. The origin of thrombin is the most complicated part of the whole story and only after a hundred years of patient laboratory work and meticulous observation of patients with various clotting disorders is the full picture being finally understood. Like a gourmet recipe, at least ten ingredients are needed to form thrombin, among them a factor from damaged tissue itself, blood platelets (the tiny scraps of cellular material that are even smaller than the thirty billion red blood cells in our body) and a number of enzymes and their precursors, such as prothrombin, and other factors. If one link in the chain of reactions necessary for blood clotting is broken then exceptionally serious consequences follow. Haemophilia (literally the love of blood) is a disease in which one link in the chain in the formation of thrombin is broken. It is an inborn, hereditary disease and it is found in horses, dogs and some primates, including humans. Dogs and horses with the disease generally die within three to six months of birth, but human beings with the disease, like Prince Leopold, can live to be adults.

Although haemophiliacs are born with the disease, they do not bleed severely during birth or when the cord is cut. It is not known why. The baby, however, may bruise easily and when he begins to crawl may bleed into the knee and elbow joints. Unlike the normal person, relatively slight damage, perhaps not even recognized by the individual, may set off an episode of haemorrhage. Once the child begins to walk bleeding incidents become more common. Bleeding may be external or internal and can take place from practically any site, including the nose, mouth, gums, intestine, brain, kidney, skin or joints. Bleeding into the joints is common and excruciatingly painful. It gives rise to a hard, warm swelling of the joint, restricting movements of the limb and, as the blood is absorbed, causes a bodily fever. The victim is afraid of even the smallest movement and an accidental jarring of the bed can make a child scream with pain. Eventually, the blood in the joint will clot, but then it is partially replaced by fibrous tissue and repeated damage leads to severe deformities and lifelong handicap.

The problems caused by haemophilia are not the same for all individuals, and may change during the life of the sufferer. Victims of the disease recognize 'bleeding phases', even though there is no physical explanation of why the condition should get better or worse. Some hardly recover from one episode before starting the next. Some may bleed internally, whereas others do not, although all respond severely to trauma. A tooth extraction, for example, can lead to exceptionally prolonged bleeding. Occasionally, a patient may bleed into his muscles or loose tissue under the scalp and produce enormous swellings containing literally pints of blood. 'It doesn't take much to bruise an over-ripe tomato', commented one haemophiliac before modern therapies were available, 'and that is what haemophilia is like.' A medically qualified victim of the disease, writing about his own life in a medical journal in 1949, described episodes of bleeding as merely a dramatic worsening of a miserable condition and even when he was 'well' he had to live with contractures of his muscles, nerve pain, damaged joints, impaired circulation, anaemia and 'almost constant pain'.

Haemorrhage into the brain, as occurred with Prince Leopold, is one of the most serious complications of haemophilia. Children with haemophilia are usually forbidden to play sports, but may do so surreptitiously. If what appears to be a mild head injury occurs, they may be afraid to tell their parents, only to become unconscious later and perhaps die. Living with a painful, incurable, unpredictable disease may make great demands on the sufferer and on the parents, especially as families may hand down a legacy of misery and despair experienced by earlier generations. It is difficult for a mother not to be over protective and a son passive and overdependent. But surrounded by 'don't do this' and 'don't do that', a child, particularly an adolescent, may take on a dare-devil, fatalistic attitude. Some haemophiliacs seek out potentially dangerous situations, driving dangerously, or, in one contemporary case, even deciding to be a butcher. The young tsarevitch had to be left behind at Tobolsk for a while, under the care of his sisters, after his parents had been moved to their final prison at Ekaterinburg. The daughter of the family physician, Dr Botkin, later recalled that while there he used to play a wild game, sliding down the stairs from the second floor in a wooden boat. The crash made the inhabitants of the house cover their ears. 'It was as if he were trying to prove something to himself.'[1] In the nineteenth century haemophiliacs had even more difficult times than those alive today. One artisan contemporary of Prince Leopold became a cobbler and died of haemorrhage twenty days after pricking his gum with a nail, which like all cobblers, he held between his lips. Others died from accidents involving horses or farm animals. It is possible that fear and depression react directly on blood clotting and, conversely, reassurance and a calm commanding person in charge of treatment may hasten recovery.

One of the best-documented families of haemophiliacs lived in the Swiss canton of Valais, near the source of the Rhine. The church registers of the little town of Tenna record that, 'Albrecht Gartmann, legitimate son of the late Hans Gartmann, born 11th June 1699, died in 1730 on the 26th of September at 31 years of age, after all the blood flowed out of him'. Again in the same locality a few years later. 'Samuel Walther was buried here on the 8th of May 1741. He was during 33 years a pious and honourable Councillor, lived for 26 years, 5 months, 16 days with his second wife, bled 7 days and nights continuously in the mouth and died therefore when he was 65 years and 3 months old.'

The Tenna bleeders have been followed over seven generations, and five out of twenty males had children, including twenty-three daughters, each of whom would have been a carrier. There are many records of nineteenth-century haemophiliacs marrying and having children, including Prince Leopold. One severely affected man married twice and another married his dead brother's widow. One German haemophiliac was conscripted into the Franco-Prussion War and survived being wounded in battle.

From families like the Tenna bleeders the peculiar characteristics of the inheritance of haemophilia were empirically elucidated but the complicated nature of sex-linked inheritance prevented any understanding of the details of the mechanism.

The earliest historical references to the disease relate to circumcision. A second-century Jewish writer gave permission for a woman not to have her third son circumcised after her first two died from the ritual. Another rabbi exempted a woman whose sister had sons who died after circumcision, demonstrating an emerging understanding of the inheritance of the disease. Unfortunately, these examples of rabbinical advice were not always followed and one nineteenth-century Ukrainian Jewish family lost ten sons from circumcision.

The great tenth-century Arabian physician Maimonides described a village where several of the male children bled to death, and in the eighteenth century a number of family trees of haemophiliacs were drawn up. An anonymous German writer gave a good description of the disease in 1793, and in 1803 John C. Otto (1775–1845), an American physician working in Philadelphia, gave what has become a classic description of the disease in a family whose history he was able to trace back to settlers who landed in America in 1720.

Like several hereditary diseases, the physical basis of haemophilia has become increasingly well understood over the years and this in turn has led to improved therapies. Insight into the physical basis of the disease has been closely linked to knowledge of genetics and of the chemical structure of genetic material.

The laws of genetics were first unravelled by a quiet monk who had failed his examinations to become a high school teacher, but who went on to conduct elegantly simple experiments in the pollination of sweet peas in a monastery garden. Father Gregor Mendel was born in Moravia, a province of the Austro-Hungarian Empire, three years after Queen Victoria. He chose to study sweet peas because they were easy to fertilize and possessed easily distinguished characteristics which appeared to be inherited. He demonstrated that inherited characteristics could be explained by postulating discrete factors (genes) which came from each parent and were distributed to the offspring in predictable ways. The biochemical structure of the gene was discovered a hundred years later at Cambridge University, England. Working in temporary accommodation, Francis Crick and a visiting American colleague, James Watson, used X-ray crystallography, a knowledge of the architectural rules of biochemistry and, like Mendel, a good share of genius, to arrive at an understanding of the way in which molecules carry genetic information.

All living animals are composed of cells. Between the work of Mendel and Crick it had been established that all cells have a nucleus containing chromosomes which, under the microscope, can be seen to split into identical groups at each cell division so that each cell retains a full complement. In the human being there are twenty-three pairs of chromosomes. In each pair one will have been contributed from the father's sperm and one from the mother's egg. When eggs and sperm are formed the number of chromosomes is halved so that at fertilization a full complement is restored.

When sperm or eggs are formed, the chromosomes go through an important phase when the pairs line up with each other and packages of genetic material are exchanged between individual pairs. We then pass on one chromosome of each pair to join with that of our partner in the production of the next generation. It is for this reason that our children share the genetic characteristics of the two parents and ultimately of the four grandparents, and so on back through our family trees.

The gender of an animal is determined by only one pair of chromosomes. In mammals like ourselves, females possess a pair of similar chromosomes called XX chromosomes while males have a dissimilar pair consisting of an X chromosome derived from the mother and a smaller Y chromosome derived from the father. The egg before fertilization contains one X chromosome as well as the twenty-two other chromosomes. Sperm contains twenty-two chromosomes together with either an X or Y chromosome. When two X chromosomes come together after fertilization, then a female is conceived, whereas an X and Y chromosome together will produce a male (see page 50).

Inherited characteristics may either be traced to one particular gene or may, as in the case of height, depend on the interaction of many genes.

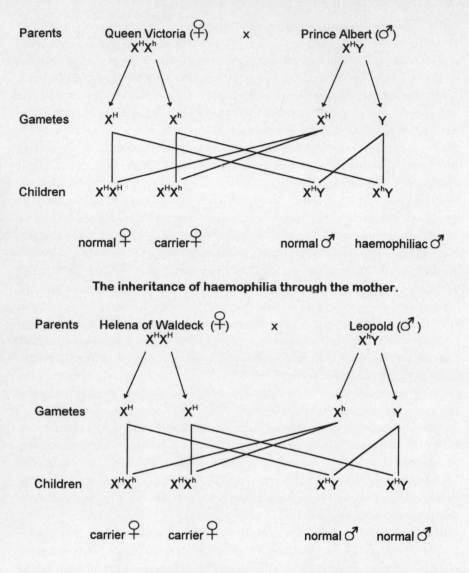

The inheritance of haemophilia through the mother.

The inheritance of haemophilia through the father.
(Note that Leopold and Helene had only 2 children, one girl and one boy).

X^H represents the normal chromosome, X^h the X chromosome carrying the defect causing haemophilia and Y, the Y chromosome.

The inheritance of haemophilia.

Some inherited factors not associated with sexual differentiation itself are carried on the sex chromosomes. This is the case in haemophilia where one of the genes controlling blood-clotting is carried on the X chromosome.

The clinical understanding of haemophilia and scientific understanding of genetics came together slowly. Once it became clear that the defect causing haemophilia was situated on the X chromosome, it explained why a woman could be a carrier but not a haemophiliac. If one of her chromosomes carried the abnormal gene then the other would be normal and would compensate for the defect. If she had a boy then he might inherit either her normal X chromosome, in which case the child would be unaffected and in no danger of passing the disease to his offspring, or he might inherit the abnormal X chromosome and manifest the disease. Being male he would have no second X chromosome to compensate for the deficiency. If an affected mother had a daughter, that daughter might inherit her mother's abnormal X chromosome together with a normal X chromosome from her father, in which case she would also be a carrier. On average, half her sons would have the disease and half her daughters would carry it to the next generation. A haemophiliac man, on the other hand, if he lives and has children, will transmit the disease to every daughter, who will be carriers, but will pass on only the Y chromosome to his sons so that they will be perfectly normal. One of the cruel aspects of the disease is that daughters of mothers who carry the gene do not know if they are carriers themselves, even if they have several normal sons. If they in turn have daughters the disease may reappear in their grandsons. Some forms of colour-blindness are also determined by genes on that part of the X chromosome that is missing from the Y chromosome. Colour-blindness is therefore more common in males but as the defects are relatively frequent and not fatal they also occur in some females.

Queen Victoria's descendants are a classic example of the inheritance of haemophilia. Two of her daughters were carriers who passed the gene to some of their sons, who were affected, and to some of their daughters who became new carriers. Prince Leopold, who was the only son of Victoria to manifest the disease, produced a daughter who was inevitably a carrier and a son who had to be free of the disease.

But how does haemophilia first arise? In order to answer that question, it is necessary to know something of the structure of genes and the nature of mutations. The genetic material which determines the structure and function of our bodies is carried as a simple biochemical code on strands of DNA. DNA is a long molecule consisting of hundreds of thousands of atoms. The molecule has a spiral thread-like structure and an ability to reproduce itself accurately so that the genetic code can be transmitted from generation to generation. If it were possible to take apart one living human cell and extract all the DNA and join the individual strands end to end, it would be about one metre long. However, in the microscopic living cell, the DNA is tightly parcelled into individual packages of genetic material which, in turn, are put together as chromosomes. The information in the chromosomes is transmitted to the rest of the cell by a complex companion molecule to DNA called RNA (ribonucleic acid) and finally translated once more into the building blocks of protein and other molecules that make up the cell and its secretions. This whole process involves millions of interactions at the molecular level but takes place rapidly, each strand of DNA being read about sixty times a second.

Whenever a cell divides, every atom on each strand of DNA must be copied exactly. Inevitably, errors occur, but there are a number of molecular processes for identifying and eliminating most mistakes. Certain chemicals and radiation, such as X-rays or cosmic rays, can damage DNA. A mistake or mutation in the DNA in the cells that will form the eggs or sperm has great potential significance.

Occasionally a mutation leads to some extra fitness and then an animal carrying such a beneficial mutation has very slightly more chance of succeeding in the struggle for existence than its brothers and sisters. Such mutations are the basis of the tiny steps by which evolution has taken place, but most mutations are so harmful that development never begins, or if it does it soon ends in a spontaneous abortion. (Abortion, although an unhappy event if the pregnancy is wanted, is a natural, necessary process that overcomes these and other errors of development and many spontaneous abortions involve embryos with chromosomal and other errors.)

In biological terms, haemophilia is a relatively mild mutation, compatible with life, and therefore can be passed on to the next generation. The fact that women have two X chromosomes and the defect only occurs in one, helps protect her against the otherwise certain death that would accompany childbirth or menstruation. There have been only two or three girls in the whole of medical history, who were the offspring of cousin marriages, who were unlucky enough to inherit two X chromosomes from both sides of the same family, each with the gene for haemophilia. They manifested the same symptoms as male haemophiliacs suffer and invariably died at puberty, when they began to menstruate.

In the nineteenth century the treatment of haemophilia was often even worse than the disease. Sometimes haemophiliac patients were bled deliberately, like everyone else. One haemophiliac died from the application of leeches, another from cupping and others from the deliberate opening of their veins. All too often in the history of medicine physicians have shown a tragic loyalty to current practices, as did the nineteenth-century surgeon who opened the knee joint of a haemophilic to let out the internal bleeding: not only did he kill that patient but he went on to try the same operation on another luckless victim, who also died. Even as late as 1894, the famous doctor William Osler, whom Victoria had knighted for his services to medicine, was still recommending blood-letting as a treatment for haemophilia.

Nevertheless, some early scientists did deduce that haemophiliacs must lack some special substance and therefore suggested blood transfusion as a treatment, not to replace blood lost by haemorrhage, but to make good whatever abnormality was preventing normal blood-clotting. Within three years of Queen Victoria's coronation, and long before Leopold was born, Samuel Armstrong Lance, a London physician, treated a twelve-year old bleeder with a blood transfusion. However, the need to give a patient blood of their own group was not recognized in the nineteenth century so transfusion reactions usually frustrated treatment, and it was only from the 1930s that blood transfusion became a real option in treating haemophilia.

In the 1940s the constituent of normal blood that makes good the deficiency in a haemophiliac was isolated and called anti-haemophiliac globulin. Nowadays, it is called Factor VIII – a name that underlines the many critical steps in the cascade of events involved in blood-clotting. It is a large molecule composed of hundreds of thousands of atoms, manufactured in the liver and passed into the bloodstream. A similar molecule is present in a haemophiliac's blood but it must have some tiny abnormality that stops it working. Abnormalities in the way in which the atoms are arranged in large biological molecules are the cause of several diseases. For example, sickle cell anaemia, which afflicts some blacks, is caused by a difference of a few atoms in the haemoglobulin molecule that makes the molecules fold in an abnormal way, deforming red cells. Blood-clotting involves many steps and factors, so there are other forms of haemophilia apart from Factor VIII deficiency. Some of these rare forms of haemophilia are named after the doctor who described them, as in Von Willebrand's disease, or after the patients in which they were first described, as in Christmas and Stuart disease.

In the 1950s and '60s, through the work of Brinkhouse in Chapel Hill, North Carolina, and others, it became possible to concentrate Factor VIII in various ways, including freezing blood plasma. Factor VIII is easy to store and a haemophiliac can inject himself at home. Factor VIII can bring about a near-miracle in the life of a person with haemophilia and Russian history and world history might have been very different if Factor VIII had been available earlier in this century.

To secure enough Factor VIII to be effective, it must be extracted from literally thousands of blood donations – fortunately the blood remains perfectly usable after Factor VIII has been removed. However, in addition to concentrating Factor VIII, the process also pools some of the infections donors may have been carrying. In the early 1980s, when Aids first appeared and before the nature of the disease was understood, many doses of Factor VIII became infected with the human immunodeficiency virus – the cause of Aids. It was a cruel twist of fate and in many places the majority of people with haemophilia now carry the virus and more and more are dying of Aids. By the middle 1980s ways were devised to test for the Aids virus and Factor VIII is again safe to use. However, a great deal of damage occurred in the brief years when the spread of the disease was not understood. Some school-age haemophiliacs with the Aids virus have been treated as lepers in their own communities, even though they pose no danger of infection to others. On very rare occasions infected haemophiliacs passed the disease unknowingly to their wives through sexual intercourse and then, when pregnancy supervenes, there is also a risk that the virus may be transmitted to the infant.

It is now possible to make Factor VIII without having to collect it from blood plasma. This is done by genetic engineering – the practice of isolating critical sections of the DNA message and programming cultured mammalian cells or bacteria to produce the associated unique proteins. At first sight it would seem an almost unachievably complex task but bacteria and even human cells can be grown by the billion in the laboratory, and techniques are being developed to select out desired characteristics. Now, although haemophilia has not been cured, the ways of helping those who suffer from this unhappy disease have improved to the point where they may lead an almost normal life.

It is also now possible to find out whether or not a woman is a carrier. If she only has one X chromosome making Factor VIII she has measurably less in her blood. Women from haemophiliac families who may be carriers can now be advised on their chances of passing the disease on to their children. It is also possible that quite soon screening of pregnant women at risk as carriers will become common. It is already possible in the laboratory to identify genes associated with haemophilia from foetal cells collected in the tenth week of pregnancy, and ante-natal testing is likely to become easier with the passage of time. Women who carry the gene will then be able, if they wish, to abort any offspring with haemophilia, or who are carriers of the disease.

However, modern scientific insights also prompt some questions about the past: where did Queen Victoria's gene come from?

CHAPTER SIX

Mutation or Bastard?

Haemophilia is a dramatic, easily identified, lifelong affliction. The history of the royal houses of Europe is recorded in meticulous detail, both in public records and in innumerable pages of gossip found in private letters, magazines and newspapers. The course of the gene in Victoria's descendants is easily traced; its origin is much more obscure. The Duke of Kent's history is well documented and, whatever his defects, he was certainly not a haemophiliac. The gene Victoria transmitted has several possible origins. Her mother, Victoire, might have been a carrier herself; it might have arisen as a new mutation in Victoire; it might have been inherited from a haemophiliac father who was not the Duke of Kent; or the mutation might have occurred in the X chromosome of the Duke of Kent. These explanations will be examined in turn. The gene could not have come from the Prince Consort Albert as haemophiliac fathers cannot have haemophiliac sons, yet Leopold, Victoria's youngest son, was a haemophiliac.

Was Victoire a carrier? Victoire had a son and daughter by her first marriage. The son was normal but Victoire could still have been a carrier, in which case one might expect to find cases of haemophilia among her ancestors. Her family tree on her mother's side has been put together in exceptional detail and a deliberate search has been made for haemophilia. The relevant data still exists, although in an unpublished form. The story of why the work was done and how it has survived is an odd byway in medical history.

The writings of Darwin and speculation about the reasons for the different achievements of various groups of people stimulated an intense interest in all aspects of human heredity. Francis Galton, Charles Darwin's first cousin, was a prolific writer and thinker in the area he called eugenics – 'The science which deals with all influences that improve the inborn qualities of a race'. Galton played a leading role in demonstrating that each person has a unique pattern of fingerprints, and he was the first person to study identical and non-identical twins as a way of unravelling hereditary from environmental influences. One of his more original researches was into the efficacy of prayer, arguing that as the monarch and archbishops were prayed for every day in church, then if prayer were efficacious they should live longer than the average citizen. Galton's statistical analysis showed that they did not. One of the first products of the Eugenics Society was a series entitled 'Treasury of Human Inheritance' and in 1911 William Bullock and Paul Fildes brought out the first volume, *Haemophilia*.[1] Bullock and Fildes surveyed every article they could find on haemophilia from Britain, continental Europe and the United States and produced numerous well-documented family trees setting out the inheritance of the disease.

Queen Victoria is not mentioned in the Treasury volume, but her case was too obvious to miss and Bullock spent a great deal of time in private producing a handwritten genealogy that traces Queen Victoria's mother's ancestry back over eight generations. It is written in Indian ink in Bullock's careful, round hand, on two linen scrolls 7 ft 6 in long, attached to 5 ft 6 in wooden rollers. We found these tied with red tape, and housed in a carefully morticed wooden box kept on the top shelf of the librarian's office of the Royal Society of Medicine Library in Wimpole Street, London. The scrolls are unsigned but we checked the handwriting against letters and manuscripts signed by Bullock now in the Eugenic Society papers in the Wellcome History of Medicine Library in London. The first scroll carries the names of about 500 individuals. Victoire, Victoria and Victoria's descendants are listed and the haemophiliacs and haemophilia carriers clearly marked.

If Queen Victoria's mother had carried the haemophilia gene then her son, Charles, by her first marriage to the Prince of Leiningen, would have had a 50 per cent chance of manifesting the disease. Charles (1804–56) was a normal, healthy male. Her daughter, Feodora (1807–72), who would have a 50 per cent chance of being a carrier, married Ernest IV, Prince of Hohenlohe Langenburg, and had five children. None of the three sons of this second generation – Charles (born 1829), Herman (born 1832) and Victor (born 1833) – showed any signs of haemophilia. There is still a chance that Feodora might have inherited the gene and passed it to Victoire's granddaughters, Adelheid (born 1835) and Feodora (born 1839). Adelheid married Frederick, Duke of Holstein (1829–80) and bore him four daughters and three sons. The eldest daughter, Augusta (born 1858), married into the German royal family, becoming the wife of Kaiser Wilhelm, of whom more later. The second child, Caroline Matilda (born 1860) married a duke of Holstein and a third daughter, Louise Sophie (born 1866), a duke of Prussia. The last daughter, yet another Feodora, died in infancy in 1874. Caroline was to have nine children, yet again no trace of haemophilia is apparent in any of her children or grandchildren, now four and five generations removed from Victoire. Two of Adelheid's sons, Ernest Bernhard and Frederick, grew to be healthy adults, while Ernst Gunther died in infancy, although there is no suggestion that haemophilia was the cause. Finally, Victoire's youngest granddaughter, Adelheid's sister Feodora, the last child of Feodora and Ernest (born 1839), had two healthy sons.

In short, Queen Victoria's half-brother and -sister did not carry the haemophilia gene. Of course, with a 50 per cent chance of each carrying the disease, there is a one in four possibility that they might have escaped even if their mother did carry it. While the gene was not present in Victoria's half-sister and half-brother, what of her mother's antecedents?

The second of Bullock's scrolls in the Royal Society of Medicine Library covers Victoire's ancestors over seventeen generations. One, Ludovicus II, was called 'Ohne Haut' (literally 'skinless' or 'hideless') and lived in Hungary from 1506 to 1526. He himself left no descendants. However, his sister Anna (born 1503), the wife of King Ferdinand I, had fifteen children who married into several royal lines and who included among their descendants Charles II of Spain (1661–1700), Louis XV of France (1710–44) and Charles I of England. Among this whole vast, historically visible family, William Bullock found no bleeders. Neither did he among any of the ancestors of Ludovicus II, whom he followed back to the thirteenth century. It must be concluded that however Ludovicus got the epithet 'Ohne Haut' it was not because of haemophilia.

Information for the Royal Society of Medicine scroll was collected within a few years of Queen Victoria's death. The scholarship involved was never published because Bullock failed to find a bleeder among Victoria's ancestors and thus deepened the puzzle of the royal disease. If there are no haemophiliacs among Victoria's ancestors, then either the gene was a new mutation, or Victoria was not the child of Edward, Duke of Kent. Both explanations appear at first sight unlikely; the historical question is which explanation is the least implausible.

It is possible to calculate the chance of a mutation for haemophilia in Queen Victoria or her parents within broad limits. The disease tends to disappear eventually, for the simple reason that haemophiliacs fail to reproduce as frequently as other people. Victims sometimes die before puberty and those who do survive may be crippled and, overall, are less likely to marry and father children. On average the survival rate of the haemophiliac gene is somewhere between two-thirds or three-quarters per generation, so a quarter or more of all haemophiliacs are due to new mutations. In the early nineteenth century the birth and death rates were both higher, but the proportions may have been similar. In the USA there are approximately 10,000 haemophiliacs and this number is roughly constant. If a genetic disease is rare but consistently present, then every gene lost, on average, must be replaced by a newly mutated one. Based on this argument it is estimated that the mutation for haemophilia occurs between 1 in 25,000 and 1 in 100,000 people per generation. So, while the individual with the condition has a 1 in 2 chance of getting the disease if his mother is a carrier, he has only 1 in 25,000 to 1 in 100,000 chances of developing the disease as a result of a mutation in his mother's ovary, or if his mother were a carrier, in his grandfather's testes. If Victoria's mother was not a carrier or the Duke of Kent really was Victoria's father, the mutation is most likely to have occurred in the Duke of Kent. Mutations and chromosome damage increase slowly with age and the Duke was over fifty when Victoria was conceived. This would have increased the chances of a natural mutation slightly.

In the case of Queen Victoria, we have an interesting detective problem. One in 25,000 is a rare event; it is not impossible, but has about the same probability as being killed by lightning. By contrast, extramarital sexual relations, perhaps particularly among eighteenth- and nineteenth-century European aristocrats, were very considerably more common.

As we have seen, the Duchess of Kent's marriage was not a love match. Edward courted his bride partly with the intention of meeting some of his £200,000 debt, and partly to produce an heir to the throne. Indeed, soon after Princess Charlotte's death the *Morning Chronicle* reported on 'the intended marriage of the truly amiable and excellent Duke of Kent with a Princess of the House of Saxe-Coburg, one of the sisters of Prince Leopold'.

Edward was a rather old fifty, pot-bellied with dyed, receding hair, while Victoire, Princess of Leiningen, was thirty-two. Before their marriage they had only met once. More importantly, the duke had previously lived with a mistress for many years. Madame de St Laurent had been procured for the duke's pleasure in 1790 and he had been faithful to her for twenty-seven years. Yet significantly for our story, she never seems to have borne him any children. Was she or the Duke of Kent sterile?

To answer this question we need to trace the lives of both the Duke of Kent and his mistress prior to the establishment of their liaison in 1791. It is difficult to track down illegitimate children in any age and in the case of early nineteenth-century royalty, malicious commentators were as likely to invent fictitious offspring as parents were to conceal them. Any test of Edward Duke of Kent's fertility is further complicated by the efforts Queen Victoria and her mother appear to have made to obliterate the record of Kent's long liaison with Madame de St Laurent. Missing records and odd financial payments, which two centuries later can no longer be accounted for, have encouraged the suggestion that the duke and his beloved mistress had up to seven children. However, Mollie

Gillen[2] makes a convincing case that the twenty-seven years of partnership were sterile. In a world where the duke's younger brother, the Duke of Clarence, could have his bastard children received by the queen, there seems no reason why Kent would have been reticent in according recognition to any issue of an obviously loving relationship. Canadian traditions that the duke left several illegitimate children, or that he selected a family called Whyte to provide shelter for Madame de St Laurent and her children, are shown by Gillen to be false; both claims can be demolished by careful scrutiny of existing Canadian and British records. If the union with Madame de St Laurent was sterile was it the duke or his mistress who was infertile?

Thomas Creevey, a member of Parliament, recorded the following conversation with the Duke of Kent, held in 1817, when he was contemplating marrying Victoire:

> . . . It is now seven and twenty years that Madame de St Laurent and I have lived together; we are of the same age, and have been in all climates, and in all difficulties together; and you may well imagine, Mr Creevey, the pang it will occasion me to part with her. . . . Before anything is proceeded with in this matter, I shall hope and expect to see justice done by the Nation and the Ministers to Madame de St Laurent. She is of very good family and has never been an actress, and I am the first and only person who ever lived with her . . .

Taken at its face value this would suggest that Madame de St Laurent was a virgin when she met the duke and, in turn, must raise the suspicion that perhaps the duke was infertile. However, the actual history of both the duke and his mistress is a bit more complicated than the duke himself romantically described to Creevey.

While it seems certain that the duke and Madame de St Laurent had no children, neither came to the relationship a virgin. In January 1790 the duke, who was then just past his twenty-second birthday, returned prematurely from studies in Geneva, had a stormy meeting with his father, George III, and was dispatched to Gibraltar, all in under a month. The *General Evening Post* wrote:

> The return of an Illustrious Gentleman to this country has, it is said, excited some displeasure in very Great Persons. Permission was not given for this visit, and the departure of the young gentleman, it is thought, will be the necessary step to appease the resentment! An incident of a pathetic nature operated in a degree to induce him to leave Geneva: a young lady, of French birth, is said to have engaged a

share of his attachment, and after an intimacy of some duration, she appeared in a state of pregnancy. Her death happened a short time since; she died in childbed, and left a charming little girl behind her. During her indisposition, the unremitted [sic] care and solicitude shewn by her admirer, demonstrated a heart rich in the finest feelings of nature![3]

The historian Paul Turnbridge identified the 'young lady' as Adelaide Dubus and dates her death in childbirth as 15 December 1789. The child, christened Adelaide Victoire Auguste, was cared for by Adelaide's sister, Victoria, whom the duke also invited to become his mistress, but when this failed he paid her an allowance. It is an odd coincidence that both of Edward's daughters were christened Victoria. The last traceable payment from Coutts, the London bankers, was made as late as 1832.

If the duke fathered a child in 1789 but none for twenty-seven years with Madame de St Laurent, then several possibilities exist. The first and most obvious is that his mistress was infertile and we will examine the evidence for this in a moment. Secondly, he might have avoided pregnancy by the use of condoms, *coitus interruptus* or Madame de St Laurent could have had one or more induced abortions. Thirdly, the duke might have suffered from secondary infertility. On the whole, secondary infertility in men, that is where a man fathers one child but not a second, is less common than the corresponding condition in women. There is no evidence of the duke having mumps as an adult and even if he picked up a sexually transmitted disease it is unlikely to have made him infertile. He might have developed a varicocele which, by allowing the blood to enter the testis at body temperature, would curtail sperm production, but this is also relatively unlikely for a man in his twenties.

Contraception and abortion were available. Condoms, made from animal intestines, not latex, had been available for many years. In the previous century King Louis XV of France had instructed his London ambassadors to obtain a supply. However, consistent and effective use of voluntary family planning over twenty-seven years is unlikely, even with today's improved methods. Abortion through a variety of mechanical techniques was used, but in view of the duke's openness in recruiting his mistress and in living with her, it would seem out of character to have avoided children.

Was Madame de St Laurent infertile? Thérèse Bernardine was the middle child of a family of five born to Jean and Claudine Montgenet of Besançon near the Swiss border, and was christened on 30 September 1760. The family was prosperous and why she became a high-class courtesan is not clear. Perhaps she was seduced, perhaps she fell in love. It does seem likely that she had at least two sexual relationships before responding to Duke Edward's practical and unromantic invitation.

The second affair was with a revolutionary nobleman, the Marquis de Permangale. Mollie Gillen draws attention to a legal record sold at public auction in Paris in 1864: Item 3210 in Catalogue No. 176 of Saint-Helion as 'Action of the Baron de Fortisson against the Marquis de Permangale who lured away his mistress, 1786, piquant details given by the plaintiff, contemporary manuscript'. Unfortunately, it is not known who bought this manuscript and what piquant details it contained. There is no direct link to Thérèse Bernardine, then twenty-six years old, but today's descendants of the Marquis de Permangale claim the family acknowledged an association with the Duke of Kent's mistress, and personal letters to this effect existed until the 1900s when the grandfather of the current marquis destroyed them. We do know that by 1790 the marquis had lost his estates in the French revolution so he may have had to economize by dropping his mistress, and if Thérèse Bernardine is the woman in question, then she would have been willing to accept the duke's invitation.

Madame de St Laurent was also directly linked to the Marquis de Permangale by Colonel Symes, a conscientious observer who was given the task of watching over the Duke of Kent when he was posted to Gibraltar. In the Royal Archives (Add. 7/1485) for 15 December 1837 is a List of Simple Contract Creditors of the late Royal Highness the Duke of Kent presented to the young Queen Victoria, which includes an item referring to Alphonsine Thérèse Bernardine de St Laurent, Countess Mongenet and Mqs de Permangale. The relationship is further confirmed by the fact that after Madame de St Laurent had parted from the Duke of Kent, she met the marquis once again in Paris. He was then sixty-three and his name appears in the registration of her sister's death in 1818. The marquis, like Madame de St Laurent, had led an adventurous life, having been imprisoned in 1793 and actually prepared for the guillotine in 1794, only to be secretly rescued by a former student. English newspapers and Canadian groups in 1800 also associated her name with Baron de Fortisson. The de Fortisson family was a large one but Pierre, Baron de Roquefort, married in 1786 and, interestingly, was childless.

There is, therefore, convincing evidence that Madame de St Laurent was not a virgin when she met the Duke of Kent. Judging by her portrait, she was a woman who in face and figure could be called beautiful and who history suggests was sexually experienced, but there is no evidence that she had ever been pregnant. Did she acquire a sexually transmitted disease from her first lover or lovers? Biologically, women are more at risk than men to infertility after gonorrhea or chlymidial infection. Or did she abort one or more pregnancies by Edward or a previous lover? Aristocrats and their mistresses were certainly no strangers to abortion. Later in the nineteenth century Edward VII's mistress Lillie Langtry and Lady Elcho, mistress of James Balfour, Foreign Secretary in the First World War, both had abortions.

Victoire, unlike her predecessor in Edward's bed, was obviously fertile and had had two healthy children. However, the duke grieved after parting from his mistress and wrote to a friend just before the wedding in decidedly unromantic phraseology: 'I hope I shall have the energy to do my duty'. Victoire, for her part, approached the wedding with amiable pragmatism. The ceremony took place at Coburg on 29 May 1818, and there was a honeymoon in Coburg before a slow journey through Brussels to Dover and on to London. There was great pressure on Victoire to conceive and we can assume that she at least was eager for sexual relations. Her newly acquired elder brother-in-law, the Duke of Clarence, later William IV, married Adelaide of Saxe-Meiningen on 11 July 1818, and Edward and Victoire were married a second time, in the Church of England, in a double ceremony. Her brother-in-law, Adolphus, Duke of Cambridge, became engaged only one month later. If Adelaide failed to conceive, any child Victoire bore would be heir to the throne of the richest and most powerful nation in the world at that time, and her own and her family's future would be ensured.

For two months the new duke and duchess were together in London living in Kensington Palace, and Victoire's continuing menstruation must have been both a disappointment and a worry. In September the duke and duchess left London and travelled slowly to Amorbach, the German estate of the duchess' first husband, the Duke of Leiningen, which her son would one day rule. Parliament granted only £6,000 of the £25,000 promised, and to economize the duke had borrowed another £10,000 to bring the palace at Amorbach up to his discriminating standard, but before they had time to settle in the duchess found she was pregnant. At the same time both his elder brother, the Duke of Clarence and his younger brother, the Duke of Cambridge, who were also living on the continent in Hanover, found that they were to be fathers. While his brothers were content that their children should be born on the continent, the Duke of Kent insisted that his heir must be born in London. At this time he was so impecunious that he had difficulty in finding the money for the return journey, but eventually he succeeded in raising a small loan. Unable to afford a coachman he put his wife, his stepdaughter, a nurse, a maid, two lap-dogs and his wife's canaries, in the coach and took the reins himself. The other maids, his doctor and the midwife, Madame Sicbold, followed in other vehicles. An English tourist could hardly believe her eyes when she recognized the duke on the box driving 'an unbelievably old caravan'.

The future Queen Victoria was born on 24 May 1819, and was a healthy and apparently full-term baby. Therefore, her mother's last period was probably about 17 August 1818. In fact, 17 August had been Victoire's birthday and a dinner was held in her honour at Carlton House, London. Queen Victoria was probably conceived in London, or possibly on the continent as the duke and duchess had sailed from Dover in early September. If Victoire, keen to produce a child who might well be heir to the British throne, had suspected her husband's fertility, she might well have tried to improve her chances with another man.

The main outline of the Kents' activities in London during the relevant time, and their continental itineraries, can be reconstructed from the Court Circulars. On 6 August, they visited Victoire's brother Prince Leopold at Claremont and stayed until the 12th. On that day it was announced that the Duchess of Cambridge was pregnant. The child would be heir to the throne unless the Clarences or Kents had children. It is interesting that the Duke and Duchess of Kent returned that evening to Kensington Palace, while Prince Leopold visited the Cambridges the same day and then dined with Edward and Victoire that evening. As they had already spent six days together, the topic of conversation must have been the new potential heir. On 15 August Leopold left Claremont in order to visit Germany for the first time in several years. On 22 August *The Times* reported that the Kents would also remain in Britain until Leopold returned, but on the 28th this was contradicted by the announcement that the Kents would leave for Germany on 6 September. Their last three weeks were spent at Kensington Palace and the duke visited his mother, Queen Charlotte, who was dying, at Kew, almost every day. The couple also exchanged visits with the duke's brothers and sisters and their spouses, the Duchess of Cambridge on 17 August, the Prince Regent on 30 August, Princess Sophia on 6 September. In between, they visited a penitentiary at Millbank (22 August) and a commercial premises on 18 August. On 7 September they sailed from Dover, reaching Cambrai on the 8th and Valenciennes on the 10th, when they reviewed the British troops who were still stationed in Belgium following the defeat of Napoleon. By the 16th the Duchess was indisposed with a cold caught at the review, which detained them in Brussels until 3 October when they were scheduled to leave for Amorbach, but from 15 October to 25 October they visited Switzerland. Prince Leopold had visited Switzerland earlier, but by 5 October he was in Coburg.

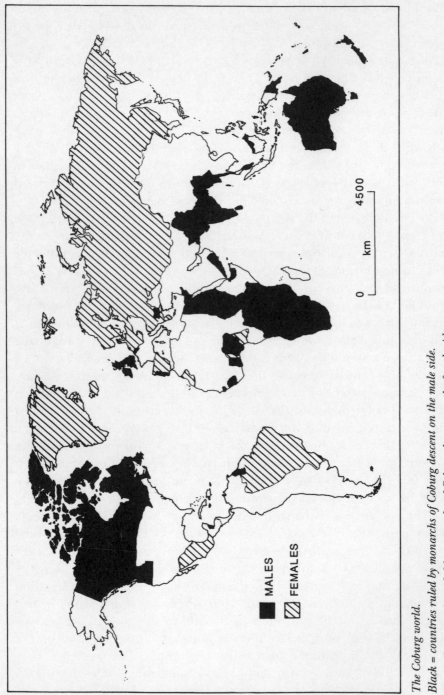

The Coburg world.

Black = countries ruled by monarchs of Coburg descent on the male side.

Hatched = countries ruled by monarchs of Coburg descent on the female side.

The Brazilian monarchy was deposed before Isabella could ascend the throne. When Victoria became queen the territory of Columbia, now part of the USA, was under British control.

MALES

FEMALES

0   4500

km

Victoria's conception must be viewed against the extraordinary dynastic ambitions of her uncle, Prince Leopold. Prince Leopold was particularly eager to see his sister pregnant. He was, by any measure, the most successful dynast the world has ever seen. The younger son of a minor German duke, he might have been expected to have passed a life of total obscurity, yet by determination and personality he had gained the hand of the Crown Princess of Britain. When Princess Charlotte and her baby died, a lesser man might have settled down to enjoy his pension of £50,000 a year, but he arranged instead to marry his widowed sister to the Duke of Kent, consequently becoming uncle to the British queen, and then married a nephew, Albert (who was possibly his own son), to her. His position as uncle to the British heir apparent helped him to gain the throne of Belgium for himself. He married another nephew to the Crown Princess of Portugal and in a generation raised himself and his family to a unique position of power and influence. The foundation of his success was his close kinship with the heir to the British throne. The ambition was there; would he have accepted defeat if the Duke of Kent had been infertile or inadequate, or would he have encouraged his sister to take corrective action when they learned that the younger brother's wife was expecting a potential heir or heiress?

Victoire might have slept with another man on one of these August or September days in London, but would she have chosen a haemophiliac? The chances are small, but substantially greater than the chance of a mutation. Many male haemophiliacs have fathered children.

There is nothing in the character of the Duchess of Kent to suggest that she would have baulked at sleeping with another man if she had decided the duke was unable to give her a child, and several aspects of her behaviour would fit with a secret knowledge that Victoria was illegitimate. As we have seen, William IV had a large brood of ten children by Mrs Jordan – the FitzClarences – who were given titles, entertained at court and generously accepted into the royal household by Queen Adelaide. In marked contrast the Duchess of Kent had an almost hysterical fear and hatred of the royal bastards and the contemporary diarist, Charles Greville, recalls how when the court was at Windsor or St James she would rise and ostentatiously withdraw from the room whenever one of her illegitimate nephews or nieces entered. Victoria's mother told the Duchess of Northumberland, 'I never did, neither will I ever, associate Victoria in any way with the illegitimate children of the royal family; with the King they dine. Did I not keep this line, how would it be possible to teach Victoria the difference between vice and virtue?' This sanctimonious behaviour might have been overcompensation for a guilty conscience, and is all the more hypocritical as she was having an affair with her secretary Conroy at the time.

Greville records, 'I said I concluded he [Conroy] was her lover. And he [Wellington] said he supposed so.' He backed up this inference by two observations. One was Victoria's obvious hatred of Conroy and her total exclusion of him once she ascended to the throne, and the second was the sudden and otherwise inexplicable dismissal of Baroness Spaeth from the Kensington Household in 1829, which may have been due to Spaeth's knowledge of circumstances which Victoire wished to conceal. The baroness had been with the Duchess of Kent for twenty-five years. Spaeth had been Victoire's closest companion when Victoire was a young and somewhat neglected bride of the Prince of Leiningen. She was with her on the journey from Germany when she was seven months pregnant with Victoria; she loved and played with Victoria and kept the duchess company after the duke died. Then suddenly, when Victoria was ten, Spaeth was summarily sent away to be a lady-in-waiting to Princess Feodora and to live in the cold and relatively isolated Langenburg Palace. It was a painful episode in the tight community that had grown up at Kensington. The Duchess of Clarence said it would kill Spaeth to send her away. One gentleman-in-waiting burst into tears and said, 'Going! Impossible!' and Spaeth herself said she 'would endure any privation' as long as she could see Victoria.

Wellington's explanation of the otherwise inexplicable dismissal seems cogent. 'Victoria had seen her mother and Conroy in some sort of intimate situation. What She had seen She had repeated to the Baroness Spaeth and Spaeth not only did not hold her tongue, but . . . remonstrated with the Duchess herself on the subject. The consequence was that they [Conroy and Victoire] got rid of Spaeth and,' continued Wellington, 'they would have got rid of Lehzen too if they had been able.' This last remark is independently verified by Prince Leopold in a confidential letter he wrote to Lehzen, Victoria's governess, in 1836. 'Had I not stood firm', he wrote, 'you would have followed Spaeth.' Baroness Lehzen, 'best and truest friend', according to Victoria's private journal, had been with the family for many years, having previously been Feodora's governess. It must have been painful for the duchess, who could on occasion be genuinely kind-hearted, to lose her faithful companion of twenty-five years, but if Victoria were a bastard, it would have encouraged her to accept Conroy's arguments to be rid of her old friend, who more than anyone else might have had embarrassing knowledge of the heir to the throne's parentage. It seems most likely that Conroy and the duchess were physically intimate. Victoria herself was quick to suspect the worst of Conroy and when, ten years later, her lady-in-waiting, Flora Hastings, appeared to be bulging in the wrong places under her crinoline, Victoria confided in her journal: 'We have no doubt that she is – to use psalm

words – *with child*! . . . the horrid cause of all this is the monster and
Demon Incarnate, whose name I forbear to mention . . .' The monster
was Conroy, who had travelled back alone with Lady Flora in the post-
chaise from Scotland some months earlier. Lady Flora had in fact been
appointed to the houschold as a 'companion' for Victoria, but Victoria
had always disliked her. The accusations against Conroy and Lady Flora
turned out to be mistaken and Lady Flora, who was only thirty-three, had
an enlarged liver and probably had episodes of ascites, or the
accumulation of fluid in her abdomen. The accusation was to damage
Victoria's political credibility and helped to bring down Lord
Melbourne's government, but it is noteworthy how quickly Victoria was
willing to think the worst of her mother's closest friend and advisor.
Greville comments, 'Whether she secretly suspects the nature of her
mother's connection with him or is only animated by a sort of instinctive
aversion is difficult to discover'[4], but after Victoria ascended the throne
Wellington provided further details. 'The cause of the Queen's alienation
from the Duchess and hatred of Conroy the Duke said was
unquestionably owing to having witnessed some familiarities between
them'.

The possibility that the young, ambitious duchess was unfaithful to her
elderly husband must also be considered against the background of
contemporary behaviour. Even from our own more lax times it is difficult
to comprehend the sexual mores of the aristocracy in the first half of the
nineteenth century when viewed through the window of Victorian moral
standards. A memorandum in the Royal Archives from the Duke of
Clarence (later William IV) to the Prince Regent reads, 'Last night I
fucked two whores – I hope I don't catch a dose'.

The Duke of Cumberland, one of the sons of George III and Victoria's
uncle, was widely believed to be the father of his sister's illegitimate child,
and one morning he attempted to rape the wife of the Lord Chancellor.

Letters from Princess Sophia, sister of the Duke of Cumberland and
Victoria's aunt, to her elderly confidant General Garth, about her
brother's [Cumberland] behaviour created a scandal. Taylor, the king's
secretary, told Greville that Garth was paid £1,500 p.a. and had half his
debts paid in return for the letters.[5] Garth handed over the letters but
kept attested copies of the papers in a box which he showed widely. 'Lord
Bathurst told me likewise that Taylor [the King's secretary] had
discovered that Garth had retained copies of the papers when he gave up
the originals, that General Garth certainly is the Father (which I believe
he certainly is not) and that the letters which affect the Duke of
Cumberland are letters from her to Garth complaining of his having
made attempts upon her person. It is notorious that the old Queen

forbade the Duke's access to the apartments of the Princess. There is another story which I am inclined to believe, that he is not the son of the Duke of Garth, but of some inferior person (some say a page of the name of Papendy).' One must conclude either that the duke was the father or that he made an unsuccessful assault upon his sister while she was having an affair with someone else.

Greville also recounts an attempt by the Duke of Cumberland to rape Lady Lyndhurst. Lord Lyndhurst was born in Boston but the whole family fled to England during the American Revolution. A self-made man, he became Master of the Rolls and later Lord Chancellor and was so well respected that he could have displaced Wellington as leader of the Tory party.[6] 'There is a story current about the Duke of Cumberland and Lady Lyndhurst which is more true than most stories of this kind. The Duke called upon her, and grossly insulted her; on which, after a scramble, she rang the bell. He was obliged to desist and go away, but before he did he said "By God, Madam, I will be the ruin of you and your husband, and will not rest till I have destroyed you both".'[7]

A few days later[8] Lady Lyndhurst gave Greville her account of the affair. 'I took a long drive with her, . . . and asked her to tell me about it. . . . She said that the Duke called upon her and had been denied [entry to the house] . . . that on a subsequent day he had called so early that no orders had been given to the Porter and he was let in, that he had made a violent attack upon her, which she had resisted, that his manner and his language were equally brutal and indecent, that he was furious at her resistance and said he would never forgive her for putting him to so much annoyance.'

When a report appeared in the press the duke, in order to preserve the proprieties, wrote to Lyndhurst to ask for the authority of Lady Lyndhurst in contradicting it. A heated correspondence followed, but the Lord Chancellor, in consultation with the Duke of Wellington, refused to let Lady Lyndhurst issue any denial. It is clear that the Duke of Cumberland was prepared to sexually assault both his sister and the wife of the Lord Chancellor of England. The most that can be said in his defence is that he was not a very successful rapist.

The following year Lord Chancellor Lyndhurst himself was pursuing Lady Fitzroy Somerset, writing her note after note while on the bench, and was so preoccupied with her that he was unable to follow the legal arguments put before him.[9] In January of the same year the Duke of Cumberland was discovered in an affair with Lady Graves which led to the suicide of the unfortunate Lord Graves. Lord Graves was perhaps exceptional in taking these matters so seriously. A year later the forgiving Lyndhurst was of the opinion that the Duke of Cumberland would make a very good king. Fortunately, Victoria intervened.

Princess Sophia's baby and the Lyndhurst case are relevant as far as they throw light on the mores of the royal circle at that time. It seems unlikely that any moral scruples would have prevented Victoire from being unfaithful to her husband shortly after her marriage. If Queen Victoria were not the daughter of the Duke of Kent the remarkable difference in her attitude to her English and her German relatives, and indeed to England and Germany, would be more easily understandable. The Queen's proclivity for Germans and Germany was notorious and Greville[10] had complained, 'However it shocks the people of England that the Queen takes no notice of her paternal relations, treats English ones as alien, and seems to consider her German uncles and cousins as her only kith and kin'. Her predilection for all things German was grotesque in an English queen, even though her mother and husband were German. When her first son (later King Edward VII) was born in 1841 she desired that his armorial bearings should quarter the arms of Germany with the royal arms of England, and when the baby's arms were gazetted the absurd title Duke of Saxony, to which neither his father nor he had claim, was given precedence over his English and Scottish titles.[11] During the Danish-Prussian confrontation she supported the Prussians, in defiance of both popular and informed opinion. When the British government attempted to rally Sweden, Russia and France to counter the Prussian and Austrian threat to Denmark in 1864 she protested, 'This draft seems to the Queen to commit the Government too strongly to the Danish view of the Question (of Schleswig-Holstein) and to encourage too much hope of material assistance from England. The imputation also upon the motives of the German powers seems impolitic and uncalled for.'[12] She even reprimanded (in English) the unfortunate Prince of Wales for having the temerity to write to his Danish fiancée in English, rather than in German. 'The German element is one I wish to be cherished and kept up in our beloved home – now more than ever' (after the death of Albert) . . . 'as Alix's parents are inclined to encourage English and to merge the German into Danish and English and this would be a dreadful sorrow to me.'

Some other factors are in favour of legitimate descent. Victoria had some facial resemblance to the Duke of Kent and perhaps a closer resemblance to George III. All three had round faces with receding chins and foreheads and protruding noses, particularly when elderly. The similarity is most marked in profile, as a comparison of George III and Victoria 'old head' coins will confirm, but this might be due in part to artistic licence in fitting the profile to a round coin. The Duchess Augusta wrote of Victoria that, 'Her face is just like her father's, the same artful blue eyes, the same roguish expression when she laughs', but it is impossible to recognize a roguish expression in the stolid features of the Duke of Kent, in any of his portraits.

Greville's diary provides evidence that Albert had no doubt of his wife's Hanoverian ancestry. When Queen Victoria bullied and harassed her daughter after her marriage to the German Crown Prince, Stockmar courageously intervened, writing to the Queen 'such a letter as she probably had never had in her whole life'. Prince Albert had not dared to control his wife because 'the Queen is so excitable that the Prince lived in perpetual terror of bringing on the hereditary malady and dreaded saying or doing anything which might have a tendency to bring on the effect'. As Victoria was not a porphyriac his forbearance was uncalled for but even if she had not been the Duke of Kent's daughter, nothing would have been gained and much might have been lost, if Albert had been informed by Leopold of any irregular features of his wife's ancestry.

It is not possible to distinguish between a mutation and unfaithfulness on the basis of the historical evidence. There are, however, no records of a haemophiliac candidate. The puzzle is even more complex because there is another genetic defect, porphyria, which was prevalent in the British royal family for many generations, and which increases the probability that the Duke of Kent was not the father. Of course, modern DNA 'fingerprinting' techniques could settle the question if bone fragments or tissue samples from the Duke of Kent and Victoria were available.

For centuries before Victoria's descendants suffered from haemophilia the Stuarts and Hanoverians were plagued by porphyria. Unlike haemophilia, porphyria is genetically dominant, that is, all those who carry the gene may display the symptom to some extent. Porphyria arises from a defect in the synthesis of porphyrin, a component of all cells and particularly of the blood pigment haemoglobin. Sufferers have one defective and one normal gene; two defective genes would prevent any porphyrin synthesis and would be fatal. Porphyrin is produced by a chain of complex reactions. The defective gene produces a bottleneck in the chain and the precursors may build up, causing the attacks. Attacks may be brought on by drugs, alcohol or anaesthetics. Some porphyriacs never have attacks and are unaware that they are at risk. During attacks the victim's urine darkens on standing and may assume a deep purple-red colour. This conspicuous and unusual symptom helps to identify sufferers in earlier centuries, even when the medical records are very limited. The disease may also cause many other symptoms including severe abdominal pains and constipation, due to loss of muscular tone caused by inhibition of the autonomic nervous system. This may also complicate childbirth. Other symptoms include extreme sensitivity of the skin which may make clothing very uncomfortable, and nervous excitement characterized by rapid, continuous talking. The symptoms usually begin to appear in the second or third decade of life. The intensity of the disease fluctuates, severe episodes alternating with symptom-free interludes. Attacks may prove fatal but recovery from attacks is usually rapid.

The diagnosis of any disease in the long dead, from inadequate records, is always hazardous, but the peculiar nature of porphyria, the good documentation of royal diseases and the occurrence of the disease in several living descendants of George II make the diagnosis of royal sufferers of porphyria very convincing. There is little doubt that Mary Queen of Scots was a sufferer, as was her son James I of England and VI of Scotland and his son Prince Henry (Charles I's elder brother), who died of the disease. It can probably be traced back to Margaret Tudor, the sister of Henry VIII, who married James IV of Scotland. Many descendants of James, including Queen Anne, Frederich the Great of Prussia, his father Frederich I and George III of Britain, were also affected.[13] George III's attacks of 'madness' were due to this condition. George IV was also affected, as was probably his wife Queen Caroline, who was descended from Frederich the Great. Princess Charlotte could therefore have inherited the disease from either her father or mother. From the age of sixteen she suffered from abdominal pains and periods of nervous excitement, and porphyria may well have been a factor in her sudden collapse and death. At the age of sixteen she wrote, 'I am far from well . My spirits rally but for a very short time'. Later it was reported, 'The Princess is really not well. She looks ill – and has complained for some time past but more lately of a pain in her left side . . . the pulse is quick.' When she was eighteen Dr Mathew Baillie wrote, 'Her pulse is still too frequent, for it was yesterday 84 . . . Her Royal Highness complains of distension of the stomach from indigestion . . .' Her own comments show that she was mystified by her symptoms, 'Last night I had a slight nervous attack again, which always affects my spirits as well as my side . . . what I feel on these occasions is oppressed like as if my heart would burst or sigh itself out . . . I must say that I get every day more ignimatical to myself . . . At times I laugh and talk away as fast that you would think I had no cares at all.'[14] She frequently suffered pain in her side, and colic. At her post-mortem her stomach and intestine were found to be dilated with fluid and air.

Edward Duke of Kent, like his brother George IV, Frederick Duke of York and Augustus Duke of Sussex, also suffered from porphyria. While a young man at Gibraltar he suffered frequent bilious attacks which were recognized as being similar to his father's complaint. In a letter to his father he observed, 'by my remaining here another summer season my health would be exposed not only to the most prejudicial but perhaps the most fatal attacks of a complaint, the severity of which, is, I believe, not unknown to your majesty'. A few years later his skin was so sensitive that he complained of 'being unable to wear anything but a pair of loose trowsers'. Abdominal pains due to porphyria may well be the origin of the tale that he developed symptoms of couvade while his wife was carrying Victoria. Some of the symptoms of his last illness may also have been due to this affliction. If Queen Anne's inability to bear a healthy child was due in part to porphyria, then this disease played a part in both the origin of the Hanoverian succession and its end.

MacAlpine and Hunter, in their pioneering study *George III and the Mad Business*, found no evidence of porphyria in Queen Victoria or among her numerous descendants. However, it has recently been demonstrated that Charlotte, the sister of Kaiser Wilhelm, and a granddaughter of Victoria, was a sufferer – 'itching of the skin, constipation, abdominal trouble and, the clinching symptom, orangey dark-red urine'.[15] Unfortunately this does not confirm her descent from the Duke of Kent, as she might well have inherited it from her father's family, the House of Prussia, descended from the porphyriac Frederick the Great. This is the more likely hypothesis because if Victoria had carried the gene it should be common among her progeny, even allowing for the fact that it can remain dormant in many individuals.

To summarize: the case cannot be closed as there is insufficient evidence to decide whether Victoria's gene was a recent mutation or derived from an illicit union. Certainly there is no evidence of haemophilia among the putative ancestors of either Victoria or the Duke of Kent. The disease either appeared as a new mutation in Queen Victoria's mother or in the Duke of Kent, or her father was a haemophiliac who was not the Duke of Kent. The probability of a mutation for haemophilia is 1 in 25,000 to 1 in 100,000, and Victoria's failure to inherit the porphyria of the Duke of Kent lengthens the odds. A mutation could have occurred during her early development in the cell line leading to her ovaries or in either of the cell lines leading to the eggs or sperm from which she came. The peculiar circumstances of Victoria's conception, the unrivalled ambition of her uncle Leopold and some aspects of her mother's behaviour make it possible that Victoria was not the daughter of the Duke of Kent but was the child of some haemophiliac who has gone unrecognized or, as all the explanations of her haemophilia are by their nature statistically improbable, the third possibility is that she was a bastard but the haemophilia came from a mutation that occurred in either the sperm or the egg from which she came. On the other hand, about a quarter of all haemophiliacs are the result of mutation, not inheritance, and if Victoire had been unfaithful the chances of choosing a haemophiliac as father are about 1 in 20,000. In the absence of a haemophiliac candidate Victoire must be given the benefit of the doubt. If not, then the true line of British kingship would have passed through Victoria's uncle, the Duke of Cumberland, the unsuccessful rapist and later King of Hanover.

CHAPTER SEVEN

Crowns Rolling about the Floor

The First World War laid the foundations of the modern world. It changed the political map of Europe, altered the social order irrevocably in Western Europe and brought Lenin to power in Russia. By its very destructiveness, it left the USA as the richest and most powerful nation in the world. The battles of 1914–18 also set the stage for another even more bloody conflict twenty-five years later. It was also a feud between Victoria's grandchildren and relatives – both those with and those without the haemophilia gene.

By 1918 the world Queen Victoria had known and helped to shape had fallen apart, abruptly and catastrophically. At the beginning of the twentieth century, Coburg descendants ruled Europe and much of the rest of the world. By the time the First World War ended the emperors of Germany, Austria and Russia had all lost their thrones, while Britain had lost its pre-eminent position to the USA. Among all the cataclysmic changes that occurred between August 1914 and November 1918, the greatest were in Russia, and here the role played by the tsar in the destruction of his throne was directly influenced by his son's inheritance of Victoria's gene.

So much has changed in the past seventy-five years that it requires some effort to appreciate the world of 1914. At the turn of the century twenty kings sat on the thrones of Europe. Victoria's son King Edward VII had been called the 'Uncle of Europe' When he died in May 1910, nine kings, seven queens, five royal heirs and forty other royal personages followed the dead monarch's cortège to Westminster Abbey. In 1914 his son King George V had first cousins on the thrones of Germany, Russia, Norway and Spain and other cousins were heirs to the crowns of Sweden and Romania. The kings of Denmark and Greece were his uncles. The Dowager Tsarina of Russia was his aunt and his sister was Queen of Norway. Other relatives, through the British king's Coburg ancestry, reigned in Bulgaria, Belgium and numerous principalities of the German Empire, while a Coburg had recently abdicated in Portugal. It was a tangled knot of interrelated families who exchanged state visits and called on one another in sumptuous yachts.

George V assumed the British throne on the death of Edward VII in

1910. He was a solid, unexciting, not too intelligent king. He had none of his father's European focus, skill in languages or diplomatic interest, although he did have a proud interest in the British Empire. Like his grandmother he could be quick tempered, but unlike her he could also swear like the seaman he had been in his youth. Whereas Edward VII had gained the nickname 'Edward the Caresser' as a result of his active sex life, George led a spotless domestic life, having married Princess Mary of Teck in 1893. They had six children and the Tsar Nicholas of Russia and Tsarina Alexandra were godparents to the first born, who later briefly became Edward VIII.[1] Victoria's direct male descendants, other than Leopold, were free of the haemophilia gene, but as we will see shortly, the gene was very nearly reintroduced into George V's generation.

Kaiser Wilhelm II of Germany was also a grandson of Queen Victoria and, as he never ceased telling people, it was in his arms that she breathed her last. Wilhelm's mother, Queen Victoria's eldest child, the Princess Royal, had been promised to the Crown Prince Frederick at the tender age of fourteen and was married to him – amidst floods of royal tears – at seventeen. Her liberal ideas were to make her unpopular in conservative Prussia. Fortunately, she was not a carrier of haemophilia, but she was unlucky in her first delivery. She had a long labour complicated by a breech presentation and a placenta praevia, and while her German and English obstetricians quarrelled over how to treat her, both mother and child nearly died. Baby Wilhelm did survive but his left arm was always paralysed. He had a spartan education and as he grew up his arm was encased in a variety of torturing – but purposeless – iron and leather devices. To his parents' dismay, he turned into an egocentric, impetuous, loquacious militarist, made all the more dangerous by a hearty dose of Coburg energy and intelligence. He told the British ambassador in Berlin: 'My mother and I have the same characters. I have inherited hers. That good stubborn English blood which will not give way is in both our veins.'

Wilhelm became emperor at the age of twenty-nine, on the death of his father from throat cancer. He made a bombastic monarch: he erected thirty-two statues to his Hohenzollern dynasty, kept a wardrobe of over three hundred uniforms and called on God as his 'Celestial Ally'. Constitutionally he was less restrained in his powers than his cousin George. The Reichstag, or Germany's parliament, was described by one member as 'the figleaf of absolutism'. The nation Wilhelm ruled was growing fast in wealth, overtaking British industrial production in the 1890s.

The third giant of Western Europe was France, glorying in its past but uncertain about its future. The distant United States and France were the only significant nations on the globe without a monarch. Like Germany, France took pride in its powerful land army, almost too big for its borders.

In the now half-forgotten map of Europe in 1914 the Russian frontier was a mere 180 miles east of Berlin but the country stretched eastwards halfway round the world, covering one-sixth of the world's land mass. Tsar Nicholas II came to the Russian throne in October 1894. Nicholas's mother was the daughter of Christian IX of Denmark and her sister, Alexandra, had been married to Edward VII; thus George V of Britain and Nicholas II of Russia were first cousins and boré a striking resemblance to one another.

Not only was Nicholas styled Emperor of Russia but he was also King of Poland, Grand Duke of Finland and Lithuania and Prince of Estonia. Unlike all other contemporary monarchs, his powers were absolute; his formal titles included that of Autocrat and Lord and Master of All Northern Countries, and he personally owned 600 million acres of land. His powers inside Russia were limited only by his conscience. While Victoria was Defender of the Faith and constitutionally Head of the Anglican Church, the Tsar was literally a priest. At his coronation he crowned himself – no one else was worthy enough. Only the emperors of China and Japan were as close to divine as Nicholas. The post office officials were even reluctant to frank the royal portrait on Russian stamps.

'Everyone in Russia', observed a British diplomat, 'is a little mad.' Russia produced great literature, ballet and theatre, and was the birthplace of Tolstoy, Chekhov, Kandinsky, Chagall, Rachmaninoff, Scriabin and Stravinsky, but the peasants had only been freed from the last vestiges of serfdom in 1906 and lived their lives, in Tolstoy's words, 'in want and heavy work'. Before 1906 many were still bound to their communal farms. Although the land was the property of the farmers the farms were in debt to the state. Peasants could buy themselves out, but in practice few could afford the capital. Byzantine tradition lingered in the church which, as in medieval Europe, was part of the state. Daily life was invested with religious rituals: a cross was hung around a child's neck at birth and never removed throughout life; the church prescribed strict fasts and gluttonous feasts; an icon hung in every house and was saluted by everyone even before they greeted their own family. The bulk of the people followed the Orthodox Church, but there were significant Nonconformist sects and three million Jews. There were atheists in the cities and extreme fundamentalist sects in the countryside. One believed in total abstinence and self-castration: the castrates were subject to the 'little seal' where they removed the testicles and scrotum with a razor, or the 'second degree of purity' or 'great seal' when they also sliced off the penis. Nikitian, in imitation of Abraham, cut his children's throats and when exiled to Siberia for his religious zealotry, managed to nail his feet to a cross on Good Friday, wielding his hammer with his right hand while he held on to the cross with his left. The Holy Ghost Worshippers breathed especially deeply while praying, in hope of swallowing the Third Person of the Trinity. Even older traditions survived, including the popular and ecclesiastical belief in the half-mad, half-divine miracle-working holy man, whose ancestry went back to the pre-Christian shamans of the northern forests. Even the most educated believed in medievally quaint miracles. Prince Zhevakhov observed that St Petersburg preferred to mistake a sinner for a saint than to fail to recognize a saint. Nicholas ordered the digging up of a long dead cleric and although his body had decomposed, which saints traditionally are not supposed to do, Nicholas argued that the state of preservation of his bones, teeth and hair was sufficient to justify canonization.

Terrorist acts resulted in 2,691 deaths between 1905 and 1909 and in turn thousands of terrorists were executed or sent into exile. As a thirteen-year-old, Nicholas had stood at the end of the bed in which his grandfather was dying from an assassin's bomb, both his feet blown off and his belly ripped open. As tsar, Nicholas remained afraid of liberal changes, yet for once Lord Acton's aphorism that all power tends to corrupt and absolute power tends to corrupt absolutely was not fulfilled. Nicholas was not a sadistic tyrant, but a reserved, frequently indecisive ruler: the kaiser described him as 'only fit to live in a country house and grow turnips'.

The only European dynasty not directly related to Victoria and the Coburgs was that of the Habsburgs. The Austro-Hungarian Empire was composed of what is now Austria, Hungary, Czechoslovakia and parts of Romania, Poland, Slovenia, Croatia and the Ukraine. The Emperor Franz Joseph was born thirteen years after Victoria, and was the only monarch to equal her in longevity (he died in 1916) – or to approach her in majesty. Constitutionally he had more authority than Victoria, but his government had no secure roots in democracy and the parts of the empire were united only in their common crown. To the south of Franz Joseph's empire, geography and history had broken the uninterrupted land mass of the Balkans into small, unstable units – Serbia, Bulgaria, Montenegro, Greece, Albania and Romania – which were still in turmoil following the collapse of the Ottoman Empire. In his long reign Franz Joseph saw his wife assassinated, his only son commit suicide, his brother executed, his sister-in-law go mad, his heir assassinated, and before he died he was to fire the diplomatic salvos that triggered the First World War.

Prior to 1914 Germany's foreign policy was dominated by the fear that some day it might have to fight a war on two fronts. In 1882 Bismarck had completed a Triple Alliance between Germany, Austro-Hungary and Italy, where each nation guaranteed the others' borders if attacked. Britain, with borders protected by the sea, was less inclined to sign treaties with continental blocs. However, as Germany deliberately built a battle fleet to rival the British Royal Navy, Britain shifted from relative isolationism to join Russia and France in a Triple Entente. The kaiser particularly disliked King Edward's role, calling him 'Edward the Encircler'.

When war eventually came it was brought about by a combination of changing technology, human idiosyncrasies and family pettiness among the royalty of Europe. Militarism had become an obsession. Generals believed whichever side mobilized first would win and planned endless paper wars, moving millions of pretend men by rail and winning quick victories with imaginary cavalry charges. They forgot that the machine-gun had been invented and overlooked the experience of the American Civil War when massed formations had been massacred by men behind muzzle-loading guns in trenches. If war broke out Germany planned to knock out France by a lightning attack before Russia could intervene effectively. The German military strategy of attack had been designed by the late General Count Alfred von Schlieffen, who planned to carry his troops to the French and Belgian borders on 11,000 carefully scheduled trains.[2] Diplomats and military theorists had prepared for war for so long that it became a self-fulfilling prophecy, the apparent advantage of striking first once a crisis had arisen adding dangerously to the instability of the system of alliances. It took only the murder of a royal personage to start the guns firing in August 1914.

The Emperor Franz Joseph's only son and heir, Crown Prince Rudolph, had killed his mistress and then committed suicide in 1889, making the emperor's nephew Franz Ferdinand heir to the Austro-Hungarian Empire. Franz Ferdinand, in turn, had annoyed his uncle by entering into a morganatic marriage with a mere countess, and any heir they produced could not inherit the Austro-Hungarian throne since their mother was not of royal blood. However, unlike most Habsburg marriages, it was an unusually happy union and it rankled with Franz Ferdinand that his wife could not be accorded the protocol due an archduchess. On Sunday 28 June 1914, the royal couple's fourteenth wedding anniversary, they visited Sarajevo in Slavonic Bosnia, which had recently been annexed from Turkey. It was a well-known hotbed of militants who would have preferred to become Serbian citizens, and a group of six young men, funded by the Serbian secret service, were planning to assassinate Franz Ferdinand. Bosnia was under military control. The Archduke, as Commander-in-Chief, had extensive powers and, for once, could arrange that his wife was treated with full honours. In order to give his wife the prominence he thought she deserved the Archduke published the itinerary for his visit in great detail, while the officials organizing the tour, taking their cue from the disgruntled Emperor, provided only light police protection. As the heir apparent approached the town hall a bomb was thrown, injuring two officers. The royal visit continued but secret changes were agreed in the route. Unfortunately, the royal chauffeur was not informed and began to drive down the previously announced route. When the motorcade had stopped and was trying to reverse, one of the Serbian nationalists – a nineteen-year-old youth called Gavrilo Princips – who had given up his assassination attempt and dropped into a coffee shop to steady his nerves, suddenly and unexpectedly found himself 10 ft from the Archduke, who was sitting bolt upright in an open-topped car. He shot Franz Ferdinand and his wife, who both died within 15 minutes, Franz Ferdinand mumbling, 'It is nothing'. His life might have been saved had he not taken such pride in his military bearing that he insisted on being literally sewn into his uniform – and no one could find the scissors quickly enough to staunch his wounds. When the news reached the old Emperor in Vienna, he coldly remarked, referring to the dead couple's despised marriage, 'The Almighty does not allow Himself to be challenged with impunity . . . A higher Power has restored the old order, which I unfortunately was unable to uphold'.

Whatever Franz Joseph thought about divine retribution privately, publicly Austria reacted to the murder briskly: Serbia was to be punished. But first the Austro-Hungarian ambassador was sent to visit the German kaiser who, acting alone, gave explicit and personal indications that Austria could depend on Germany's backing. He hoped that Austrian bluster, backed by German military might, would win the Emperor Franz Joseph a diplomatic victory and the kaiser vicarious glory, without any call to arms. Serbia, Orthodox in religion and Slavonic in language, looked to Russia for support.

On 23 July 1914, Austria delivered a blistering and humiliating ultimatum to Serbia, which submitted within 48 hours. The kaiser's gamble had apparently paid off handsomely, but stupidity and malice were eventually to turn diplomatic victory into military defeat. The Emperor Franz Joseph, now eighty-four-years old, was tricked into declaring war by false tales that Serbian troops had fired on Austrians, while the kaiser was not told of Serbia's submission until 60 hours after it occurred: '. . . every reason for war has been removed', he wrote when it was too late. Unfortunately, in Vienna, war had already been declared on

Serbia and the troop trains were starting to roll. When the kaiser saw what had happened, he was shaken by the imminence of full-scale conflict. He cabled his cousin Nicholas, who was treaty-bound to support Serbia: '. . . with regard to the hearty and tender friendship which binds us both from long ago with firm ties, I am exerting my utmost influence to induce the Austrians to deal straightly to arrive to a [sic] satisfactory understanding with you. . . Your very sincere and devoted friend and cousin – Willy.'

The tsar had already sent a similar message: 'in this most serious moment I appeal you to help me. . . . To try and avoid such a calamity as a European war, I beg you to stop your allies from going too far. – Nicky.' Poignantly, both telegrams were written in stilted English, but sadly, common descent and fraternal feelings could not avert war. Later, thinking of Queen Victoria's reign, the kaiser declared, 'To think that George and Nicky should have played me false. If my grandmother had been alive, she would never have allowed it.'

Once the German war machine was set in motion it continued inexorably to the invasion of France and Belgium. The British guarantee to Belgium, originally intended to support Victoria's uncle Leopold against the French, allowed Britain to intervene but was not obligatory. The British premier, Asquith, had already promised France support against Germany but needed an excuse. The German invasion of Belgium provided it.

But although Victoria was dead her genes lived on and were to play a critical role as the war ran its cruel and immeasurably destructive course. As noted earlier, the Romanovs had had close ties with the Coburgs since the days of Napoleon. Victoria's second son, Alfred Duke of Edinburgh, had married the tsar's daughter and it was not surprising that Nicholas II married one of Victoria's granddaughters, Princess Alexandra, the daughter of the German Duke of Hesse.

Princess Alice, Queen Victoria's third child, was the first to inherit the defective gene. In due course a German husband, Ludvig Grand Duke of Hesse, was selected for her. The marriage took place in circumstances which foreshadowed the tragedies to come. Prince Albert died shortly before the wedding and Victoria insisted that the whole congregation, including the unfortunate bride, should wear only black or purple in respect. Depressed by the atmosphere and the loss of his elder sister, Prince Alfred sobbed loudly throughout the ceremony and even the Archbishop of Canterbury, who was conducting it, broke down. Victoria herself commented that it was more like a funeral than a wedding. Two of Princess Alice's daughters, Irene and Alexandra, and her son Frederick were in turn to inherit the gene.

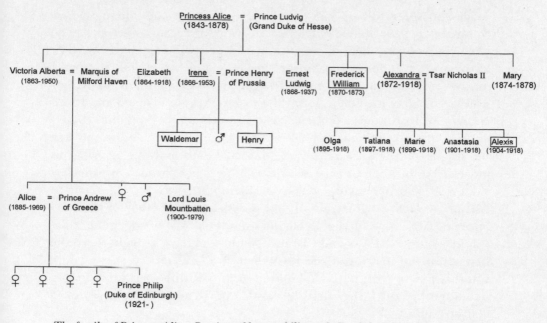

The family of Princess Alice. Carriers of haemophilia underlined, haemophiliacs boxed.

Alexandra Victoria Helena Louise Beatrice was born on 6 June 1872 in Darmstadt, near Frankfurt. Her mother, Princess Alice, knew that her German relatives would never pronounce her English name correctly so called her Alix. What she could not know was that at her conception the egg that was fertilized contained an X chromosome carrying the gene for haemophilia.

Alice wrote to her mother Victoria that Alix was 'a sweet, merry little person, always laughing with a dimple in one cheek'. When she was six Alix and her siblings went down with diphtheria. In the nineteenth century, with neither vaccination to prevent it nor antibiotics to cure it, diphtheria could be a deadly infection: today a whole nation may go for years without a single case. Queen Victoria sent her personal physician, but first Alix's younger sister and then her mother died. The sunny little princess turned into a sullen, obstinate, sometimes bad-tempered child. Her grandmother poured affection on her and Alix became her favourite granddaughter. She frequently holidayed with Victoria at her summer palace in Osborne, on the Isle of Wight.

At first, Victoria hoped Alix would marry the Duke of Clarence, the elder brother of George V and then heir to her own throne. The duke was an unsavoury young man. His tutor Dalton[3] referred to the 'abnormally dormant condition of his mental powers', but his problem may have been aggravated by deafness inherited from his mother. A coach appointed to help him enter Trinity College, Cambridge, said he could not 'possibly derive much benefit' from attending university as he hardly knew 'the meaning of the words to read'. He was bisexual, frequenting a homosexual brothel in Cleveland Street[4] but sharing a mistress with his younger brother George, later King George V, while they were in the navy together.[5] According to Knight[6], he married and had a child by an Irish Roman Catholic girl who worked in a shop immediately opposite the brothel and this led to a blackmail attempt and to the Jack the Ripper murders. Clarence providentially died in 1892, allowing his more stable brother George as heir to inherit the throne. Appalled by Victoria's plans for Alix, her sister Elizabeth, who was married to Nicholas's uncle Serge, wrote, 'I find the idea [of the Duke of Clarence marrying Alix] quite dreadful. He does not look over strong and is quite stupid.' A union of Alix and Clarence might well have brought down the British throne instead of the Russian had not Elizabeth steered Alix towards the unfortunate Nicholas. The possibility of reintroducing haemophilia into the British royal family was evidently not a consideration.

No one in St Petersburg considered the possibility of haemophilia either, even though the risks were plain. No royal family took the risks into account until 1913 when the tsar offered his eldest daughter Olga to Crown Prince Ferdinand of Romania. Ferdinand's mother was flattered by the idea but scotched it because of the risk of bringing haemophilia into the family.[7] The disease was apparent in Alix's family long before her marriage. Her mother Alice had seven children; two daughters, Alexandra and Irene, proved to be carriers and Alix's brother Frederick William was a haemophiliac. One morning, when he was three years old, 'Frittie' dashed into his mother's first floor bedroom and ran straight through the open window, which reached to floor level. He fell to the terrace below and although no bones were broken he was dead by evening of a brain haemorrhage. Alix's sister Irene had two haemophiliac sons.

The failure of the tsar's family to appreciate the genetic risks was not due to ignorance in Russian scientific circles. More likely it was due to the isolation of the royal family from the intellectual life of the country and the scientific ignorance of the narrow circle of aristocrats and politicians with whom they associated.

Alix's courtship was encouraged by her sister Elizabeth who invited her to St Petersburg for two summer seasons.[8] During the second the 23-year-old Nicholas confided to his mistress, an imperial ballerina, that 'of all possible fiancées he liked Princess Alice [sic] the best'. They were married in November 1894, one week after Nicholas's father Alexander

III had died from kidney disease. Nicholas quickly forgot the supple ballerina and after his wedding night wrote, 'Never did I believe there could be such happiness in this world, such an utter feeling of unity between two mortal beings.' Alexandra had been brought up more as an Englishwoman than a German, spending much of her adolescence in Britain, and all her correspondence with her husband was conducted in English. Like Victoria and Albert – and unlike a great many of their relatives – Nicholas and Alexandra enjoyed a lifelong, faithful, loving, dependent, passionate relationship, all the more remarkable because they were also the rulers of a vast, brutal, totalitarian state.

Despite their love the marriage was also a mismatch. Alix, unlike her English cousins, was an ambitious, stubborn young woman with a will of iron and a passion for politics. She was a firm believer in the absolute right of monarchs, but she was married to a weak, almost will-less, monarch with little wisdom or discretion, but with almost absolute power. It was to prove a dangerous combination.

They lived in the Alexander Palace, started in Catherine the Great's reign. Smaller than some other Russian palaces, it had more than a hundred rooms. Alix did her best to become a Russian. She converted to the Russian Orthodox Church, literally spitting on her old Protestant faith, and made a great effort to become word-perfect in Russian, but despite her efforts, Alexandra remained an outsider. Her mother-in-law did not like her and refused to pass down the imperial jewellery. The aristocracy was offended when she cut down the number of pompous palace balls.

The first duty of the tsarina was to provide the dynasty with a male heir. Instead, Alix bore a succession of daughters: Olga in 1895, Tatiana in 1897, Marie in 1899 and Anastasia in 1901. As daughter succeeded daughter, Alix resorted to a variety of quacks, in particular to a 'Dr' Philippe Vachot, who began as a butcher's assistant, and was thrice convicted in his native France for practising medicine without the necessary qualifications. He claimed to be able to communicate with the spirit of Alexander III, the previous tsar, and to foresee the future. He convinced Alix that he could help her bear a son. In her desperation she believed him and in 1902 it was publicly announced that she was with child. When, after six months, it became apparent that it was imaginary, the official embarrassment caused 'Dr' Philippe to leave Russia. It is a measure of the total lack of judgement of the imperial pair that following this débâcle Nicholas wrote to the French President commending Philippe for the French Academy. As he left, Philippe forecast to Alix that 'One day you will have another friend like me to speak to you of God'. This prophecy helped to prepare the way for Rasputin.

On 12 August 1904 the guns of St Petersburg boomed out a salute of three hundred guns. In Nicholas's words, it was 'a great never-to-be-forgotten day when the mercy of God has visited us so clearly. Alix gave birth to a son at one o'clock.' In a symbolic and belated attempt to civilize a primitive society, Nicholas chose the birth of his son as the occasion to abolish corporal punishment in the army and navy.

For a few weeks after his birth all seemed well with the little tsarevitch but on 8 September Nicholas noted in his diary: 'Alix and I are disturbed by the constant bleeding of little Aleksei. It continued from his navel until evening.' At first they could not admit that he had inherited the fateful disease, but eventually the truth had to be faced. His mother was naturally stricken. Anna Vyrubova, her closest confidante, later wrote, 'She hardly knew a day's happiness after she knew her boy's fate'. Her health and spirits declined and she developed heart trouble. Although the boy's affliction was in no conceivable way her fault, she dwelt morbidly on the fact that the disease is transmitted through the mother and that it was common in her family. 'Although it was no one's fault, the Russian people regarded any defect as a divine judgement for some sin. So the affliction of the future Tsar and supreme priest was concealed from all except the immediate family. It was understood that the child was frail but some trouble was obvious. 'The emperor aged ten years overnight,' said the Grand Duke Aleksander Mikhailovic. He commented that the courtiers were 'afraid to smile in the presence of the Tsar and Tsarina', and noted that Alexandra especially 'turned all of her thoughts towards religion and her face took on a hysterical character'. The secret forced the family even closer together and deepened their isolation. They rarely met their subjects. Nicholas rotated between his palaces, from St Petersburg to Tsarskoe Selo to Lavidia, near Yalta on the Black Sea, seeking homeliness amid great opulence.[9] Part of the summer was spent on the gigantic yacht, *Standart*, surrounded by a large part of the imperial fleet.

He and Alix called each other 'Hubby' and 'Wifey' in fashionable English. Like his cousin the King of England, the tsar smoked the increasing popular machine-made cigarettes. The effort to protect the young child from trauma turned him into a spoiled brat believing his father was only half-joking when he called him 'Aleksey the Terrible'. Alix had tastes like Imelda Marcos, and her favourite colours were mauve and cream. She filled the imperial apartments with solid Edwardian furniture selected from the mail-order catalogue of Maples in London. Her friends were mystics and nonentities and she valued loyalty and devotion above intelligence. Her friend, Anna Vyrubova, saw visions and was described by the tsarevitch's tutor as having 'the mind of a child lacking either intelligence or direction'.

13   *The Russian royal family with Kaiser Wilhelm on their yacht the Standart in June
1909. Kaiser Wilhelm is holding Aleksei and the daughters are holding the dolls that the
kaiser had brought as presents. KEA Publishing Services Ltd – CSAOR.*

14   *The tsar's daughters. From left to right Olga, Tatiana, Marie and Anastasia in
Peterhof, 1906. KEA Publishing Services Ltd – CSAOR.*

15 *Tsarevitch Aleksei and the sailor Derevenko at Friedberg, 1910. The tsarina was so concerned that the boy might injure himself that he was not allowed a bicycle of his own, although a tricycle was permitted. KEA Publishing Services Ltd – CSAOR.*

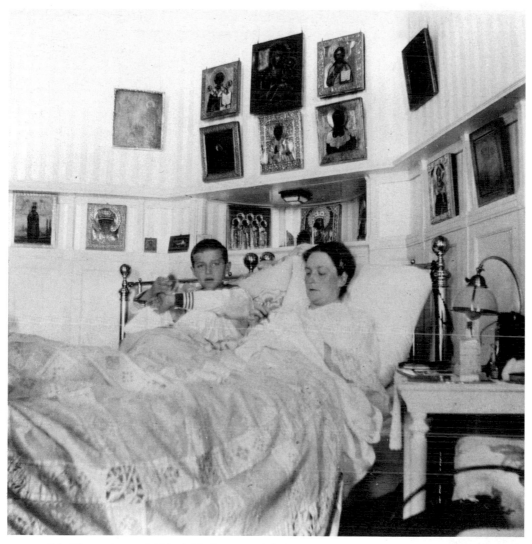

16 *The tsarina and Aleksei. Mother sews while Alex plays. KEA Publishing Services Ltd –*
CSAOR.

17   *The tsar's children, 1910. Left to right: Marie, Tatiana, Anastasia, Olga and Aleksei. Hulton Deutsch Collection Limited.*

18 *The Russian royal family at the tsarina's childhood home of Wolfsgarten, in Germany,*
November 1910. In the front row the tsarina's sister Irene with Marie, Tatiana and Aleksei
and the Grand Duke of Hesse's two sons. Second row extreme left, Eleanor, second wife of
the Grand Duke of Hesse, Anastasia, the tsarina and Olga Slightly further back between
Anastasia and the tsarina are Prince Henry of Hesse and the tsar and, behind and between
the tsar and tsarina, wearing a bow tie, sits the Grand Duke. KEA Publishing Services Ltd
– CSAOR.

19   Rasputin taking tea with wealthy Russian ladies. David King Collection.

20   Four of the royal children after the abdication, relaxing after tending the vegetables.
KEA Publishing Services Ltd – CSAOR.

21 The tsar and his family in captivity at Tobolsk, 1917–18. Left to right: Olga, Anastasia, the tsar, the tsarevitch, Tatiana, Marie. Hulton Deutsch Collection Limited.

22　*The Ipatiev house in Ekaterinburg in June 1918. The photograph shows the wooden fence erected to screen the royal family. The tsar, his family and entourage were assassinated here. The house was demolished on the orders of Boris Yeltsin, now President of Russia, on instructions from Moscow. David King Collection.*

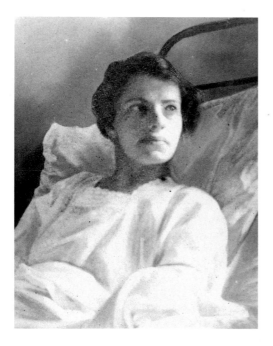

23　*'Fraulein Unbekannt' in Berlin in 1925. Hulton Deutsch Collection Limited.*

Following Russia's defeat by Japan and the civil disturbances that followed in 1905 a new constitution was introduced under which the tsar reluctantly agreed that his previous 'autocratic and unlimited powers' should be somewhat curtailed, but he still insisted on retaining his 'autocratic powers'. Under the intelligent and able statesman Stolypin, a kind of tsarist Gorbachov, tragically and mysteriously assassinated in 1911, all political prisoners were freed and many reforms were introduced. The redistribution of land was so extensive that Lenin complained, 'If this should continue . . . it might force us to renounce any agrarian programme at all'.

In 1905 Gregorii Rasputin[10] came into this unhealthy and isolated family circle. Rasputin was a Siberian peasant who bore a scar on his head, the result of a beating he had received for horse stealing. His appearance was savage. He stank like a goat, ate with his fingers, which he wiped in his beard, and dressed in baggy peasant clothes, but was distinguished by his brilliant, penetrating, pale blue eyes. In his favour it should be added that he had a genuine sympathy for the conditions of the Russian peasant and strongly opposed the war with Germany, whose consequences he foresaw. Rasputin was filled with exuberant coarseness, the Siberian ability to drink himself and others under the table, and unrestrained lechery. He was also shrewd, forceful and possibly sincere in his preaching and had an hypnotic power, particularly with women. Women of all stations were not only willing to sleep with him but were curiously moved by his sexuality. Even his enemies credited him with an extraordinary power to withhold orgasm for long intervals. Sometimes he would sleep with one or more naked women to test his and their ability to resist temptation. He would kiss young girls to help them in their struggle against sin.

In 1891 Rasputin decided to become a wandering pilgrim; according to his father, this was because he was too idle to live as a peasant. Leaving his wife and children, he claimed he had had a vision of the Virgin and was to be under her guidance. He preached an unorthodox doctrine of salvation through sin, especially to the female members of his flock. 'Man must sin in order to have something to repent of . . . If God sends us temptation, we must yield to it voluntarily and without resistance so we may afterwards do penance in utter contrition.' Rasputin provided the temptation, the sin and the absolution.

Rodzianko, the President of the Duma, complained that he had files of letters from mothers 'whose daughters had been dishonoured by this insolent rake'. The Minister of Finance described him as 'the sort of Siberian tramp I encountered in Tsarist prisons'. Rodzianko read a report on his activities and said 'Some of the details were so repulsive that they could not be read without abhorrence'. Undoubtedly, he had an hypnotic personality and the French ambassador referred to his 'magnetic pupils' that 'seemed to read one's inmost thoughts'. Stolypin, the Chairman of the Council of Ministers, and one of the few really intelligent men who ever served Nicholas, described meeting him: 'I felt an irrepressible repulsion to that horrible being rise in me. But, I realized that the man had great hypnotic power and was producing a strong psychic impression, truly one of repulsion. Mastering myself, I shouted at him. . . .'

Rodzianko had a similar experience: 'Rasputin turned his face towards me and his eyes began to move over me: at first over the face, then over the region of the heart, and again over the eyes. This lasted several seconds. Personally, I am not in the least subject to the influence of hypnosis – I have tested it many times – but this time I experienced a tremendous and incomprehensible force. I felt a purely animal rage rising in me, blood rushed to my heart, and I realized I was approaching a state of genuine madness.'

When orthodox medicine could offer no hope Alix had resorted to quacks. Following the departure of Philippe she turned to Badmaev, a Buddhist Mongol from central Asia, described by Palaeologue, the French ambassador, as an ignorant fanatic. Without any medical qualifications he took obscure cases of a psychological or gynaecological nature for which he invented expensive new treatments with herbs and magic potions. These were supposed to be specially imported from Tibet but were, in fact, purchased from the nearest grocers and chemists.

Theofan, the royal family's private bishop, distrusting the Lutheran background of the tsarina and the non-Orthodox faiths of her medical advisors, decided that if Alix wanted to be surrounded by quacks they should at least be Russian Orthodox ones. He appointed Rasputin 'Imperial Lamp Tender' in charge of the lamps burning before the numerous icons in the royal palaces. While tending the lamps he became acquainted with Badmaev, who unwisely called him in for consultation during a bleeding episode. Rasputin rapidly rose from wick-trimmer to royal physician, displacing Badmaev.

Rasputin not only met the tsarina's proclivity for fakes and charlatans but in a unique way offered the royal couple the only therapy available for their child's bleeding episodes. Torn blood vessels will heal, but movement prevents healing and stress raises blood pressure, which increases bleeding. First, Rasputin was able to calm and even put to sleep an often hysterical child and reassure his family – and this was a considerable advantage during a bleeding episode. Second, as the British geneticist J.B.S. Haldane suggested, Rasputin's hypnotic presence may actually have helped the tsarevitch constrict the arterioles, which are controlled by the autonomic nervous system. The Grand Duchess Olga was a witness of one of Rasputin's 'treatments' at Tsarskoe Selo:

> The poor child lay in pain, dark patches under his eyes and his little body all distorted, and the leg terribly swollen. The doctors were just useless . . . more frightened than any of us . . . whispering among themselves . . . It was getting late and I was persuaded to go to my rooms. Alicky then sent a message to Rasputin in St Petersburg. He reached the palace about midnight or even later. By that time I had reached my apartments and early in the morning Alicky called me to go to Alexis's room. I just could not believe my eyes. The little boy was not just alive – but well. He was sitting up in bed, the fever gone, his eyes clear and bright, not a sign of any swelling in the leg – Later I learned from Alicky that Rasputin had not even touched the child but merely stood at the foot of the bed and prayed.

Whatever the physiological basis of Rasputin's power his ability to help the only male heir to the throne, when orthodox medicine was helpless, gave him absolute power. Rasputin's most dramatic intervention was performed at a distance and was clearly purely coincidental. The royal family was on a hunting expedition to Belovehi in Poland in 1913 when Alexis had two serious bleeds, the second forming a large hot painful lump in his groin. The child screamed with pain and the doctors feared the mass of blood becoming infected. Consideration was given to draining the unclotted mass but the doctors were afraid they would precipitate uncontrolled bleeding. Anna Vyrubova telegrammed Grigorii who had returned to his ancestral village of Pokrovskoe east of the Urals. He cabled back, 'the illness is not serious, don't let the doctors tire him'. Next morning the tsarevitch had recovered and Rasputin's place in the royal household was unassailable. The tsar explained to Kokovtsov, the last peace-time prime minister, 'Rasputin is a simple peasant who can relieve the suffering of my son by a strange power. The Empress' reliance upon him is a matter for the family and I will allow no one to meddle in my family's affairs.' This attitude was the more unaccountable and unacceptable to the Russian people because no one outside the most immediate family circle was allowed to know the nature of the tsarevitch's affliction. Even Pierre Gilliard, who was tutor to the four princesses between 1905 and 1913, did not discover the fact until he was appointed tutor to the tsarevitch himself. That many Russians would have seen the illness as a judgement of God made concealment even more important, but to outsiders the tsarina's absolute faith in Rasputin was as inexplicable as it was deplorable. It was taken as evidence of her total unfitness for the position to which marriage had brought her.

Rasputin was one of the few people who went into the domestic apartments at Tsarskoe. He incongruously called the royal couple Momma and Papa and they called him their Friend sent by God. To the royal children he brought a glimpse of the outside world they had not seen before and they obviously liked the bearded eccentric. While the tsarina had complete faith in Rasputin and was completely under his will, the tsar retained more independence. He declined to discuss affairs of state with him but admitted that at times of stress or anxiety Rasputin could soothe him and raise his spirits: 'Five minutes conversation is enough to feel myself calm and resolute. Rasputin can always say what I need to learn at the moment and the effect of his words lasts for weeks.' As Rasputin's control of the royal family, and particularly the tsarina, grew, he began first to meddle in church affairs and then in politics. In 1911 the church leadership turned against him and in one confrontation a more eccentric than usual priest suddenly lunged at Rasputin, grabbing at his penis, while Bishop Hermogenes attacked him with a heavy cross.

Over the years the imperial couple gradually exhausted all their subjects' reserves of loyalty, respect and trust. They were rarely seen but it was universally known that they consorted with a drunken lascivious peasant. An intelligent, outgoing tsar might well have converted Russia into a respectable liberal democracy. Unfortunately, Nicholas was weak, timid and suspicious. During the next ten critical years, under the influence of his wife and Rasputin and continually worried by the young tsarevitch's bouts of bleeding, he shed all intelligent or forceful ministers. A month before the revolution, Rodzianko warned him, 'Your Majesty, there is not one reliable or honest man left around you; all the best men have been removed or have retired. There remain only those of ill repute.'

Protopopov, Minister of the Interior when the first revolution broke out, was typical of the people who were placed in positions of eminence by the malign influence of Rasputin. The British ambassador described him as certifiably insane.[11] The French ambassador reported that Protopopov was in the early stages of general paralysis of the insane due to syphilis. Protopopov himself claimed that he could communicate with Rasputin by telepathy. When the riots began in Petrograd in 1917 Protopopov, who was responsible for the maintenance of law and order, locked himself in a darkened room and sought advice from the spirit of Rasputin, by then assassinated.

Rasputin was probably too shrewd to have tried to seduce the tsarina but inevitably rumours abounded, and lascivious letters purporting to have passed between Rasputin and the tsarina were in circulation. Rasputin added fuel to this speculation by his drunken boasts. It was widely believed that he took part in orgies involving not only the empress but also her four growing daughters. Alix certainly encouraged them to write most remarkable letters. At the age of fourteen, Olga addressed him as her 'dear darling beloved friend', and signed 'ardently loving you, your Olga'. 'My Dear and true friend', wrote the Grand Duchess Tatiana, 'God loves you so. And, you say God is so good and kind that he will do anything you ask. So visit us soon. It is so dull without you. Mother is ill without you and it is so sad to see her ill.' Alix clearly loved the man who appeared to heal her son. In one letter she wrote: 'My beloved, unforgettable teacher, redeemer and mentor! How tiresome it is without you! My soul is quiet and I relax only when you, my teacher, are beside me. I kiss your hands and lean my head on your blessed shoulder. Oh how light, how light do I feel then. I only wish one thing; to fall asleep, to fall asleep, for ever on your shoulders and in your arms. . . . I am asking for your holy blessing and I am kissing your blessed hands. I love you for ever. Yours, M [Mama].'

Protected from arrest by the tsarina his behaviour became more outrageous. Russian secret police reported regularly on his behaviour. On one occasion he exposed himself to a number of women in a public restaurant. He followed this by giving his audience a vivid description of his amorous adventures, naming the women involved, and boasted that he could do anything he liked with the tsarina, whom he referred to as 'the old girl'.

Rasputin's apartments were the scenes of the wildest orgies. 'They beggared all description', wrote the American ambassador, 'The . . . infamies of the Emperor Tiberius on the Isle of Capri are made to seem modest and tame.' Even though the secret police documented his wild adventures outside the palace in great detail, the tsar merely took the criticisms as a breach of etiquette. 'Better one Rasputin than ten fits of hysterics a day', he let slip on one occasion. Even when a detailed account of Rasputin's activities in the restaurant were sent to Nicholas such was Alix's obsession that nothing could be done. In 1911 the able Stolypin, shocked by reports of Rasputin's behaviour, attempted to have the latter sent back to his home. When he tried to warn Nicholas of the effect Rasputin was having on his reputation Nicholas replied 'Perhaps everything you say is true. But, I must ask you never to speak to me again about Rasputin. In any case, I can do nothing at all about it.' Alix was so enraged by Stolypin's attempts to remove Rasputin that when Stolypin was assassinated she regarded it as a divine judgement on him: 'Those who have offended God in the person of our Friend may no longer count on divine protection.' Alix habitually referred to Rasputin as 'our friend'.

The effect on the morale of those classes on whom the emperor depended is illustrated by an entry in the diary of General Bogdanovich: 'I took up my pen feeling crushed and wretched. I have never known a more disgraceful time. It is not the tsar but the upstart Rasputin who governs Russia, and he states openly that the tsar needs him even more than the tsarina: and then there is that letter to Rasputin in which the tsarina writes she only knows peace with her head on his shoulder. . . . The tsar has lost all respect and the tsarina declares that it is only thanks to Rasputin's prayers that the tsar and their son are alive and well; and this is the twentieth century!'

Even so, the bizarre ramshackle system of tsarist rule might have survived indefinitely had it not been for the stresses of the First World War. Conversely, it is just possible that the war might not have started if the tsar had not been so exercised by his son's suffering. Three days before Franz Ferdinand's assassination, the tsarevich had slipped on a ladder on the *Standart*. The boy's ankle swelled rapidly and the internal bleeding led to great pain. To add to the royal family's distress, a few hours before Franz Ferdinand's murder in Sarajevo a syphilitic ex-prostitute, Chionya Gusyeva, had attempted to assassinate Rasputin in his home village in Siberia. For the first time for a year Rasputin had returned home to visit his family. Gusyeva stabbed him deeply, exposing his intestines. Remarkably, Rasputin survived even though surgical repair had to be delayed for six hours and he refused an anaesthetic during the operation. It is curious to think how different the history of the world might have been if Franz Ferdinand had been slightly tougher and Gregorii Rasputin a trifle weaker. But it was Rasputin who lived, although he had to remain in Siberia for some time.

Ironically, June and July 1914 were perhaps the only times when it might have been useful for Rasputin to be near the tsar. If he had alleviated the heir's suffering it would have taken a weight off Nicholas's mind at a crucial time. More importantly, Rasputin was strikingly perceptive of the danger of war. He wrote shakily from his sick bed: 'Thou art the Tsar, the father of the people, don't let the lunatics triumph and destroy themselves and the people. If we conquer Germany, what in truth will happen to Russia? When you consider it like that there has never been such a martyrdom. We all drown in blood. "Terrible is the destruction and without end the grief." Gregorii.' – and he always believed: 'Had I been there, there would have been no war. I would not have permitted it.'

It may have been an idle boast, but in view of Rasputin's power over the royal family in other ways, it was quite possible. The tsar knew his country's weaknesses and had no stomach for a patriotic war. He tried to compromise by limiting mobilization to the south of the country, hoping that support could be given to Serbia without bringing about a confrontation with Germany. But he was overtaken by the pace of events. Germany attacked France through Belgium and Britain went to the assistance of Belgium, in response to the guarantee that Victoria had renewed to her beloved Uncle Leopold over seventy years earlier.

Russia entered the war badly equipped, but the speed of its mobilization surprised the Germans. Russia immediately invaded East Prussia and in doing so relieved pressure on the western front. Germany hoped to defeat France first and threw seven-eighths of her army into the invasion. German mobilization went according to plan until the tsar's invasion of East Prussia. Due to greatly superior German staffwork and an acute shortage of ammunition on the Russian side, the Russian invasion ended in disaster at the battle of Tannenberg, but the attack forced Germany to switch two army corps, a cavalry division and their best commander from the west to the east. The hoped-for breakthrough into France never occurred. General Dupont, one of the French General Joffre's aides, wrote of the diversion from the Schlieffen Plan, 'This was perhaps our salvation'.

Early in 1915 Hindenburg persuaded the kaiser to transfer more troops from the stalemate on the western front in order to mount a major offensive against Russia. The tsar had a superfluity of soldiers but too few officers to lead them and a gross deficiency in guns and ammunition: one soldier in three had no rifle and some had no boots. In a series of hideous encounters, in which the Germans used poison gas for the first time in warfare, the Russians lost 100,000 killed and 130,000 taken prisoner. Winter snows, frost and mud added to the misery. The Germans made considerable advances but failed to meet their strategic goals and the Russians achieved considerable success against the Austrians on the southern front.

Allied warships bombarded the Dardanelles in an attempt to break open the route between the Mediterranean and the Black Sea, which Turkey had blocked since the beginning of the war. Had they succeeded the Russians could have received supplies of arms from the west, but both the naval attack and the later landings failed miserably. German reinforcements on the Austrian front eventually drove the Russians back. The retreat became general, Warsaw fell, essential railways were cut and numberless columns of refugees packed the roads beside the fleeing troops. To his credit Grand Duke Nicholas, the Russian Commander in Chief, aided by the onset of winter, managed to slow the German advance later in 1915 but in one year Russia had lost about one million men in battle and three-quarters of a million captured by the enemy.

In August 1915 the Minister for War reported: 'One can expect irreparable catastrophe at any time. The army is no longer retreating, it is simply running away.' 'But', he concluded his report, 'there is a far more horrible event which threatens Russia. I feel obliged to inform the government that this morning . . . His Majesty told me of his decision to remove the Grand Duke (Nikolaevich) and to personally assume supreme command of the army.' In spite of a collective appeal by the Council of Ministers, Nicholas arrived at the Headquarters although he was persuaded to leave the not very competent grand duke in effective command. Alix bombarded him with letters of advice: 'Being firm is the only saving', and reassuring him, 'our Friend's prayers arise night and day for you to heaven and God will hear them'. As he left for the Headquarters she gave Nicholas one of Rasputin's combs with the advice, 'Remember to comb your hair before all difficult tasks and decisions . . . it will help you in the future and give strength to the others to fulfil your orders'. Such was the Russia which faced the most powerful and best organized army in the world.

For a while it seemed that Nicholas's assumption of command might pay off. In 1915 and 1916 Russian industry was reorganized on a war footing and the supplies of shells and equipment became adequate. Although the Russians were driven back by the Germans and lost all of Poland in 1915, they advanced against the Turks with tragic consequences for the Armenians under Turkish control. In 1916 in a brilliant campaign led by General Brusilov, planned to coincide with the catastrophic British campaign in Flanders and an Italian attack at the head of the Adriatic, the Russians broke the Austrian line over a 200-mile front and took 350,000 prisoners. Germany was hard pressed on all fronts and even Romania rashly declared war on the Teutonic giant, but the Germans reinforced the Austrians yet again and the Brusilov offensive was halted after the loss of 350,000 men. As the emperor was in command he also took the blame.

As the war progressed, Alix became increasingly involved in her husband's affairs: she was obsessed with strengthening his will. When dealing with his Headquarters staff, she instructed him, 'Be Peter the Great, Ivan the Terrible, Emperor Paul – crush them all under you'. He replied, 'God bless you, my Darling, my Sunny! Your poor weak-willed little hubby Nicky.' 'Don't laugh at silly old wifey, she has trousers unseen', she encouraged him. She returns to her trousers metaphor repeatedly. Sometimes they were 'black trousers'. Once 'I yearn to show these cowards my immortal trousers'. 'He is a man, not a petticoat', was a high compliment. In a different culture she might have become a militant feminist, in early twentieth-century Russia she had to work through and on her husband. Her attitude inevitably made her many enemies 'who fear that I interfere too much in the affairs of state'. In September 1916 the empress cabled, 'Our Friend begs you not to worry too much over the question of food supply, says things will arrange themselves'. A letter told Nicholas, 'This must be your war and peace. . . . They have not the right to say a single word on these matters.'

When the tsar was at Headquarters, he relied on Alix for information. 'Yes, truly you ought to be my eyes and ears there in the capital', he suggested, and 'you really help me a great deal by speaking to ministers and watching them', he encouraged. She took up the task enthusiastically. 'I am no longer the slightest bit shy or afraid of ministers and speak like a waterfall in Russian', Alix boasted to her husband. Gradually she used her influence to ease out the more independent members of the Council of Ministers and replaced them with Rasputin's nominees. The incompetent Sturmer was made president, 'Warmly recommended to the Emperor by Rasputin'. According to the liberal and pro-western Foreign Minister Sazonov, however, Sturmer was 'A man who has left a bad memory whenever he occupied an administrative post'. When Sazonov advised the tsar to offer the Poles autonomy if the allies won Alix, fearing that her son's domain would be diminished, hurried to Headquarters with Sturmer and persuaded the tsar to dismiss Sozanov and make Sturmer foreign minister as well as premier.

Soon Rasputin, through Alix, began to give Nicholas military advice. 'Move up our cavalry a little to the north, in the direction of Libau', she ordered, and a little later, 'I must pass on to you the following request from our Friend, suggested to him by a vision. He asks you to order an offensive near Riga. . . . He says that we can and must attack, and for me to write you that immediately.' Nikolaevitch threatened to hang Rasputin if he ever set foot in the Headquarters but Alix eventually succeeded in having the grand duke dismissed.

By the end of 1916 the demoralization of the nation and the army was complete. 'The Tsar offends the nation by what he allows to go on in the palace', wrote one right-wing politician. In a desperate effort to remove one cause of their troubles, a group of conspirators, including Prince Yussopov and the Grand Duke Pavlovitch, resolved to kill Rasputin. After the tsar, Felix Yussopov was the richest man in Russia[12] and Dmitri Pavlovitch was a nephew of the Emperor Nicholas himself. Using the beautiful Princess Irma as bait, the plotters enticed Rasputin, in secret, to the Yussopov palace where they fed him with cakes and wine which were supposed to be laced with cyanide. To their amazement and consternation he ate and drank with gusto and called for music and song – a gramophone played 'Yankee Doodle'. In desperation Yussopov finally shot him twice in the chest. Rasputin at first appeared to be dead but to Yussopov's horror rose up and almost escaped to the street. Purishkevitch shot him twice more in the back of the head and dragged him back into the house where the prince beat the body with a large brass candlestick until he was exhausted. Finally, Rasputin was pushed through the ice into a canal. Remarkably an autopsy showed he was still alive at this point and when death finally came it was from drowning. The body was secretly buried in a church near Alexandrovsk but was later exhumed by the army, burned, and the ashes scattered to prevent the development of a Rasputin cult.

The conspirators were hailed everywhere as heroes and in spite of Alix's hysterical letters, escaped serious punishment. Grand Duke Nicholas Mikhailovitch wrote of Rasputin's murder, 'although it has cleared the air, everything they have accomplished is but a half measure since Alexandra Feodorovna [the Empress] and Protopopov must be got out of the way'.

Even at this stage, if Nicholas had appointed a competent ministry acceptable to the Duma, the regime might possibly have survived; but when the tsar's brother-in-law, Grand Duke Aleksander Mikhailovitch, urged this course on the imperial pair, Alix speaking on behalf of the royal couple ridiculed him, while Nicholas smoked and said nothing. Stubbornly, the tsar returned to be with his generals at the front.

The army commandeered far more trains than it required and although there was food enough in the country, the citizens of St Petersburg were left cold and increasingly hungry. Protopopov had been placed in charge of the distribution of food at the request of Rasputin. On 23 February 1917 large crowds began to converge on the city centre and, although there were occasional cries of 'Down with the police' and 'Down with the war', they remained orderly. The Cossacks were called out but were obviously reluctant to break up the crowds. At this crisis, when the fate of the Empire was poised in the balance, Protopopov, Minister of the Interior in charge of security, in a darkened room, was desperately trying to contact Rasputin's ghost for advice.

When news of the disturbances eventually reached Nicholas, he cabled General Khabalov: 'I order you to bring all of these disturbances to a halt as of tomorrow.' Khabalov took this as an order to fire on the crowds if necessary. Forty demonstrators died the next day but some troops were clearly reluctant to fire. One detachment of Guards in barracks seized their rifles and ran out into the streets, possibly intending to stop the bloodshed. Confronted by a detachment of police they exchanged a few shots and returned voluntarily to their barracks. When news of this minor incident spread it had an electrifying effect as it led to the belief that the army was joining the revolt. A last appeal that night to Nicholas to appoint a Ministry acceptable to the Duma was rejected. Next day the Guards regiment which had briefly clashed with the police mutinied. The February Revolution had begun.

At this critical juncture the three older girls and the tsarevitch caught measles. Alix devoted so much time to nursing them in Tsarskoe Selo that she became even more out of touch than usual with events in St Petersburg twenty miles away. She advised her husband, 'You must tell the workers that they must not declare strikes, if they do they will be sent to the front'. On 27 February[13] Rodzianko ended a cable to the tsar: 'The last hour has come when the fate of the dynasty and the fatherland is being decided'. 'That fat-bellied Rodzianko has written me a lot of nonsense again, which I won't even bother to answer', the tsar commented to his wife, but by the 28th even Alix was worried. 'Concessions are necessary. The strikes continue; many troops have gone over to the strikers', she cabled, but by now it was too late. The next day Nicholas declared martial law and sent a single battalion to the capital, unaware that the 100,000-strong garrison had joined the revolt. Nicholas started back to St Petersburg in the imperial train. Too late, he offered the very concessions which earlier might have restored the situation.

The Provisional Government demanded that the tsar step down in favour of his son, with his brother Grand Duke Michail as Regent. At 3 p.m. on 15 March 1917, in the imperial train, which had been literally halted in its tracks, Nicholas signed the instrument of abdication. It is possible that this solution might have prevented further revolutions but the saga of Victoria's gene had one more twist to it. While the imperial staff waited for a train to take the papers to the capital, Nicholas began to question his physician, Dr Fedorov, about the tsarevitch's future. Fedorov said, 'Science teaches us, Sire, that it is an incurable disease. Yet those who are afflicted will sometimes reach an advanced old age. Still, Alexis Nicolaevich is at the mercy of any accident.' The deposed tsar began to realize that he and Alexandra might well be exiled, while his son would be kept in Russia. At 9 p.m. on the same day he hand-wrote an abdication paper with the words, 'Not wishing to part with our dear son, we hand over our inheritance to our brother, the Grand Duke Michail Alexandrovich . . .'. A few days later he rejoined Alix and sobbed on her breast like a child. By disinheriting his heir Nicholas further weakened the throne. Much of the residual loyalty that would have passed to the tsarevitch was not transferable to the tsar's brother Michail, who was not in line to the throne. The new government, which was prepared to accept the boy as a constitutional monarch, feared that the grand duke might be as autocratic as his brother. Realizing that his position was hopeless, Michail abdicated after only one meeting with his ministers. The 300-year-old Romanov dynasty was at an end.

A moderate government under Kerensky attempted to continue the war alongside the Allies, but in November, the Communists seized power in St Petersburg and several other cities. The Communist government soon made peace with Germany, allowing German troops to be transferred to the western front. For a while the war shifted in Germany's favour but eventually the great German offensive of 1918 was driven back. King Alfonso XIII of Spain and Queen Wilhemina of the Netherlands, as neutral sovereigns, tried to bring about peace but although the European monarchs had played a role in starting the war, they were unable to end it. By November 1918 German resistance was collapsing, the Armistice was signed and the kaiser abdicated.[14] At the end of the First World War, the crowns of the European monarchs, in the words of one commentator, 'were rolling about the floor'. Although many new republics were created, few were more democratic than their monarchical predecessors. Germany, Spain and Russia sooner or later became dictatorships.

The war had achieved nothing – except unprecedented death and destruction. It aborted the economic and political leadership of Europe. The origins of the disaster lay not in the need to set right some intolerable injustice, in unacceptable commercial tensions, or even in some dark, longstanding religious division. It was a diplomatic folly and militaristic adventure where old men totally misunderstood the effects of new technology: the kaiser told his troops they would be 'home before the leaves fall'. It was a war where the cry 'King and Country' was heard often. Kings played a major role in starting the conflict – especially the jingoism of Wilhelm, Franz Joseph's desire to crush the Serbs and Nicholas's dithering, which was exacerbated by his genuine love for a congenitally sick son.

Russia had been an anomaly even in 1914, a modern European power with a medieval government. Change of some kind was inevitable, a communist revolution was not. Indeed, the Marxists themselves expected to come to power in one of the older industrialized states first. Both by virtue of his background and his limited mind Nicholas was an obstacle to change, but he was also very weak, and in different circumstances he might easily have accepted change. The real misfortune was Alix. She might have proved the tsar's evil genius even if the tsarevitch had not been a haemophiliac and even without Rasputin, but it is clear the tsarevitch's illness gave Rasputin his power. Rasputin's power, in turn, ensured that the throne was surrounded by scoundrels, nonentities and idiots – and when the crisis came the royal family had lost the natural reservoir of loyalty and goodwill among all classes of society which had supported the throne down the previous centuries.

Without doubt, the haemophilia gene Nicholas's wife carried, through its political side-effects, hastened his family's end. Whether any part of the lineage lived on is the subject of the next chapter.

CHAPTER EIGHT

The Pretenders

When a king dies violently pretenders to the throne quickly volunteer to fill the vacancy or overthrow the usurper. After Richard III died at Bosworth both Lambert Simnel and Perkin Warbeck falsely claimed to be the rightful heirs. The circumstances of the murders of the tsar and his family were particularly obscure. For seventy years after the deaths the scene was closed to the rest of the world by Communist paranoia. The family was murdered at a remote spot during the chaos of a civil war, while the world's attention was distracted by the climactic battles of the First World War, then taking place on the western front. Although the anti-Communist White Russians captured Ekaterinburg eight days after the murder they did not appoint Sokolov to hold an inquiry until six months later and his incomplete report only became available four years later still when he fled to the west. Only recently has perestroika, and later the collapse of the Communist regime, made new evidence available. In the years following the murders a variety of pretenders appeared. Some were rapidly exposed but one, variously known as Mrs Anderson, Mrs Manahan or Anastasia, was a cause célèbre for much of the twentieth century. The story filled cheap gossip columns and reached the highest judicial circles of Germany, producing 8,000 pages of legal documents in the longest legal case of the century. It was the subject of a government inquiry, numerous books, three films – including one with Ingrid Bergman – and enough newspaper and magazine articles to bring Fleet Street or Times Square to a halt. Recently the most sophisticated genetic tests of bone, hair and tissue samples of Mrs Manahan, the skeletons of the Russian royal family and of living relatives, have demolished the claims of Mrs Manahan but the status of at least one other possible survivor of the massacre remains in doubt, and as long as the exact fate of the tsarevitch and one of his sisters is unknown, speculation will continue.

Where thirty years of legal argument were inconclusive modern scientific technology has recently proved, ten years after her death, that Mrs Manahan was not the daughter of the tsar, but her story was a remarkable one and shows clearly how it is difficult to make sufficient allowance for coincidence. Facts are often stranger than fiction. As social beings we are intensely interested in other people's lives and enjoy romantic interpretations of the data. It would have been more exciting for Mrs Manahan to have been the daughter of the tsar, mysteriously snatched from a firing squad, than a munitions worker – and her claims were corroborated by so many remarkable coincidences that many who had known the real Anastasia were prepared to accept her. She bore such a remarkable physical resemblance to the real Anastasia that some experts on physiognomy, after examining her ears, skull and body scars, declared her to be Anastasia. Like Anastasia her middle fingers were short, her big toes were deformed and even her handwriting was similar. She seemed to have had detailed information on the Winter Palace, and to know enough of court etiquette to fool some of the surviving relatives of the tsar. She had a good knowledge of English as well as German and some arcane knowledge of the activities of the royal families of Europe. How a munitions worker who had been certified insane, after being seriously injured in an explosion, managed all this is a mystery in itself. Finally, when the grave of the Russian royal family was opened the remains of only three of the daughters were found. The Russians first announced that it was the skeleton of Anastasia that was missing, adding circumstantial credibility to her claim.

While Mrs Manahan was still alive we attempted to check her identity by determining whether she carried Queen Victoria's gene for haemophilia. In the event we were thwarted by an obstructive lawyer and her sudden death, although the more recent tests have shown that the results would have been negative.

The real Anastasia was born in 1901. She inherited her father's intense blue eyes, was slightly plump, with fair hair and, in the words of a cousin, 'frightfully temperamental'. Much is known about Anastasia's court life and even her school books survive, with lessons neatly written in English, German and Russian. She was the daughter of the absolute monarch of the world's largest nation and life at court instilled in her a strict observance of protocol. At the same time she expected the world to do her bidding and as a child she was sometimes a tomboy, rough and spoiled, who kicked and tripped up the servants.

The early months of 1917 were the last of Anastasia's old way of life. The previous year had ended inauspiciously, as Rasputin's corpse was dragged from the frozen canal on 19 December, yet few had guessed the country would be on the verge of revolution only three months later. In Switzerland, Lenin could still write, 'we older men may not live to see the decisive battles of the approaching revolution'.

With solid reason, the tsar was blamed for Russia's woes. Worse, in St Petersburg the tsarina was said to have betrayed Russia to her German relatives – a false but understandable accusation. Following their abdication the Kerensky government decided to keep the imperial family out of harm's way at their summer palace, Tsarskoe Selo.

After the abdication the tsar appealed to King George V for political asylum and the Kerensky government made a formal application via the British ambassador in St Petersburg, who wrote, 'I earnestly trust that, in spite of the obvious objections, I may be authorised, without delay, to offer his majesty asylum in England'. At first the king reluctantly agreed and even the kaiser volunteered safe conduct for a vessel through the Baltic, but the war on the western front was going badly and government opinion turned against the imperial family. 'The Empress is not only a Boche [German] by birth', wrote the British ambassador in Paris, 'but in sentiment.' Prime Minister Lloyd George was anxious to quarantine the virus of Lenin's revolution, even if this meant persuading King George to turn his back on his own cousin. The king himself also feared that 'the presence of the Imperial Family (especially the Empress) in the country would raise all sorts of difficulties', and started to raise all sorts of difficulties himself. He demanded that the impoverished Kerensky government should meet all their expenses in Britain, had misgivings about the sea voyage and even suggested that Balmoral Castle, a possible refuge, was not a suitable residence in winter, although Aberdeenshire must be almost tropical compared to Russia. The decisive influence seems to have been the king's private secretary, Lord Stamfordham. Eventually, the king persuaded the British government to withdraw their offer. The weak but loyal autocrat and his family were left to their fate.

In August 1917 the Kerensky government moved the royal family and their immediate servants from St Petersburg to Tobolsk in Siberia, where they thought the local population would be less hostile. Two months later the Communists under Lenin seized the reins of government and in March the following year concluded the Treaty of Brest-Litovsk with Germany. Russia had suffered an unprecedented defeat and Brest-Litovsk ushered in a brutally unequal peace: Russia ceded one-third of its population, half its industry and nine-tenths of its coal mines to Germany. One Russian delegate to the treaty was so humiliated that he shot himself. On hearing of the treaty the tsar said, 'I should never have thought the Emperor William and the German Government could stoop so low as to shake hands with these Bolshevik traitors'.

Lenin had no love for the tsar – his own brother had been executed by Nicholas's father. Soon after Brest-Litovsk the German ambassador to Moscow was assassinated and Lenin was terrified that the Germans might use the episode as an excuse to attack again. Civil war was breaking out in several parts of the country where White Russians loyal to the tsar were fighting the Bolsheviks. Lenin ordered the family to be moved again, this time to Ekaterinburg, later known as Sverdlovsk,[1] in the Urals, where he felt confident of the loyalty of the local Soviet. At his accession the twenty-year-old Nicholas had wept, 'What am I going to do? What is going to happen to me? . . . I am not prepared to be a tsar. I never wanted to become one.' As a middle-aged man he had brought his country into the war to honour a treaty with Serbia, he had mobilized one and half million men in a week and seen half of that first draft killed or wounded. He had perhaps saved the West in 1914 but he had destroyed his own country in the years that followed. Now he was a prisoner, alone with the family he loved, except for a few loyal servants including his personal physician Dr Botkin and a cheerful sailor, Nogorny, who carried the haemophiliac child around in his arms. Once again Alexis had a bleeding episode and he and his sisters made a delayed entrance into their new prison, three weeks after their parents, on 24 May. At Ekaterinburg, the royal family was guarded by a Soviet commissar called Alexander Avadeyev, who drank heavily, stole from the family, invaded their privacy and drew obscene pictures of the tsarina and Rasputin on the lavatory wall, where the grand duchesses and the tsarevitch would see them. Nogorny, the loyal sailor, was murdered and the tsar now had to carry his son about the house himself.

It is at this point that hard historical facts begin to fray into tattered threads of gossip and political propaganda. It was rumoured the Brest-Litovsk Treaty contained a secret clause whereby the Communists guaranteed the safety of the imperial family. The kaiser seems to have been genuinely solicitous of his cousin's welfare and he would have benefited politically by being the saviour of the tsar. The tsarina, however, claimed 'she would rather die in Russia than be saved by the Germans'. The kaiser's daughter-in-law recalled, much later, that the tsar said he would not be saved 'at any price. His attitude', she went on, 'much disturbed the German Emperor, who spent sleepless nights in mourning over the Romanovs' fate.'

Russia was vast, communications poor and the country was racked by civil war. To the west the war was entering a critical phase and each side knew that the renewal of war on the eastern front could well decide the outcome in the west. The Germans felt that they might gain the support of the monarchists if they aided them against the Bolsheviks. Many a Russian wanted to join the British and French and renew the war against Germany. Each side tried to keep its options open. Nicholas II had abdicated in favour of his brother Grand Duke Michail Alexandrovitch. The grand duke abdicated in turn but after the death of Nicholas the grand duke could still have been a centre of resistance. The Bolsheviks claimed that Michail had been assassinated in Perm on the night of 12–13 June 1918, a few weeks before Nicholas was murdered, but German diplomats in Russia continued to telegraph Berlin that the grand duke was still alive, claiming from St Petersburg on August 24, 'Completely reliable and exact news that his Imperial Highness Grand Duke Michail is healthy and has been found in safety'. To this day no corpse and no unequivocal account of his death have been found.

The last Tsar of all the Russias was killed in the early hours of 17 July 1918. That much has never been in dispute, and two days later Lenin interrupted the session of the Council of the People's Commissars on public health legislation in St Petersburg with a dramatic message, 'at Ekaterinburg, by a decision of the Regional Soviet, Nicholas has been shot'. The Council, none of whom knew any of the details, fell silent until Lenin said drolly, 'Let us now go on and read the draft, clause by clause'. The official press communiqué added to the report of the tsar's death: 'The wife and son of Nicholas have been sent to a safe place.' In spite of these comforting words it is clear that most or all of the rest of the family were also murdered. How the rest of the family died and what happened to the corpses has remained one of the greatest historical mysteries of the twentieth century.

The tsar died in a house on Ascension Avenue in Ekaterinburg, belonging to an engineer called Ipatiev. A White Russian army was at the outskirts of the town and would capture it from the Bolsheviks a few days later. Before they died, on 12 July, the tsar and tsarina 'constantly' heard the cannon along the battlefront.

Eight days later, the White Russians captured Ekaterinburg and later set up an inquiry into the fate of the royal family, chaired by Sokolov, a lawyer. Seven years later Nikolai Sokolov published a book, called *Judicial Enquiry into the Assassination of the Russian Imperial Family* (until the recent revelations this book was the basis for all later accounts). According to Sokolov, as the White Russians advanced on Ekaterinburg the family and their few remaining servants were shot in a basement room of their prison,[2] their bodies were burnt and treated with 358 lb of sulphuric acid and any remains thrown down a flooded mine shaft 30 ft deep. Certainly there were bullet-holes and blood in the house where the Romanovs had been held, but there were no reliable first-hand witnesses and human bodies are difficult to destroy completely. Even though the mine-shaft was drained and explored during the White Russian occupation of Ekaterinburg, only one human finger, a few other bone fragments (never proved to be human), and some false teeth were recovered. None of the royal family had false teeth but their personal physician Dr Botkin wore them.

Regicide, inevitably, is the stuff of drama. Those who ordered the execution and those who carried it out were perfectly aware of the historical significance of what they were doing, yet for a series of understandable reasons, the details became blurred, confused, hidden and filled with false leads.

The authorities running the Urals Soviet responsible for Ekaterinburg, the party bosses in Moscow and the Cheka (the secret police predecessor of the KGB) all played a role in controlling the execution, but each wanted the story told in a different way. The soldiers were zealous to shoot the tsar but reluctant to kill the daughters. The family was killed in a basement by a crowd of soldiers, firing partially blind, into a room rapidly filling with smoke. Several of the soldiers were drunk, almost to the point of incapacity. The women were wearing the equivalent of flak jackets, the like of which the world has never seen before and will never see again.

In the years that followed, tens of millions of Russians were to be shot, starved or beaten to death (including all but one of those who gave the order to execute the tsar). Under Stalin historical facts were subservient to propaganda needs. The key documents, particularly the diaries of the royal couple and several written statements by eyewitnesses were unread, apparently even by the bureaucrats who looked after them, and even physical evidence of the deaths was poorly analysed and went unpublished. It took the light of glasnost to unravel most – but perhaps still not all – of what had happened in the Ipatiev house in the hot summer of 1918.

Edvard Radzinsky is a major contemporary Russian playwright, who trained as an historian and who has recently had access to the Central State Archives to the October Revolution. To his astonishment he was shown all the diaries of Nicholas and Alexandra. The tsar had filled fifty notebooks on his day-to-day life, beginning shortly after the assassination of his grandfather Alexander II in May 1868, until a few hours before his own assassination. In the late 1970s a colleague who knew of Radzinsky's interest had copied a critical document from the Museum of the Revolution, although at the time she called it 'abstract knowledge' and was certain he would not be able 'to talk about all this any time in the next hundred years'. Slowly, however, material was declassified and in 1989 Radzinsky published the first eyewitness account of the tsar's death. It opened a floodgate of information from around what was still the Soviet Union. There was even a Russian version of 'Deep Throat' who telephoned and visited anonymously with key items of information. Radzinsky's book *Zhisn i smert Nikolaia II* was published in English as *The Last Tsar* in 1992.

From the Bolshevik perspective Nicholas was a danger, in the sense that if a White Russian army recaptured him he would become the focus of anti-Communist opposition. The military commissar for the Urals, Filipp Goloshchekin wanted 'Nicholas the Bloody' or the 'Crowned Hangman', as they called him, dead, but was afraid to move without Moscow's approval. Moscow wanted to be rid of the Romanovs, but was afraid of international criticism.

A trap was laid by the Cheka. Friends of the royal family were given permission to send food to the Ipatiev house. The Cheka wrote notes, hidden in milk bottles and written in bad student-French suggesting rescue. The tsar wrote in his diary for 16 June: 'Spent an uneasy night and kept vigil fully dressed. All this because a few days ago we received two letters, one after the other, telling us to prepare to be abducted by some loyal people! The days have passed, though, and nothing has happened, and the waiting and uncertainty have been very trying.'

Cleverly, the windows of the family's living quarters had been whitewashed and sealed so the family looked forward to their brief walks in the garden behind the high fence, away from the stifling conditions indoors. While they were in the garden the diary was read. Goloshchekin had his 'evidence'; he went to Moscow, saw Lenin and the execution was agreed. It was characteristic of the tsarina to insist that the notes in the milk bottles were genuine, but why did Nicholas record the plot in his diary? Was it plain stupidity, or did he believe, as Radzinsky suggests, that by sacrificing himself his family might escape, just as he believed that by abdicating he could still preserve the throne for his brother?

For the Communists the military situation was deteriorating. On 12 June the Ural Soviet agreed unanimously to the execution of the royal family. Goloshchekin didn't tell them that Moscow had already agreed. The Commander-in-Chief on the Ural front told him to proceed. Now he had authority from three different sources, but even so he sent one final telegram to make assurance doubly sure: 'To Moscow, the Kremlin, Sverdlov,[3] copy to Lenin. From Ekaterinburg transmit the following directly: inform Moscow that the trial agreed upon with Filipp due to military circumstances cannot bear delay, we cannot wait. If our opinion is contrary inform immediately. Goloshchekin, Safarov.'

The royal family had no way of knowing their assassination plans were so advanced but they were having a difficult time: Alex had migraines and sat for long hours with cold compresses on her head. Nicholas had painful haemorrhoids and couldn't sit and the young tsarevitch had another episode of bleeding and couldn't walk. A new commandant, Yakov Yurovsky, from the secret police, was appointed at the Ipatiev house. He ingratiated himself by examining Alexei's leg, and listed all the family's valuables under the pretext that the garrison might steal things. There was a lot to steal and the soldiers suspected it. The tsarina loved secrets and for years had used special codes in letters to her husband. In letters to the family in Tobolsk she called jewellery 'medicines' and said it was 'extremely important' to bring them to Ekaterinburg. Tatiana had double bodices sewn for herself and her sisters, concealing diamonds and pearls between the two layers. Yurovsky suspected, but could not prove, that other fabulous wealth existed in addition to his formal lists of family valuables. The men of the guard had all been replaced.

On the evening of 16 July the tsar and tsarina read the Bible, played bezique and went to bed early. Goloshchekin did not receive Lenin's confirmation of his telegram until about midnight. A lorry to collect the corpses arrived at the house at 1.30 a.m., and Yurovsky issued revolvers to twelve men. The royal family and their few retainers were woken and told that because of increased fighting around Ekaterinburg it would be safer if they moved to the basement. It took 40 minutes for them to dress; no doubt it took time for the four daughters to climb into their jewel-laden bodices.

Yurovsky shepherded his victims, the tsar, as he so often did, carrying his haemophiliac son, to the half-cellar, selected because it would muffle the gun-shots and the bullets would not ricochet off the plaster walls. Yurovsky seems to have allayed the group's fears by saying there were malicious rumours that the family were dead, so he was going to photograph them. Chairs were brought for Alix and her son and everyone else arranged themselves in two neat, convenient lines against the wall opposite the door. Instead of a camera, the twelve soldiers with their pistols were called to the doorway. Yurovsky now read from a scrap of paper: 'In view of the fact that your relatives are continuing their attack on Soviet Russia, the Ural Executive has decided to execute you.' 'What, what?' asked the tsar. Yurovsky repeated the statement. 'Forgive them, for they know not what they do', breathed Nicholas. Alix and Olga began making the sign of the cross, but the bullets began to fly before they could finish.

Killing people can be curiously difficult. In the middle of the night, after a bout of heavy drinking, twelve soldiers were crowded into a narrow doorway, to shoot a family they had been brought up to believe was almost divine. They held their pistols in outstretched arms and they were so close together that those at the front got powder burns on their hair and necks from the guns of those behind.

The tsar and tsarina fell quickly, but the rest of the group began running round the room, now becoming opaque with smoke. For the rest of their lives, the soldiers would argue over who had the honour of actually pulling the trigger on the tsar, but only a few minutes earlier, Yurovsky had to replace two of the soldiers because they 'refused to shoot the girls'. Something amazing was happening. In Yurovsky's written account he says 'the bullets from the revolvers bounded off for some reason and ricocheted, jumping around the room like hail' – the bodices had turned into diamond-studded flak jackets! Even the haemophiliac Alexei survived the first hysterical shooting, as did two of the daughters, the lady-in-waiting and Dr Botkin. If this seems improbable it should be recalled that the present King Hussein of Jordan owes his life to the fact that a bullet ricocheted off the medals on his chest when his father, King Abdullah of Jordan, was assassinated in 1951.

The 'Crowned Hangman' had been executed, but it was more difficult to murder the women. The commandant tried to reassert his control: firing from the doorway was stopped. Yurovsky emptied a clip of bullets into the survivors. Then he ordered the victims bayoneted. The lady-in-waiting 'grabbed the bayonet in both hands and began screaming', wrote the commander: 'Later they got her with their rifle butts'.

An effort was made to disentangle the bodies and feel for pulses. It was 20 minutes since the royal family had been brought into the room. The bodies were carried on sheets and loaded into the lorry. The soldiers began to loot watches and other valuables. Another eyewitness (Alexander Strekotin) takes up the story: 'When they laid one of the daughters on the stretcher she cried out and covered her face with her arm. The other [daughters] also turned out to be alive. . . . Ermakov took my bayonet from me and started stabbing everyone dead who turned out to be alive.'

But Peter Zakharovitch Ermakov was even more drunk than most of his comrades. Yurovsky also witnessed this resurrection, adding, 'When they tried to stab one of the girls with a bayonet, the point would not go through her corset'. Ermakov had been delegated the job of disposing of the bodies, but he seemed so incapable that Yurovsky decided to stay with the lorry. In later years Ermakov claimed he fired the first bullets that night and also wrote down his recollections, although they were inaccurate, his memory being blurred with alcohol. He began: 'The good fortune befell me to carry out the ultimate proletarian Soviet justice against the human tyrant, the crowned autocrat. . . . I was honoured to fulfil my obligation before my people and country and took place in the execution of the tsar's entire family.'

But Ermakov was also commissar of a nearby region and, privately, he had promised his companions to bring out the duchesses alive – 'We're not shooting womenfolk! Just the men!' he told them. It was the middle of the night, alcohol and adrenaline were circulating in his veins, Ermakov wanted the girls alive, the bayonet would not go through the corset of the girl who cried out: how long did she live on the lorry?

Ermakov had selected an abandoned mine about 11 miles from Ekaterinburg to dispose of the dead. When the lorry arrived near the place at about dawn, about twenty-five of Ermakov's rowdy friends were waiting: 'Why didn't you bring them to us alive?', they called, remembering the promised sexual pleasures. In the hope of finding something to loot, the local men pretended they could not find the mine-shaft. Eventually, Yurovsky ordered the corpses laid on the ground and stripped naked. He noted later, 'When they began undressing the girls, they saw a corset torn in places by bullets and through the opening they saw diamonds'. Eventually, 18 pounds of diamonds were recovered.[4] The clothes were burnt and the bodies thrown down a shallow shaft with water at the bottom: a hand grenade was thrown in. This may account for the finger later found in the mine.

Twenty-five drunken men, extras to a climactic moment in history, do not keep quiet. Within a few hours Yurovsky realized that everyone knew about the previous night's events. He spent the day looking for another hiding place and twenty-four hours after he had begun the execution he used a small party of men to recover the corpses from their wet grave. Botkin's teeth and the finger were evidently left behind.

What happened next is described in conflicting terms by three eyewitnesses. Yurovsky claims that the corpses were carried a long way. Two (Alexei and the lady-in-waiting) were burnt and disfigured with sulphuric acid and the rest were buried in a 6-foot deep grave. A lorry was finally run backwards and forwards over the site. Ermakov bombastically claims that he recovered the bodies himself and then, near the first grave, all the corpses were cremated: 'The bodies burned to ash, which was buried.' Lyukhanov, who drove the lorry carrying the corpses on both journeys, was exceedingly secretive and never wrote down his memories. His wife, a party idealist, left him shortly after the killings but 'forgave her husband' before she died. Forgave what?

One of Edvard Radzinsky's informants was a man who had known both Ermakov and Lyukhanov's son. He believed Anastasia and the tsarevitch both survived and were taken off the lorry when it stopped on the way to the first burial site. Intriguingly, two eyewitnesses uncovered by Radzinsky observed that the bodies of two of the Ekaterinburg victims were missing from the lorry that took the corpses to the burial site. Did Lyukhanov, who had been party to the escape, tell his wife, who in her zeal for Communism then left him? Ermakov and Yurovsky covered up for each other. Fourteen-year-old Alexei had probably also worn a diamond corset but it was not described by the regicides because they never undressed him. When rumours of Anastasia's survival reached Russia, Yurovsky changed the record of the names of those he cremated from Alexei and the lady-in waiting to Alexei and Anastasia.

More recently (June 1992), nine skeletons have been recovered from a shallow grave near Ekaterinburg. The skulls of the tsar and tsarina and three of their daughters, Olga, Tatiana and Anastasia, have been identified by comparison of their reconstructed faces with the computerized reconstructions of their heads from photographs,[5] and a third skeleton has been identified from its lack of teeth as that of their personal physician, Dr Botkin. Three skeletons were originally identified as those of Olga, Maria and Tatiana,[6] adding to the confusion. As one of the skulls is badly damaged the reliability of these identifications cannot be guaranteed. The bones were brought to England for mitochondrial DNA 'finger-printing'. Mitochondria, small subcellular organelles found in most cells, are inherited only through the mother. All the tsarina's children should therefore possess Queen Victoria's mitochondria. Prince Philip should possess the same mitochondria as he is also descended in the female line from Victoria, and has been used for confirmation. The identity of the remaining three skeletons remains uncertain. One was female and two male, but the tsarevitch is not among them.

The DNA tests were carried out at the Home Office Forensic Science Laboratory at Amersham, Bucks, England; preliminary results were published in July 1993 and a full report in 1994.[7] The tests confirmed that the supposed skeletons of the tsarina and three of her daughters were indeed descendants of Queen Victoria as their chromosomal DNA matched those of Prince Philip, but the results also confirmed that the skeletons of the tsarevitch and another of the daughters were not buried in the mass grave. The bones of the tsar contained two kinds of mitochondrial DNA, a rare condition known as heteroplasmy. One kind exactly matched that from two distant relatives both descended in the female line from one of his maternal ancestors. The other kind differed at one point, due to a mutation which had occurred in the tsar himself or his immediate maternal ancestors.

The new DNA evidence obviously disproves Sokolov's account but also shows that both Yurovsky, who was in charge of the execution and accompanied the bodies to the grave, and Ermakov, who was in charge of the burials, lied. Ermakov claimed that all the corpses were destroyed; Yurovsky that those of the tsarevitch and a lady-in-waiting were destroyed. Although it is remotely possible that Yurovsky confused a mature lady-in-waiting with a daughter it seems more likely that they were both trying to conceal the embarrassing absence of two important bodies. This is also consistent with Radzinsky's two eyewitnesses who insisted that two of the bodies were never put on the lorry before it left Ekaterinburg.

The grave site appears to have been identified from Yurovsky's description and to have been opened on two occasions prior to 1992, each time somewhat carelessly. In 1979 three geologists and a writer opened the grave and took out the three skulls, one of which had a gold dental bridge and was assumed to be the tsar's. They took plaster casts and replaced them. Ten years later, it was rumoured that authorities from Moscow were going to excavate the site, so the three local men, with the backing of the local police, who kept guard, opened the grave again and this time removed nine skeletons, some rope, possibly used to haul the bodies out of the mine shaft, and fragments of glass vessels which may have contained the acid.

It is beyond doubt that eleven people entered the execution chamber in the Ipatiev house. Yurovsky claimed that the bodies of Alexei and the lady-in-waiting were burnt but it is difficult to destroy a body totally and this tale might have been an effort to cover up the discrepancy between the eleven in the cellar and the nine buried bodies. Radzinsky does not identify his informant although he reproduces a drawing and two photographs: was he himself involved as one of the grave robbers? Did his informant really keep his identity secret?

Evidence of a different story, but involving the sighting of Anastasia in European Russia, after the execution at Ekaterinburg, is contained in Anthony Summers and Tom Mangold's 1976 book, *The File on the Tsar*. They tracked down Sokolov's original seven-volume dossier on the murder, as well as the files of Nikander Mirolyubov, the public prosecutor of the Ekaterinburg district. These original documents differ surprisingly from Sokolov's published report. Sokolov's paper contains evidence that the tsarina and her four daughters were evacuated west to Perm, where they were kept as pawns in negotiations over the fate of the German Communists, particularly Karl Liebknecht, then held by the Germans. Summers and Mangold argue that the royal survivors were probably executed after Germany collapsed in 1918, when they ceased to be of value to the Russian Communists.

At first sight it all sounds like a badly written detective mystery but there are interesting clues. It appears Sokolov made up his mind early in the inquiry that all the members of the family had been slaughtered at Ekaterinburg, even though he later accumulated a great deal of evidence that the women were evacuated to Perm. After the White Russians recaptured Perm Sokolov's agents visited the town and interrogated a number of witnesses. His belief that the tsarina and the three elder daughters survived is clearly wrong, but it may be significant that most of his evidence relates to sightings of Anastasia, and that this evidence is earlier than her 'reappearance' in Germany. Sokolov recorded that in February 1919 a Jewish doctor, Pavel Ivanovich Utkin, made a long statement to White Russian investigators. He described how, on 20 September 1918, he had been called by a group of Bolsheviks in Perm to care for a young woman 'somewhat average in height, very well educated, in appearance about eighteen or nineteen years old . . . her hair was cropped and did not reach her shoulders'. She was sick 'and had been beaten', and had a series of superficial face wounds. He cared for her wounds and visited her on three occasions, once staying for an hour. When Dr Utkin asked her who she was she replied, 'In a trembling voice but quite distinctly . . . "I am the Ruler's daughter, Anastasia".'

Summers and Mangold give a number of reasons why Dr Utkin's evidence is credible. He was a careful, almost pedantic, witness and at the end of his statement he said, 'I request you alter my testimony in one respect. Anastasia Nikolyeva did not say to me exactly what you have written: "I am the daughter of the emperor [imperatora], Anastasia", but the following: "I am the daughter of the ruler [gosudarya], Anastasia".' Not knowing what name to write on the prescription for a medicine Utkin had simply put the letter 'N'. The prescription was traced and verified. Utkin's story is internally consistent and, as he pointed out, 'I did not have the slightest doubt that she was the daughter of the emperor, then or now. What would be the purpose, you see, of a person hastening their own end, calling themselves by their true name when someone comes upon them by chance?' The White Russians thought Utkin's evidence so important they sent him to see Sokolov who entered the data in his files but never mentioned it in his book. To add to the confusion further batches of Sokolov's papers have been auctioned more recently but have not yet been published.

Moreover, Utkin was not the only witness who saw the princesses alive in Perm or to testify to an escape attempt by one of the daughters. Eighteen individuals claimed to have known about an episode where a daughter of the tsar was captured after an escape attempt. Maxim Grigoryev, a railway signalman, reported how he ran over to see 'A young girl, who looked about 18 or 19' sitting in a sentry box 'looking very miserable'. He commented on her short cropped hair, as had Utkin, and lengths of shorn hair belonging to the royal children had been found in Ekaterinburg. Their hair had been cropped during their attack of measles. Another independent witness was the Count Carl Bonde, the Swedish representative of the Red Cross in Russia who was travelling on the Trans-Siberian railway in 1918. 'At some place, the name of which has escaped my memory,' he wrote later, 'the train was stopped in order to find the Grand Duchess Anastasia, daughter of Tsar Nicholas II. The Grand Duchess was, however, not aboard the train. Nobody knew where she had gone.'

In the years following the death of the Russian royal family several pretenders appeared. The best known and most convincing was 'Anastasia': she did not press her claim but was first identified as Anastasia by others. The written record begins when she was rescued from the Landwehr canal in Berlin in 1920, following an apparent attempt at suicide. She carried no papers, spoke German 'with a completely foreign accent' and refused to give any account of herself. She resisted physical examination but doctors found her body covered with 'many lacerations'. She weighed 110 lb, was incubating tuberculosis, her teeth needed to be pulled, she had a scar on her right temple, a wound on her foot, hammer toes and her middle fingers of both hands were very nearly the same length as her ring and index fingers.[8] She was not a virgin and responded violently to questions about a possible fiancé, screaming in fractured German, 'None of that!'

After weeks of earnest but fruitless investigations the German police had still failed to identify their patient. She was labelled Fraulein Unbekannt [Miss Unknown] and transferred to a lunatic asylum. She was withdrawn, haughty and occasionally talked to the nurses in Russian. She was labelled a working woman but talked of riding horses. She was never diagnosed as having a recognizable psychotic illness and her refusal to explain herself was noted by her doctors as 'more fear than reticence'.

After two years of institutional life at Dalldorf, not far from Berlin, she began to confide in others. Her identity was suspected, although initially she was mistaken for Tatiana. She still responded to formal inquiries with terror, hiding her face and turning to the wall. Baroness Sophie Buxhoeveden, a former lady-in-waiting, was brought to see her. Miss Unbekannt had to be literally dragged from her bed in order that she could be seen, but Buxhoeveden dismissed her as 'too short for Tatiana'. Fraulein Unbekannt said nothing to correct her, but when later identified as Anastasia she ever after accepted the diagnosis.

She was seriously disturbed. Her statements were disjointed and often contradictory and by selection or omission could be made to support almost any tale. However, she bore a striking resemblance to photographs of the real Anastasia. The Grand Duchess Olga, an aunt of the real Anastasia, after several meetings, rejected her as an impostor. So did Pierre Gilliard, her former tutor. On the other hand, Madame Botkin, the daughter of the tsar's doctor and one of the last people to see Anastasia alive, accepted her without question, as did her cousin Grand Duke Andrei and second cousin Princess Xenia Georgievna. She

offended the Grand Duke of Hesse, her supposed uncle, by claiming to
have seen him in St Petersburg in 1916, an odd but telling claim as
there is independent evidence that the kaiser attempted to negotiate a
separate peace with Russia at this time, sending the grand duke, the
tsar's brother-in-law, as his secret emissary. This claim was examined in
detail at the German Court of Appeal in the 1960s. A corroborative
witness was produced but efforts were made to discredit him and the
Court finally left the matter open. Now that the tsar's diaries are
available it should be possible at last either to confirm the story or lay
it to rest. If confirmed it would leave another enigma.[9] To discredit the
claimant the duke employed a private detective, Martin Knopf, who
identified Miss Unbekannt as Franziska Schanzkowska, a Pomeranian
munitions worker who had been severely injured in an explosion.
Declared incurably insane she had been incarcerated in various
hospitals but had escaped shortly before Miss Unbekannt had been
rescued from her canal.

In the 1920s there were half a million Russian monarchists in the
country and they had made Berlin their headquarters. In exile they were
an ill-tempered, fratricidal, leaderless group. The tsar's immediate
relatives fell into fanatically opposed camps and the rest of the exiles
took sides around them, some supporting and others dismissing the
claimant. Many of those who could have identified 'Anastasia' were dead
and the survivors stood to lose their share of any Romanov fortune
deposited in the west, if her claim were true. A number of investigations
and legal cases ensued, partly driven by her claim that the tsar had
transferred some huge fortune to a bank in England. It was almost
certainly a false rumour: the only real wealth of the tsars that did survive
after 1917 lay in the jewels relatives smuggled out of the country.[10]

Most of the Russian royal exiles were penniless, except for the dowager
tsarina who had smuggled a cache of jewels back to her Danish
homeland, where she lived in a fantasy world convinced that her son and
all his family had somehow escaped and were living in secret exile. When
she died in 1928 the jewels were sent to England where many ended in
Queen Mary's possession while the dowager's daughters, the Grand
Duchesses Xenia and Olga, received only a small part of their true worth
several years later. In 1930 Xenia and Olga, together with the Duke of
Hesse and the tsarina's sisters Irene and Victoria, persuaded the German
courts to rule that the tsar and all his family had died at Ekaterinburg,
thus excluding 'Anna Anderson' from any claim on any other
inheritance. Friends of Anna petitioned in 1938 against the decision,
leading to a case which lasted intermittently until 1968 when the courts
reached the equivocal decision that while 'Anastasia cannot be

conclusively identified . . . the death of Grand Duchess Anastasia cannot be accepted as a conclusively historical fact!'

She was shipped from hospital to castle and from palace to hotel. She continued to be exceedingly paranoiac and ever afraid of kidnapping. Eventually she came to the USA, where for a while she lived with Princess Xenia, a surviving cousin of the tsar. Once, while trying to escape prying journalists, she signed herself into an hotel as Anna Anderson. It was a name that stuck. On 23 December 1968, just as her immigrant status in the USA was being questioned, Anna Anderson was married to Dr John Manahan. The Most Revd Gleb Botkin, the son of the tsar's physician who was murdered at Ekaterinburg, was best man. Asked what Tsar Nicolas might have thought of his new son-in-law, he said, 'I think he would be grateful'. Manahan had spent a year at Harvard and then joined the wartime navy before becoming Associate Professor of History at Radford College in Virginia. 'Jack' and Anastasia made a benignly eccentric pair; he with his crumbling library and encyclopaedic knowledge of the genealogies of European aristocrats and she feeding her numerous pet cats and wearing clothes that were consistently too big for her.

As we began working on this book it occurred to us that if we could obtain a sample of Mrs Manahan's blood, it could be tested to see if she were a carrier of Victoria's gene; a daughter of the tsarina would have had a 50 per cent chance of inheriting it. If she were a carrier, it would substantiate her story beyond all doubt; if she did not carry the gene – which was the other 50 per cent chance – then her case would not be affected. The test is a highly specialized one but we were in contact with Dr John Graham of the University of North Carolina and an internationally recognized specialist in haemophilia. Only one syringe full of fresh blood, or about 10 ml, was needed for an accurate measurement of Factor VIII. The plasma of carriers contains only half the normal concentration.

We understood that Mrs Manahan had become so confused and eccentric in her old age that she might not understand what was being asked of her. We decided to approach Dr Manahan in a respectful and informed way through a medical colleague of Dr Graham who attended the same church in Charlottesville as Jack Manahan and who was also a geneticist. He explained the significance of the test to Dr Manahan who understood and agreed to what was being offered. Unfortunately, at this time, towards the end of 1983, Mrs Manahan was admitted to hospital with Rocky Mountain spotted fever. It is a rare disease, especially for an old person and in the middle of winter. Being in hospital should have made the task of getting a sample of blood a lot easier. Unfortunately, Dr

Manahan decided to take her out of the hospital one November day, even though she had not totally recovered from the disease. Eventually, the Virginian police found the couple who claimed to be the daughter and son-in-law of the last Tsar of Russia, on a snowy road bundled up in an ancient station wagon. Mrs Manahan was taken back to hospital and placed in the legal care of a Charlottesville attorney. The attorney was approached in the same way as Dr Manahan had been and on several different occasions, but he adopted a wooden and antagonistic attitude, seemingly unable to grasp what was required.

One of us read *The Times* obituary of Anastasia while on a bus in Italy. Immediately Dr Graham was contacted but the body had been cremated. In one final, improbable twist to a story which had been on the edge of solution so many times, we heard in 1992 that all patients with Rocky Mountain spotted fever had had blood samples taken and stored as part of a research project, but staff at the Centre for Disease Control were unable to find the specimen. Anyhow, a post-mortem specimen of blood might not have served the purpose.

Some time after his wife's death, we visited Dr Manahan. He remembered the request for the specimen of blood well and confirmed he had given his consent. He was still convinced the enemies of the tsar were after him and told us that only the previous week his library had been broken into by the British Secret Police and a glass case full of ancient flint arrowheads had been stolen. The whole of the bottom floor of the house was filled with his books and a further glacial mound of volumes slipped down off the outside porch. Remarkably, he still knew the ten thousand or more books well and searched for a long time until he found a passage he wanted to quote to us. As we climbed round between the bulging shelves we found we were ankle-deep in Indian arrowheads – it was not the British MI5 that had purloined the arrowheads but damp that had burst the case.

The cremation of Mrs Manahan's body and the disappearance of her blood sample left the problem of her identity open and the reported absence of Anastasia's skeleton from the Siberian grave increased interest in the problem.

Modern medicine requires blood and tissues for many kinds of tests. Recently, samples of Mrs Anderson's tissues, preserved for histological examination after intestinal surgery in 1979, have come to light in the Martha Jefferson Hospital in Charlottesville. In life Mrs Anderson was the subject of the longest legal case in Germany history, in death her five posthumous gut fragments immediately became the subject of a legal wrangle. The hospital authorities argued that under Virginian law they could only be handed over to her next-of-kin or authorized executor.

Eventually they agreed to release them at the petition of Martha Botkin, whose grandfather had died with the tsar at Ekaterinburg. As the samples were fixed and embedded in wax gross preservation was good but the chemical process of fixation made the recovery of DNA difficult. However, in October 1994 Dr Gill of the Home Office Forensic Laboratory announced the results of comparisons of the mitochondrial DNA profiles from Mrs Manahan with those of the Russian royal women and one Carl Moucher, a great-nephew on the female side of Franziska Schanzkowska, the Pomeranian munitions worker identified by the Duke of Hesse's detective. According to a television programme screened on 5 October 1994 the DNA profile did not match that of the royal women but that further work was required to determine whether or not it matched that of Carl Moucher, although it more closely resembled Moucher than three hundred other unrelated profiles. Simultaneously, it was announced[11] that tests in America of the mitochondrial DNA profiles from samples of Mrs Manahan's hair matched that of Moucher, but that profiles from a blood sample, supposed to be that of Mrs Manahan, did not. On balance it seems very likely that Mrs Manahan was Schanzkowska although a small doubt remains.

Labelled locks of hair from each of the four daughters, preserved in the Museum of Communism in Moscow, have recently come to light, and samples have been sent to the Forensic Science Laboratory. Unfortunately only the roots of hair contain cells and therefore DNA, and so far no reports have been made as to the identity of the three daughters. Individual identification would require chromosomal DNA, not mitochondrial DNA, which is identical in all children of the same mother.

Although Mrs Manahan was the best-known case, the absence of the bodies of the tsarevitch and one of his sisters increases interest in the cases of other possible survivors. Radzinsky in his recent book has provided evidence that the tsarevitch himself might have survived in Russia. This seems very improbable in view of his vulnerability to the hazards of everyday life, let alone a firing squad, however drunk. Nevertheless, in the absence of his skeleton the tale is worth repeating.

One of the people who wrote to Radzinsky after his observations became public was a psychiatrist at Karelian Psychiatric Hospital Number I from Petrozavodsk, Dr K. Kaufman. She told of caring for a mentally sick man in 1947. 'Amid incoherent utterances in a mass of other expressive exclamations the name 'Beloborodov' flashed by two or three times.' Alexander Beloborodov was Chairman of the Ural Soviet and agreed to the tsar's execution. Dr Kaufman said that the man's birth was recorded as 1904, he suffered from haematuria (or blood in the urine), had a scar on his buttocks and had one undescended testicle. Like Mrs Manahan, he knew a lot about court protocol and the layout of the Winter Palace. He claimed that his father, the tsar, had pressed his face to his chest when the shooting began and that he had later been rescued from the cellar of the Ipatiev house. The Head of the Psychiatric Hospital Number I confirmed this story when Radzinsky contacted him. The patient had gone under the name of Semyonov. Mental hospitals are notoriously home to Napoleons and Jesus Christs and some of these are superficially convincing, but one would have to have been severely deranged to have claimed to be the tsarevitch in early Communist Russia.

Haemophilia never cures itself and prior to the availability of Factor VIII few haemophiliacs lived beyond the age of forty. There could be other causes of Mr Semyonov's haematuria than haemophilia and it seems surprising that there was no additional clinical evidence of haemophilia, such as damaged joints, in a man supposed to have survived forty-three years with the disease. In July 1918 the tsarevitch was recovering from another episode of bleeding and, while he seems to have survived the first round of killing, his disease would certainly have complicated any recovery and made survival unlikely.

Dr Kaufman said she and her colleagues kept the patient's identification secret and he was eventually discharged to a Soviet labour camp. An independent witness said he had been impressed with Semyonov and all the prisoners believed his story. But would the authorities really have permitted the tsar's son to survive in Stalin's Russia?

First reports from Russia stated that the missing daughter was believed to be Anastasia.[12] More recently a Russian Government Commission has reported that the missing daughter was Marie. The results of the Amersham DNA tests have still to be published and the American historian Peter Kurth suggests that the Russian announcement is an attempt to pre-empt the Amersham report. 'They are resentful of Western scientific judgements on what they regard as their own mystery. They want it to be a purely Russian affair. If the Western scientists say Anastasia is missing, the Russian scientists will say Marie is missing.' At present, in 1995, the identity of the missing daughter is still not settled beyond question and there is a remote possibility that it was Tatiana who survived. This depends on the credence that can be given to another unverifiable and rather unreliable source, the diaries of Colonel Richard Meinertzhagen, DSO. All seventy volumes are stored in the Rhodes Library at Oxford and form the basis of Michael Occleshaw's book *The Romanov Conspiracies*.[13] At the time of the tsar's death Meinertzhagen was in charge of British Military Intelligence for Russia, Persia, Afghanistan and Romania, and reported directly to King George V.

24   *Leopold II of Belgium. The son of the enlightened Leopold I, he was a monster
responsible for countless deaths in the Congo. He also imprisoned one perfectly sane
daughter in a home for the insane, and so maltreated his wife that she prayed for death.
Hulton Deutsch Collection Limited.*

25 *The family of Queen Victoria in 1887, the year of her Golden Jubilee, by Laurits Regner Tuxen. Among those pictured are Queen Victoria herself (right of centre), the then Prince of Wales (centre, standing) and third left of him, standing at the back, Princess Alix of Hesse (later the tsarina). To the right and just behind Victoria, Princess Beatrice (Princess Henry of Battenberg) holds her baby son and, directly in front of the*

Queen, the Duchess of Albany presents her two children, Princess Alice and Prince
Charles Edward Leopold (later Duke of Saxe-Coburg-Gotha). Second from the left
(standing) is the Kaiser, and sitting almost directly in front of him, to the right of the
Duchess of Edinburgh, who is playing the piano, is Princess Irene of Hesse. The Royal
Collection © Her Majesty the Queen.

26 *Princess Beatrice, youngest daughter of Queen Victoria. She was a carrier of haemophilia which she transmitted to her daughter.*

27 *Twenty-year-old King Alfonso XIII of Spain and his fiancée Victoria Eugenie, 'Ena', who was Beatrice's daughter and proved to be a carrier of haemophilia. Hulton Deutsch Collection Limited.*

28   *The Prince of Wales, later King George V (right) and his cousin, Tsar Nicholas II in 1909. They are dressed here in almost identical clothes to enhance their similarity. The Royal Archives © Her Majesty the Queen.*

29 The nine sovereigns who attended the funeral of Edward VII. Standing, from the left;
Haakon VII of Norway, Ferdinand of Bulgaria, Manuel of Portugal, Wilhelm II of
Germany, George I of Greece and Albert I of Belgium. Sitting: Alfonso XIII of Spain,
George V and Frederick VII of Denmark. All except Haakon, George and Frederick were of
Coburg descent but Haakon had a wife of Coburg descent and George and Frederick's heirs
were married to descendants of Victoria and Albert. John Murray.

30 The Archduke Ferdinand and the Archduchess photographed leaving the town hall in
Sarajevo on 28 June 1914, shortly before they were assassinated. Hulton Deutsch Collection
Limited.

31 *'Foxy' Ferdinand of Bulgaria (left) with Emperor Karl of Austria–Hungary in 1918.
Imperial War Museum.*

32 *Charles Edward Leopold, one-time Duke of Coburg, cousin of George V and an influential supporter of Hitler. Private Collection.*

Meinertzhagen was almost a caricature of a professional army officer, dashing, moustachioed, courageous but with a liking for practical jokes. On 18 August 1918 he wrote a brief account of his activity during the previous month: 'On July 1st everything was ready and the plane took off. Success was not complete and I find it too dangerous to give details. One child was literally thrown into the plane in Ekaterinburg and brought to England where she still is.' Meinertzhagen appears to have typed his diary from earlier notes. Like most diaries it was an emotional safety valve, although he remained professionally discreet about his intelligence work. According to Occleshaw this last survivor, fearing assassination, lived under an assumed name, suffering from tuberculosis acquired in captivity. She married an English officer with the genealogically striking name of Owen Tudor but died young without children and is now buried in the north-east corner of the new graveyard at Lydd in Kent, under the name Larissa Feodorovna. When Tatiana's mother was accepted into the Russian Orthodox Church, after her marriage to Tsar Nicholas, her new baptismal name was Alexandra Feodorovna, as the service took place in St Feodor's Cathedral. Had there been any reference to this remarkable episode in the unpublished diaries of the tsar, Radzinsky would presumably have reported it, so the story is almost certainly fiction, but a comparison of the DNA from the bones in the grave at Lydd with those of the tsarina's relatives would be interesting. Colonel Meinertzhagen is a most unreliable witness. Even his later reputation as an ornithologist has recently been clouded by detailed accusations of the theft of specimens from the British Museum of Natural History and the falsification of records.[14]

Shortly after Anna Anderson moved to America, yet another individual made a public claim to be a living daughter of the tsar: her story was exceedingly odd, although not totally impossible. She was Mrs de Graaf, a resident of Dorn, the small Dutch town where Kaiser Wilhelm had lived in exile from 1918 to his death in 1941. There is no evidence that Suzanna Catherine de Graaf ever met the man she claimed to be her half-cousin. She lived a quiet life as the local faith healer and psychic, held in some affection by a group of close-knit Dutch neighbours. In October 1968 she told a reporter from *Figaro* that she was a daughter of Nicholas II: not a survivor from Ekaterinburg, but a disowned fifth daughter born between Anastasia and Alexis.

In 1903 it had been publicly announced that the tsarina was pregnant. On 1 September her doctors reported that she had a pseudocyesis, or false pregnancy (something her ancestor Bloody Mary had also experienced). Mrs de Graaf claimed her adoptive father told her in 1937 that the pregnancy really ended in a live birth, and that the imperial family had concealed the birth and abandoned the infant to the care of others. 'Russia,' she commented, 'demanded an heir to the throne. There were already four girls. . . . The reason for my repudiation: I was a girl, not a boy.'[15]

An improbable story, but Mrs de Graaf did have some curious supporting evidence. She owned a large number of crisp rouble notes, with consecutive serial numbers (although these could be bought for almost nothing after the Communists took over), some Romanov linen, china and other trinkets. The tsarina had been greatly influenced by the quack French doctor Philippe Vachot, who promised to determine the sex of her children. He complained that he had been consulted too late in the case of Anastasia: Mrs de Graaf claims Vachot spirited her out of Russia and that in 1912 she received a dowry of 12 million roubles.

The author James Blair Lowell[16] has pieced together Mrs de Graaf's history. Her legal father, Leendert Hemmes, was born in 1874 and made a living as a *piskijker* – or 'piss watcher' – a psychic who interpreted his clients' urine and whose own father had been drowned at sea when he was four years old. There is no explanation as to why or how Vachot might have chosen Hemmes, and the suggestion that Leendert's father might have travelled the Baltic or that Vachot (and Alexandra) were crazy enough to select a piss-watcher to care for a royal daughter is extremely tenuous. The most curious fact is that while Suzanna's father never showed any talent and neighbourhood psychics are rarely wealthy, he did buy himself a handsome house in Rotterdam that still exists. Could he have received money from the imperial family?

Irina Yussopov claimed to have heard of a Romanov daughter called Alexandra who 'died as a child', and Mrs de Graaf adopted the name Alexandra. Gleb Botkin knew about Mrs de Graaf and wanted her story 'thoroughly investigated' and Prince Frederick of Saxe-Altenburg[17] took the trouble to visit her.

Alexandra and Nicholas, whatever their shortcomings, were doting parents. It is unlikely that they would have abandoned a fifth daughter, however strong the political pressures. On the other hand, the tsarina was certainly desperate and certainly under the sway of Phillipe Vachot. Mrs Anderson insisted her younger sister had been kidnapped by Vachot from a drugged tsarina, adding a ludicrous touch to an improbable tale. Perhaps the best that can be said is that if Mrs Anderson had been who she claimed to be, then the strange story of Suzanna (Alexandra) de Graaf (Romanov) would have to have been taken seriously.

Could Victoria's gene help unravel her story? If true, she had a 50 per cent chance of being a carrier. Mrs de Graaf married twice, first to Antoon van Weelden by whom she had a son (also called Antoon and born in 1929) and second to Jan Barend de Graaf, by whom she had another son and then twin daughters (born in 1945). Mrs de Graaf died in 1968, so her blood cannot be examined to see if she was a carrier for haemophilia. It is certain, however, that neither of her sons were haemophiliacs, which makes it less likely that her story is true, but does not totally disprove it. One of the twin daughters died aged ten, the other is alive and according to Lovell looks remarkably like Tsarina Alexandra does in her photographs. It is possible, although not likely, that she is a carrier. If she were it would prove her mother's claims beyond reasonable doubt.

A gentleman styling himself Prince Alexis d'Angou de Bourbon Conde Romanov-Dolgoruky, presently resident in Madrid, claims to be the son of Anastasia's sister Maria, and heir to the Russian throne. His claim depends on the survival of Maria, rather than Anastasia or Tatiana, and her marriage to a Prince Nicholas Alexandrovitch Dolgoruky, a descendant of the Ukrainian royal house, both of whose parents lived lives of total obscurity. Even if his descent were verified his claim would not stand as Tsar Paul I introduced Salic law into Russia, that is descent through the male line only, as in Hanover, and this law has never been repealed. This would also exclude Georgi, the son of the Grand Duchess Maria, daughter of the last tsar's uncle Grand Duke Vladimir. People in some parts of the former Soviet bloc, especially in Romania, have talked about restoring their monarchies. In the travail that has overtaken Russia as she struggles from Communism to a free market, Tsar Nicholas has been a source of pride for some groups. So, if all the pretenders' claims are proved to be false, who is the real heir to Tsar Nicholas's kingdom? According to Salic law the heirs would be Major Paul Romanov, one-time US marine major, and his eldest son. The major's grandfather was Grand Duke Paul Romanov, brother of Tsar Alexander III. Grand Duke Paul was murdered by the Communists but his son Dimitri escaped because he had been banished from Russia for his part in the murder of Rasputin. Here Queen Victoria's gene played a part in the survival of the royal line as well as the death of the last tsar and his family.

CHAPTER NINE

The Coburgs and Haemophilia in Iberia

After the defeat of Napoleon Belgium was united with Holland to provide a barrier to French expansion to the east, but the Roman Catholic Belgians, and particularly the French-speaking half of the population, were not happy under the rule of the Protestant House of Orange. When the Belgians revolted in 1831, they first offered their crown to a son of Louis Philippe, the King of France, but the other powers were not prepared to tolerate such an expansion of French influence only sixteen years after Napoleon. Knowing that, as Baron Wessenburg aptly put it, 'He had a strong liking' for a throne, the Belgians then offered it to Leopold. Although brought up a Protestant he was flexible in matters of religion; the throne of Greece would have required him to become Greek Orthodox. The cautious Leopold agreed to accept the throne if the London Conference of 1831 would guarantee the neutrality of Belgium. This guarantee was incorporated into the London Treaty of 1839. 'Belgium of its own accord bound itself to remain neutral and its very neutrality is based upon that neutrality which the other powers guaranteed and are bound to maintain if Belgium kept its engagements.' It was this guarantee which drew Britain into the First World War and which led eventually to the destruction of both the British and German empires and most of the thrones on to which Leopold was so carefully to introduce his relatives, but the guarantee was to secure the borders of Belgium for nearly a century. Being avaricious as well as ambitious, he also demanded a settlement of £83,000 from the British taxpayer to cover various imaginary debts, as a condition of surrendering his £50,000 p.a. pension, and in spite of ferocious opposition in the House of Commons, he had his way.

Spain and Portugal, with their Roman Catholic orthodoxy and Mediterranean culture, would seem to be unfavourable ground for Coburg ambitions, yet both were incorporated into the Coburg domain.

A few years after gaining the throne of Belgium Leopold expanded the Coburg empire again by marrying one of his numerous nephews,

Ferdinand, to the Crown Princess of Portugal. The background to this coup was curious. After a brilliant period of expansion in the fifteenth and sixteenth centuries Portugal entered a long period of decline, and by the eighteenth century was the most isolated and backward country in Western Europe. The Portuguese royal house of Braganza produced the most inept, bizarre and eccentric kings in Europe, a succession of fairy-tale or black-pantomime characters. Under the medieval conventions prevailing at the Portuguese court the royal infants were brought up on a diet of flattery and servility, without any form of discipline. The royal tutors could do no more than humbly entreat their charges, and consequently some of the kings could not spell their own names but displayed an extraordinary range of behaviour from altruism to sadism, unrestrained by education or morality, further deformed by the inbreeding frequent in the family.

John V, nephew of Catherine of Aragon, wife of Charles II, built a fantastical palace where 9,000 were banqueted for a week on end and 10,000 troops were reviewed on the roof. His successor kept a seraglio of 300 nuns in the convent of Adivelas which became famous for the pornographic literature it produced. When Miguel (1828–34) wanted some amusement he would break into the home of one of his unfortunate subjects with a gang of friends and smash up all the furniture and crockery. To cap the joke he would then make his victim kneel in homage, under pain of instant execution. Alternatively, he would ride down the main street of Lisbon knocking off the hats of all the pedestrians with his stick while those in carriages were made to alight and kneel in the mud. When these frolics palled he would toss young pigs into the air and catch them on his sword or pluck chickens alive. The country was ripe for a Coburg takeover.

When a small force of French troops invaded in 1806 King John the Runaway and practically all the aristocracy fled to Brazil, leaving the defence of Portugal to the British. The king returned to Portugal when Napoleon had been defeated, but his son Pedro remained behind to become the first Emperor of Brazil. When John the Runaway died in 1826, Pedro made his younger brother Miguel Regent of Portugal on condition that he should marry his seven-year-old daughter, Maria de Gloria, Miguel's niece, when she came of age. Once in power, Miguel began a reign of terror, imprisoning 40,000 people. When the chief jailer in Oporto refused to take any more prisoners because the cells were full the governor asked 'Are they full to the ceiling?' 'Not quite', the jailer replied. 'Then how dare you tell me they are full; put more men into them', he was told.

Several years after he had appointed Miguel regent, Pedro invaded Portugal and expelled him, not because of his outrageous behaviour but because he refused to carry out his side of the bargain and marry Pedro's daughter, but the prolonged campaign exhausted Pedro who died shortly afterwards. On his death his daughter Maria succeeded in Portugal, while in Brazil her brother Pedro II became emperor. When Maria's first husband providentially died shortly after the wedding, Leopold of Belgium saw the chance to extend the Coburg domains and persuaded Ferdinand to propose. Before Ferdinand set out for Portugal his uncle Leopold wrote him a small book entitled *Directions and Advices*. This contained his uncle's advice for most situations and problems which a young king might encounter. Victoria was most impressed and noted in her diary that 'Ferdinand simply cannot fail to succeed, thanks to Uncle Leopold's instructions!'

Soon after the marriage Ferdinand, now prince consort, plotted to seize power and overthrow the Portuguese constitution with the aid of troops to be supplied by Leopold, but Britain blocked the attempt. After bearing Leopold eleven children, Maria died in 1853 and Ferdinand became regent until his son, another Pedro, came of age. Queen Victoria was most favourably impressed with young Pedro and made strenuous efforts to persuade Charlotte, the daughter of Leopold of Belgium, to marry him, thus binding Portugal even more firmly into the Coburg orbit. 'You may rely on our divulging nothing', she wrote to Leopold. 'We are, however, both very anxious that dear Pedro should be preferred.' Even when Charlotte obviously preferred Archduke Maximilian of Austria, a younger son of the emperor, she wrote again to Leopold, 'I still hope by your letter that Charlotte has not finally made up her mind – as we both feel so convinced of the immense superiority of Pedro over any other young Prince even *dans les relations journalistes*, besides which the position is so infinitely preferable.' However, her efforts were in vain. When Charlotte insisted on marrying Maximilian they had to find him a throne, as befitted the husband of a Coburg. Leopold bombarded his relatives with letters full of advice, generally sensible but occasionally disastrous. He advised his unfortunate son-in-law Maximilian, 'In America there are still splendid opportunities and I should like to see the Coburgs endeavouring to realise them'. Note that a son and possible heir of the ancient House of Habsburg had been promoted to an honorary Coburg. When Maximilian, setting out for Mexico, was asked to renounce his rights to the Austrian throne if his brother were to die childless, Leopold advised him, 'My refrain is to surrender nothing'. With a little luck the Austro-Hungarian empire might fall into Coburg hands as well. Unfortunately, the Mexicans did not appreciate European monarchs and with inadequate European support Maximilian was defeated and executed, and poor Charlotte went mad.

For sixty years after her husband's execution in 1867 Charlotte lived in a Belgian palace, conversing with her dead husband, issuing orders to her imaginary soldiers and screaming in terror of being poisoned. Nutshells had to be unbroken as a precaution. Her brother 'Leopold the Unloved' used her private fortune to subsidize his Congo adventure so that the Coburg Congo empire grew from the ruins of their Mexican one.

On the accession of young Pedro his father Ferdinand retired and went to live with an opera singer. When his uncle Leopold of Belgium successively tried to interest him in applying for the thrones of Greece, Spain and Mexico, he declined gracefully. He was sadly lacking in the true Coburg spirit. Leopold wished Ferdinand to exploit the progression from minor nobility to blood royal via prince consort, as he had done. He observed, 'In my day, I had built upon my English hopes and Portugal was to do for Ferdinand what England had done for me.' As Pedro was obviously deficient in ambition, Leopold tried sex. When offering Greece Leopold later confided, 'I even went so far as to say that the beauty of Levantine women was known to be very great', but they evidently could not compete with his opera singer.

Having brought the throne of Portugal into the family Leopold then tried to incorporate Brazil. Pedro II of Brazil had married a Bourbon of the two Sicilies but this marriage produced two daughters, Dona Isabella and Dona Leopoldina. As Isabella was heir to the throne it was arranged that she should marry Augustus Saxe-Coburg, brother of the Tsar of Bulgaria. Unfortunately, Isabella was not enamoured of Augustus, and said that he had a face 'like a Dutch cheese illuminated by a leer'. She married instead his cousin the Comte d'Eu, whose mother happened to be Victoria of Saxe-Coburg, so Augustus married Leopoldina, in case Isabella died childless. In the event Leopoldina died first and childless but Pedro II was deposed in a bloodless revolution before Isabella could succeed. Pedro II was an enlightened monarch who fostered the arts and sciences, but by abolishing slavery he created a host of enemies who eventually evicted him. After over a century of republican rule involving thirty-seven presidents, nineteen military revolts, nine dictators and six constitutions, the monarchists are still strong, although they failed to win a plebiscite on the restoration of the empire in 1993, in part because the monarchists were divided among several pretenders. A leading contender for the throne is Don Philippe de Saxe-Coburg & Orleans and Braganza, in private life, Philippe Braganza, an insurance salesman from Pittsburg.

Apologists for the Coburgs have argued that they brought a more modern and enlightened view of kingship into the degenerate house of Braganza, but this view is hard to sustain. Pedro II of Brazil, who had no

Coburg blood, was an enlightened and civilized monarch, a Braganza only in the extreme degree to which he showed these virtues, while the later kings of Portugal, of Saxe-Coburg descent, behaved like the old Braganzas, plundering the state treasury, cooking the books and cavorting with dancing girls until the Portuguese people, tiring of their monarchs after many centuries, finally threw them out.

When Romania became independent of Turkey Leopold attempted to settle his second son, the Count of Flanders, on the new throne, but the Romanians went elsewhere for a king. Romania had to wait for a Coburg until 1893 when Marie, the daughter of Prince Alfred, Queen Victoria's second son, married King Ferdinand. The relationship was reinforced in 1921 when their son King Carol II married Princess Helene of Greece, Kaiser Wilhelm's granddaughter and therefore great-great-granddaughter of Queen Victoria.

The Coburgs first attempted to marry into the Spanish royal house in the 1840s. In 1833 the three-year-old daughter of Ferdinand VII became Queen Isobel II of Spain with her mother Marie Christina as regent. The marriage of such a well-endowed heiress was a matter of international concern and the Coburgs were quickly in the field. In 1846 Prince Leopold of Coburg was negotiating with Marie Christina for Isobel's hand but the French objected strenuously and the scheme collapsed. A few years later another Coburg, 'Foxy' Ferdinand, succeeded in obtaining the throne of Bulgaria. As Victoria's children matured new possibilities opened up and Leopold lived to see his great-niece, Victoria's eldest child, married to the German heir apparent. Before the century was out, among the major European royal families only the Spanish and Austrian were Coburg-free but Spain was to succumb a little later, gaining not only a queen of Coburg descent, but also haemophilia.

Queen Victoria's youngest daughter, Beatrice (1857–1944) transmitted the gene to three of her four children, a circumstance that was to have a significant effect on the history of Spain at a critical time. Beatrice remained at Windsor with Queen Victoria when her brothers and sisters had departed and even after her marriage at the age of twenty-eight to Prince Henry of Battenberg, son of Prince Alexander of Hesse, she continued to live with her mother.

As the old queen's sight began to fail Beatrice read to her aloud the contents of the official boxes. Sir Frederick Ponsonby, one of the official secretaries, complained, 'The most absurd mistakes occur and the Queen is not even *au courant* with the ordinary topics of the present day. Imagine Beatrice trying to explain the vaccination question or our policy on the East. Bigge or I may write out long precis of these things but they are often not read to HM as Beatrice is in a hurry to develop a photograph or

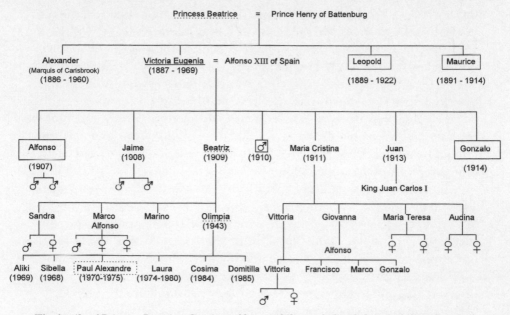

The family of Princess Beatrice. Carriers of haemophilia underlined, haemophiliacs boxed. Dotted lines or boxes indicate an uncertain diagnosis.

wants to paint a flower for a bazaar.' Victoria bequeathed all her private journals to Beatrice with instructions to censor them before publication. For forty years she copied the journals page by page eliminating anything of a controversial nature and produced a bland, emasculated version. The originals were burned.

When her husband Henry died of fever off West Africa in 1896 his body was returned to England pickled in rum, but before the tragedy she bore him three sons and a daughter. The eldest, the Marquess of Carisbrooke (1886–1960) was fortunately free of the disease. The second son, Major Lord Leopold Mountbatten (1889–1922) was a sufferer; nevertheless, he joined the Kings Royal Rifle Corps and was gazetted in March 1914. 'Physical delicacy', according to his obituary in *The Times*, prevented active service, but he was mentioned in despatches! He suffered a serious illness in 1910 and was lame and 'constitutionally delicate'. He died following a hip operation. Haemophilia is never mentioned. Her third son, Maurice, born in 1891, was also a haemophiliac according to McKusik, but was fit for active service. He gallantly joined the King's Royal Fusiliers and died of wounds received at Ypres. Her daughter, Victoria Eugenie (1887–1969), who married Alfonso XIII, King of Spain, proved to be a carrier and the danger should have been obvious.

At the beginning of the twentieth century Spain was wracked by fanaticism and extremism on both Left and Right, which was to lead to the horrors of the Civil War. Victoria Eugenie's inheritance was one of the factors which weakened the forces of moderation.

During the nineteenth century Spain lagged behind the rest of Western Europe both economically and politically. The Industrial Revolution came late to Spain and hardly affected the south. In the middle of the nineteenth century Spain had been divided by the Carlist wars fought between the supporters of two branches of the royal family and more recently had been humiliated by the loss of Cuba, Puerto Rico and the Philippines to the USA. Moderate Spanish opinion looked to France and England for inspiration but the middle class was small and was threatened on the Left by an anarchist tradition devoted to bombing and assassination, which has continued down to the present, and by powerful Marxist and Socialist movements of several descriptions which inspired a succession of strikes and riots. On the right stood the Carlist traditionalists, a reactionary church and an army whose officer corps were confident that the interests of the state were identical with their own and reserved the right to intervene whenever they felt they were threatened.

Officially, Spain was a constitutional monarchy and the constitution was based on that of Britain; even the two major political parties were named the Conservatives and the Liberals – but the political reality in Spain was very different. The parties were weak and divided. Governments rarely had the support of the majority of the Cortes and were short lived. The task of finding a new government fell on the king who was therefore continuously involved in politics and was held responsible for the governments he appointed.

Spain was further divided by local independence movements in the Basque country and Catalonia and by the rival influences of the great powers of Western Europe: Britain, France, Germany and Austria. The officer corps admired Germany. Austrian influence went back to the days of the Habsburgs, and the queen mother was an Austrian. France, though Roman Catholic, was republican and the rival of Spain in Morocco.

In the early years of the twentieth century Alfonso XIII had the difficult task of balancing these centrifugal forces. His father, Alfonso XII, had been restored to the throne following a republican interlude. After the early death of Alfonso XII, his Austrian queen, a Habsburg cousin of the Emperor Francis Joseph, became regent for his posthumous son Alfonso XIII, until he came of age at sixteen in 1902. Alfonso XII had been educated at Sandhurst but accepted a colonelcy in a German Uhlan regiment. German influence suffered when a German gunboat attempted to seize the Spanish island of Yap in the Pacific.

The new king continued the delicate balancing act, but the pattern of forces in Western Europe was changing. During the reign of Victoria

Britain and Germany were very close, although Britain never joined the Triple Alliance of Germany, Austria and Italy. With the accession of Edward VII Britain drew nearer to France and established the Entente Cordiale. This change of policy was primarily due to the growing threat from the German fleet but was also made possible by Edward's antipathy to his mother and her pro-German leanings. Edward's pro-French feelings were extreme. During the Moroccan crisis of 1906 he told the French ambassador in London, 'Tell us what you wish on each point and we will support you without restriction or reserves'.[1] This is in interesting contrast to his father's comment on the French in 1860, 'I clearly foresee the day when this vainglorious and immoral people will have to be put down'.[2] The Anglo-French Entente inevitably polarized influences in Spain. The army and the traditionalists looked to the Triple Alliance, while the Centre and moderate Left looked towards London and Paris. In 1904 the kaiser visited Spain with his fleet. To maintain the balance the young Alfonso visited Paris the following year, where he narrowly escaped an attempt on his life.

The king's choice of bride was of considerable symbolic importance. In spite of his restricted background and upbringing, Alfonso, though weak and unable to resist the temptation to intervene continuously in politics, was relatively liberal. While trying to maintain Spain's neutral position he favoured a British bride, in spite of the religious complications that this would cause in Protestant Britain. In this he was probably influenced by his erstwhile Prime Minister Moret.

Alfonso first contemplated marrying Princess Patricia, the daughter of HRH Prince Arthur. As Prince Arthur was not a haemophiliac Princess Patricia could not have been a carrier. However, the British Prime Minister Balfour consulted the Archbishop of Canterbury who objected on the grounds that the princess was too close in succession to the throne, although it would have required a quite extraordinary series of epidemics and disasters to have eliminated the two dozen or so claimants who came before her. Princess Patricia eventually married Admiral the Honourable Sir Alexander Ramsay. While her father was Governor-General of Canada, after the death of her mother and before her marriage, she acted as hostess to her father. A Canadian regiment, the Princess Patricias, and two geographical features were named in her honour.

It is a sign of Alfonso's determination that the rebuff did not deter him. In 1905 he paid an official visit to Britain, the first Spanish monarch to do so since Philip II in the sixteenth century. His visit was the more heroic as he was a bad sailor, and having sailed from Cherbourg to Portsmouth at Edward's invitation, so that he could be shown the Channel Fleet, he insisted on returning home by the shortest sea route possible, from Dover to Calais. It was probably on this visit and through the influence of the old Empress Eugenie, the widow of Napoleon III, that Alfonso met Victoria Eugenie, otherwise known as Ena, the daughter of Princess Beatrice. Eugenie was Spanish herself and was the young Eugenie's godmother.

The premature death of Prince Leopold, Ena's uncle, and the occurrence of haemophilia in her twin brother made it likely that Ena was herself a carrier and according to Sencourt, Alfonso was warned of the risk. Unfortunately, in the medieval rituals of twentieth-century monarchs the royalty of their ancestry was more important than their genetics and this risk was ignored. Princess Patricia, who was free of the defect, would have been a much better choice.

When Princess Beatrice and Ena stayed at Biarritz on the Spanish border in January 1906, the suit became a matter of public knowledge. Extreme Protestant opinion in Britain was again opposed to the marriage as Ena would have had to desert the Protestant faith, but Edward VII favoured the match and refused to interfere. Ena was received into the Roman Catholic church by a Bishop of Nottingham with the reliable English name of Brindle. Following the *Entente Cordiale* with France, Edward saw the possibility of drawing Spain towards England and France and away from the Triple Alliance. In 1907 Britain and Spain reached a formal agreement following a meeting of Edward and Alfonso.

On the return to the palace after the wedding of Alfonso and Ena, a bomb was thrown at the carriage which killed about twenty people but did not injure the bride or groom. Inevitably the new queen became the social focus of liberal society and of those sympathetic to the Anglo-French influences in Spain, while the Austrian queen mother's court was the social centre of right-wing and pro-German society.

The queen's first son, Alfonso, was born in May 1907 and unfortunately inherited his great-grandmother's gene. When it became known that the unfortunate child was a haemophiliac, anti-British circles in Spain claimed that the British had defiled the blue blood of Spain by imposing a genetically defective wife on the Spanish king, an argument which became increasingly difficult to refute when the second son, Jaime, was born a deaf mute and the third, who died at birth, was probably also a haemophiliac. Only the fourth son, Juan, the father of the present king Carlos, was healthy; the fifth son, Gonzalo, was again a haemophiliac. Many Spaniards believed the gruesome story that a young soldier had to be sacrificed every day so that his fresh blood could keep the haemophiliac sons of the king alive. Under Spanish law a physically defective son was excluded from the succession. The ever-growing list of disinherited heirs discredited the marriage and the liberal democratic forces which had engineered it. The humiliation was particularly embarrassing because the Spaniards placed greater importance on the purity of their royal blood than any other nation in Europe. 'Blue blood' is a Spanish term and the Spaniards required that their kings were of royal descent on both sides of the family.

It is impossible to measure exactly the effect of these tragedies on the Spanish throne. Spanish society was so deeply divided and flawed that civil war might have been unavoidable, but they undoubtedly helped to weaken the position of the throne and of the anglophile liberal sections of Spanish opinion.

Disaster was postponed for a while. During the First World War Spain remained neutral and prospered remarkably while her trading rivals devoted their industries to armaments. Alfonso gained considerable personal prestige by his efforts to locate and protect prisoners of war on both sides, while Spanish doctors sailed on allied Red Cross ships as guarantors to German submariners that they were not being used for military purposes. The queen busied herself with good works such as encouraging the modernization of the Red Cross Hospital in Madrid and arranging for its nurses to be trained in Britain, thus bringing the influence of Florence Nightingale into the unbelievably backward medical services of Spain.

After the war the tensions in Spanish society remained. Strikes, assassinations and a military disaster in Morocco further destabilized the state and when General Primo de Rivera seized power as dictator the king weakly acquiesced. The failure of the king to uphold his own constitution in the long run destroyed his raison d'etre. During the dictatorship the king was overshadowed by the dictator and when eventually Primo de Rivera lost the support of the army both the king and the old constitution had been discredited.

When the king finally dismissed de Rivera in 1930 republican forces had grown in strength. In the local elections of 1931 republicans of various persuasions carried the major towns, though they were a minority in the country as a whole. Alfonso's government panicked and collapsed before street demonstrations in Madrid. The king refused to abdicate but rather than subject the country to a bloody civil war he left his kingdom, rather curiously leaving his queen and family in the hands of the provisional republican government. They were treated with every courtesy and soon followed him. Under the succeeding republican regime Spain suffered from exactly the same tensions and eventually the extremes of Left and Right overwhelmed the Centre. Revolts from the right and strikes and murders from the Left culminated in the horrific carnage of the Spanish Civil War in which 400,000 died in battle while 800,000 were executed, murdered or assassinated behind the lines on both sides and in the reprisals which followed Franco's victory.[3]

Haemophiliacs must be acutely aware of the unfairness of the natural world. To be excluded from a throne because one is a haemophiliac would embitter a saint and the young princes sought consolation where they could, mainly in fast cars, fast women and wine. Alfonso blamed his mother for his misfortunes. After his father's abdication Alfonso, the eldest son, married a Cuban without his father's consent but divorced her a few years later. His second marriage, in a registry office, lasted only six months. In 1938 he was being driven by a Miami night-club singer when she crashed into a telegraph pole. Although he was not severely injured the bleeding could not be checked and he died a few hours later. He left no family. Don Jaime, the king's second son, the deaf mute, also married twice but died young leaving two sons, who could not inherit the haemophilia gene. Alfonso's third son had died as a baby. The fifth son, Gonzalo, also died of the 'Royal Haemophilia'[4] following an accident. He was a passenger in a car driven by his sister Beatrice, which hit a wall. Although his injuries were not severe he only survived a few days. The fourth son, Don Juan, was the healthy one. He made a dynastic marriage to a Bourbon princess and his son Carlos is now King of Spain, recalled after thirty years of Franco dictatorship. With considerable skill he has returned Spain to democratic rule. Although still troubled by bomb throwers the horrors of the Civil War have discredited the extremists on both sides while industrialization in the north and the tourist trade in the south have transformed the economy.

CHAPTER TEN

Later Generations

As each royal generation receives only half of its genes from its dynastic royal parent the chances of any gene being inherited by the monarch halves at each generation, providing that marriages with affected relatives are avoided. The haemophilia gene, however, continued to recur in succeeding generations and in this chapter we trace its descent and consider whether it survives today.

Statistically Queen Victoria's gene did remarkably well. Natural selection operates powerfully against it yet from an occurrence in a single individual, Victoria, it spread to three of her children and at least seven of her forty grandchildren. Information is incomplete for later generations; we shall never know how many of the tsarevitch's sisters were carriers, but statistically it is likely that there were ten haemophiliacs and carriers among Victoria's numerous great-grandchildren. In later generations the numbers have declined but it is likely that there are still some bleeders or carriers among her descendants. Male haemophiliacs are easier to trace. Here the record in succeeding generations was: Victoria's children, one (Leopold), grandchildren, three, great-grandchildren, six. There are no known bleeders in the next generation but the negative evidence is not conclusive because of the secrecy which often surrounds sufferers, and there has been a report of at least one haemophiliac in the fifth generation (see page 125).

The rapid expansion of this gene at first sight contradicts the theory that natural selection should continuously erode the proportion of any disadvantageous gene, but the apparent paradox arises from two special factors. Royal children and their mothers may have had a better than average chance of survival until recently, although before the days of scientific medicine, medical treatments were as likely to kill as to cure. More importantly, the great improvements in food and hygiene during the nineteenth century greatly increased the chances of survival of most children in Europe and led to a rapid growth in population, until the spread of contraception brought the birthrate down. When population growth exceeds selective pressure against the gene the number of bleeders in a family may increase. It should be remembered also that there is no selection against the women who carried the gene, although they benefited from the improvements in medical services and hygiene.

It is not always easy to trace the later occurrences of the gene for a variety of reasons. The condition is often concealed from public knowledge, even from obituary notices, although it had been a major feature of any victim's life. Until the recent development of special laboratory tests women who were carriers could not be identified unless they had male descendants who were haemophiliacs. As many of Victoria's descendants declined socially from royalty to commoners they became less conspicuous and eventually disappeared from public record.

The first of Queen Victoria's children to carry the gene, Princess Alice, had two sons and five daughters. The eldest son, who inherited the dukedom of Hesse, was not a haemophiliac. His younger brother Frederick, as already mentioned, was a bleeder and died in childhood in consequence. Of the five daughters at least two proved to be carriers, Irene and Alexandra, the latter Tsarina of Russia. The youngest daughter, Mary, died in childhood and Elizabeth, wife of a Russian grand duke, died childless. Either might have been a carrier.

Alice's eldest daughter, Victoria, married a Battenberg, who was created the Marquis of Milford Haven, and she had four children including Lord Louis Mountbatten and Alice, the mother of Prince Philip, Duke of Edinburgh. Fortunately, haemophilia has not appeared in any of Milford Haven's descendants, although that leaves a one in sixteen chance that Alice was a carrier but did not pass the gene on to any of her children.

Irene, Princess Alice's second daughter, married her cousin, Prince Henry of Prussia, who was a brother of Kaiser Wilhelm. She bore him three sons, Waldemar, Sigismund and Henry. Waldemar and Henry were both haemophiliacs, Henry dying at the age of four, but his brother Waldemar survived until he was fifty-six, when he died childless. Fortunately Sigismund did not inherit the defective gene. Prince Henry of Prussia was evidently as ill-advised on the dangers of marrying the sister of a haemophiliac as his brother-in-law the tsar. Some commentators have suggested (e.g. the authors of some recent *Encyclopaedia Britannica* articles and McKusick[1]) that Waldemar and Sigismund may have inherited the gene from Victoria's eldest daughter through their father, Prince Henry of Prussia. However, there is no evidence that Henry was a bleeder and even had he been, he could not have passed the gene to his sons, while, on the other hand, his wife Irene had a haemophiliac brother and a sister who was a carrier.

The massacre in the cellars of the Ipatiev house eliminated at least two and possibly as many as six carriers of the gene. The exclusion of Mrs Manahan from the list of Queen Victoria's possible descendants removes almost all possibility of the survival of the gene in the tsarina's line, but as long as the exact fates of the tsarevitch and the missing grand duchess, who were not buried in the grave near Ekaterinburg, remain unknown, a remote possibility remains that the gene still survives. The exclusion of Mrs Manahan from the survival stakes also eliminates the son she is supposed to have left behind in Romania and one Anastasia Romanov who lives in St Petersburg, a suburb of Tampa, Florida. This Anastasia claims to be a daughter of Mrs Manahan or Anna Anderson, but even if this claim were correct, she could not have inherited the gene.

If the gene still exists it is most likely to be found among the descendants of Princess Beatrice, Queen Victoria's youngest daughter. Her eldest son, Alexander, Marquess of Carisbrooke, was not a carrier. The fates of his two younger brothers, both haemophiliacs, has already been mentioned. One died of wounds in 1914, the other died following a hip operation in 1922. Neither left descendants. Beatrice's only daughter Victoria Eugenie, who became Queen of Spain, left a large family in her efforts to produce a healthy heir. Two of her sons, Alfonso and Gonzalo, were haemophiliacs and died young following car accidents. The haemophiliac Alfonso left two sons but neither could have inherited the gene. His sister Beatriz had two sons and two daughters. There is no evidence that either of her sons, Marco Antonio and Marino, were haemophiliacs, but as cadet branches of royal families decline in social status information becomes more difficult to obtain and concealment easier. Her daughter Olimpia had a son who died in 1975. According to Dr Magallón his death was due to 'un problema de sangre'. This need not necessarily have been haemophilia, but if it were then Olimpia must have been a carrier and either her mother Beatriz a carrier or her father a haemophiliac. If this were the case, each of Olimpia's daughters would have had a 50 per cent chance of being a carrier in turn, and even if Sandra had had a healthy son there would still have been a chance of one in four that her daughter would carry the gene as well. In fairness we should mention that another correspondent, Marlene Eilers of Virginia, has written to us that Olimpia herself and the boy's great-aunt (Maria Cristina) had told her that the boy was not a haemophiliac.

In an echo of her great-grandmother's wedding to Alfonso XIII, ninety years before, Sibella married Prince William of Luxemburg at Versailles in 1994. The wedding took place in the presence of the King and Queen of the Belgians, Queen Fabiola of Spain, the Queens of Norway and Greece, the exiled Empress of Iran and numerous HRHs. It is to be hoped that the bride and groom have been better advised medically than were the earlier generations of royalty and that there is no danger of haemophilia appearing in their descendants.

Eugene's second daughter Maria Cristina had four daughters and three grandsons, none of whom were haemophiliacs, but there is a small possibility that the gene might still survive in the granddaughters.

The families of both Olimpia and Victoria live quietly in Italy. It is to be hoped that neither has inherited the gene but statistically it is more likely than not that at least one and possibly several have. Queen Victoria passed the gene to three of her children. Five generations later the gene still survives in one, possibly two descendants and may be present in three of the next generation. In spite of the immense disadvantages the gene confers natural selection is surprisingly slow in eliminating it.

The gene for haemophilia almost certainly does not survive among the descendants of Victoria's son, the unfortunate Leopold. By the laws of genetics his daughter, another Princess Alice, had to be a carrier, while her brother, Charles Edward Leopold, could not. Alice married Prince Alexander of Teck who was created Earl of Athlone in reward. The earl was the brother of Queen Mary, the consort of King George V. Of the Athlone's three children, one son Maurice died as a baby but it is uncertain whether or not he was a haemophiliac. His brother, Viscount Trematon, was a haemophiliac and died at the age of twenty-one without issue. He was involved in a motoring accident in France while overtaking at high speed. The medical bulletins and *The Times* obituary make no mention of the dread word haemophilia but the evidence is clear. The accident occurred on 1 April 1928 and bleeding is mentioned on the 4th. By the 6th he is said to be much improved and to be eating and drinking. On the 7th 'recovery is assured' but a slight haemorrhage occurred on the 10th, further bleeding on the 11th, followed by repeated haemorrhaging and the unfortunate young man died on the 14th. It is obvious that he would have survived had he not been a bleeder. Before the days of seat belts and other improvements in car design the motor car was a remarkably effective agent of selection against wealthy haemophiliacs. Viscount Trematon's sister, Lady May Abel Smith, had an even chance of inheriting the gene from her mother Princess Alice. Fortunately, Lady May's son is not a haemophiliac, but each of her daughters still had a chance of being carriers. When a possible carrier has a healthy brother or son her chances of being a carrier are halved. Each of Lady May's daughters had a 25 per cent chance of inheriting the gene, but the absence of the gene in her son reduces the chance to one in eight. The chance that her granddaughter in the female line is a carrier is reduced from one in eight to less than one in a hundred by her four healthy brothers. The gene that plagued the unfortunate Leopold is therefore probably extinct. All doubt could be removed by an assay of the granddaughter's Factor VIII.

Prince Leopold's son was destined to play a significant role in twentieth-century history. After the prince's death in 1884, his wife Princess Helen bore him a posthumous son. Charles Edward Leopold was born in the old family home of Claremont, where the first Prince

Leopold and Princess Charlotte spent their short time together. While any daughter of the haemophiliac Leopold had to be a carrier, the son had to escape the gene, as it is carried on the X chromosome which is not involved in the fertilization of a male. Charles Edward was educated at Eton and seemed destined to spend his life as a cadet member of the British royal family, but in 1900 he accepted the dukedom of Saxe-Coburg-Gotha, the inheritance of Prince Albert's family. He rose to the rank of general in the German army, assisted no doubt by his close relationship with the kaiser. During the First World War he was stripped of his British titles. When the German empire collapsed in 1918 he was forced to abdicate his dukedom. He promptly gave his support to the militant organizations which sprang up in Germany in the troubled postwar years, which wished to rebuild Germany and free her from the humiliations of the Treaty of Versailles. He played a leading part in the Germany National People's Party (DNVP), which drew its support mainly from the aristocrats, landowners, retired officers and upper middle class in the Protestant or Prussian areas of Germany.

At a meeting held at Harzburg on 11 October 1931 he helped to found the Harzburg Front, an alliance between the DNVP and the National Socialist Party, the Nazis.[2] Hitler's National Socialists drew support mainly from the lower middle class and the workers. The Front was revived in January 1933 and organized a united opposition to the Brüning government. The prestige and status that this alliance gave the Nazis helped them to become the largest party in the 1933 elections. In 1932 the Nazis had gained 33 per cent of the vote. In the 1933 elections the Nazis received 44 per cent and the DNVP 8 per cent, giving the alliance a total of 52 per cent.[3] President Hindenburg, fearing that Hitler intended to establish a dictatorship, approved Hitler's appointment as chancellor solely on condition that the Nazis held only three of the nine cabinet posts, Hitler, Goering as Minister for Prussia and Frick as Minister of the Interior. The other six posts went to the DNVP and the ex-servicemen's league which were expected to control Hitler. The 1933 election took place at the depth of the Depression. As the world economy later improved unemployment declined everywhere, but the Nazis gained the credit in Germany. Had they not been elected in 1933 Hitler would probably never have come to power. A few months after the election the DNVP dissolved itself at Hitler's behest and most of its members, including the ex-Duke of Saxe-Coburg-Gotha, joined the National Socialists. Charles Edward Leopold, a grandchild of Queen Victoria, became a Group Leader in the Brownshirts.

Charles Edward first met the Prince of Wales, his half-cousin, when the latter visited Germany in the summer of 1913. In 1936 Hitler sent the ex-Duke of Coburg back to Britain, ostensibly as President of the Anglo-

German Fellowship, but in reality as an unofficial ambassador to improve Anglo-German relations and to report back to Hitler on the possibility of an Anglo-German pact. He stayed with his aunt, the Princess Alice, in Kensington Palace, where he entertained many political leaders including Duff Cooper and Anthony Eden. He had three conversations with Edward VIII, the first on the day following the death of George V. He reported to Hitler that the new king believed an alliance with Germany should be the 'Guiding principle of British foreign policy'. He conveyed to Hitler a quite false appreciation of the strength of the king's influence: 'The King is resolved to concentrate the business of government on himself. For England not too easy.' According to Charles Edward the new king dismissed the idea of talks between Baldwin and Hitler with the words, 'Who is King here? Baldwin or I? I myself wish to talk to Hitler and will do so here or in Germany.' In spite of his keen interest in international politics his obsession with Mrs Simpson gave Baldwin the opportunity to remove the uncrowned Edward VIII from the throne before he could consolidate his position by a coronation.

After abdicating in late 1936 to marry Mrs Simpson, Edward, now Duke of Windsor, visited Germany again for two weeks in 1937, ostensibly to study housing and working conditions there with a view to improving conditions in Britain, though how he could apply his new knowledge from his exile in France was never made clear. While in Germany he met Hitler, Goering and Goebbels, greeting Hitler with a Nazi salute, according to *The Times* correspondent, while his German cousin gave a gala dinner in his honour. The visit was played down by the British press, but the *New York Times* reported that, 'this gesture and remarks during the last two weeks have demonstrated adequately that the Abdication did rob Germany of a firm friend, if not indeed a devoted admirer on the British throne'. These links continued until 1940.

The popular image of Britain in 1940, a united nation heroically resisting a ferocious Hitler, who was bent on its destruction, is largely mythical. Hitler, who had fought opposite British troops in the First World War, had the greatest admiration and respect for Britain. He saw it as a fellow Germanic nation, an heroic imperial power, and consistently sought an alliance with Britain to leave Germany free to destroy Russia. In *Mein Kampf* he wrote, 'In Europe there can be for Germany, in the predictable future, only two allies: England and Italy'. Whether he would have remained a friend and ally if Russia had been eliminated is another question. In Britain there were many who either reciprocated his feelings, or felt that Britain's interests would be best served by an alliance as resistance would be futile. In 1939 Hitler had no plans prepared to invade Britain although he had detailed plans for the defeat of France. Neither did he establish a spy network in Britain, as he never planned to fight us, in marked contrast to our later Russian allies who established an extensive and efficient network in the 1930s. Even after the declaration of war in 1939 Hitler still hoped that, after crushing France, it would be possible to reach agreement with Britain. For this reason he dithered after his panzer division broke through to the coast, holding them back for two crucial days late in May 1940, while the British army retreated to Dunkirk. Goering's Chief of Staff explained, 'The Führer wants to spare Britain a humiliating defeat'.[4] During June contacts were made through Swedish intermediaries, between Lord Halifax, the Foreign Secretary and R.A. Butler, with Ribbentrop, who was confident that a settlement could be reached. Simultaneously, negotiations were carried out with the Duke of Windsor.

The Duke of Windsor was in France when the blitzkrieg began in 1940. After the fall of France he moved to Spain where he lingered for a week. The US ambassador reported 'in conversation last night with [members?] of the embassy staff the Duke of Windsor disclosed that the most important thing now to be done was to end the war before thousands more were killed or maimed to save the face of a few politicians'. The Germans contacted the duke through intermediaries and considered both bribing him with 50 million francs to stay within reach of Germany, or even of kidnapping him.

In order to persuade the duke to leave the continent, Churchill appointed him Governor of the Bahamas, but even after accepting the post, the duke dawdled in Portugal for a further three weeks while continuing to negotiate with the Germans. The Germans allowed the duchess's maid to return to their Paris residence to collect sundry personal items.

Late in July 1940 Ribbentrop effectively offered the duke the British throne. The offer was conveyed by the German Minister in Lisbon. Reasserting Germany's desire for peace with Britain he suggested, 'In such a case Germany would be willing to cooperate most closely with the Duke and to clear the way for any desire expressed by the Duke and Duchess'. To the duke's credit he chose the Governorship of the Bahamas. According to the German ambassador in Madrid, 'The Duke hesitated even up to the last moment. The ship had to delay its departure on that account.' The influence of Sir Walter Monkton finally persuaded the duke to depart, but even in the middle of August 1940, with the Battle of Britain at its height in the skies over England, the duke was still in communication with his German friends from his new base in the Bahamas.

The duke himself always believed that the war with Germany should have been avoided, but his attempt to reverse his grandfather's pro-French policy was foiled by the ease with which he had allowed himself to be manoeuvred off the British throne.

While these tentative Anglo-German contacts were being made Hitler delayed the air offensive against Britain, allowing us to rebuild our fighter squadrons, which had suffered heavily in the battle for France and over the beaches of Dunkirk. Although Hitler named 13 August as the invasion date the plans progressed only in a desultory fashion. Charles Edward Leopold's reports were a major influence in encouraging Hitler to exaggerate the strength of the pro-German party in Britain. His militaristic attitudes were in remarkable contrast to the liberal attitudes of his father and grandfather. Had Hitler had a more realistic appraisal of British opinion he might have pushed his panzers into Dunkirk with all speed and have planned and carried out the defeat of Britain with the same determination as the defeat of France.

Charles Edward paid a heavy price for his support of German nationalism as two of his four sons lost their lives in the Second World War and at the end of the war he lost most of his estates which lay in the Russian zone of Germany. He died in 1954 and was survived by two sons and two daughters.

After the occupation of Germany in 1945 George VI, with the support of Winston Churchill, took measures to ensure that the Duke of Windsor's correspondence with his cousins, Charles Edward and Prince Philip of Hesse, one time Lieutenant-General in the Storm Troops, was collected and suppressed. The man chosen for this delicate task was Anthony Blunt, himself a Russian agent, and his knowledge of this embarrassing information was his insurance against prosecution when his own treason was discovered. In the words of *The Times*[5] his treachery was trivial compared with the 'enormity of the Windsors' wartime activities'. In 1945 and again in 1953 Prime Minister Winston Churchill took action to suppress the relevant documents when the Nazi Foreign Ministry file on pre-war Anglo-German relations was published.[6]

Mention must be made of descendants of two other leading players in the story of Queen Victoria's gene, those of Leopold, later King of the Belgians, the prime mover in the drama, and those of the Duke of Cumberland, and later King of Hanover, who would have become King of Britain had Queen Victoria not been born.

When Leopold I of Belgium lay dying he could look back on an astonishingly successful life, in spite of the loss of Charlotte. He was firmly established as king of a small but prosperous country. His niece ruled the greatest empire that had ever existed and the younger members of his family were set to rule much of the rest of the world.

His eldest son, Leopold II, resembled his father in many respects. He was as ambitious and avaricious but, whereas his father had been charming and diplomatic, Leopold II was cruel and ruthless. Both manipulated their relatives' lives in pursuit of their own ambitions, but Leopold I brought success and sometimes happiness to his kin while Leopold II brought only misery to his own children. Feeling that Belgium was too small a field for his ambitions Leopold II first attempted to lease the Philippines from Spain. A year after this plan had failed he called an international conference on Africa in Brussels and joined the scramble for Africa in a unique fashion. Behind the façade of an *Association Internationale Africaine*, established ostensibly to bring the benefits of civilization to central Africa and to suppress the slave trade, he converted 900,000 square miles of the Congo basin into a private estate. Forced labour and an extortionate tax, levied in wild rubber, enforced by the bullet and the lash, made Leopold a vast private fortune. The misrule led to uprisings which were ruthlessly suppressed. Tribal levies from one area were used to put down tribes in another. Huge areas became depopulated and hundreds of thousands, possibly millions, died. No complaints were raised by the Belgians, mainly responsible for organizing these horrors, but inevitably the conscience of the English-speaking world became troubled, particularly as the result of publicity given to the problem by Roger Casement. After nearly forty years Leopold was forced to relinquish his hold and the Congo became a Belgian colony – but he was generously compensated for his sacrifice by the Belgian taxpayer.

His treatment of his family was almost as cruel. After only four weeks of marriage his unfortunate Habsburg wife, Marie Henriette of Hungary, lamented 'If God hears my prayers I shall not go on living much longer', but she survived to bear him three daughters and a son. The son died as a child but the three daughters all endured lives of misery. The eldest, Louise, was married at the age of sixteen to an elderly relative, Philip of Coburg. She literally fled from her husband on the first night, hiding in the palace greenhouse. She wrote later, 'I am not, I am sure, the first woman who having lived in the clouds during her engagement, has been suddenly hurled to the ground on her marriage night and who, bruised and mangled in her soul, has fled humanity in tears'. With Coburg resolution, she returned to her husband, learned to enjoy sex and its many variations and soon accumulated her own lovers. She eventually left her husband for a handsome cavalry officer, Count Mallachich. After a financial scandal the count was imprisoned in wretched conditions and Louise, who was quite sane, was confined in a lunatic asylum. Ignoring his daughter's pleas for help, Leopold instructed the jailer 'to keep strict watch upon the madwoman'. Eventually she escaped, but spent a long life in poverty only to inherit a fortune on her deathbed from her aunt Charlotte, the widow of Maximilian of Mexico. Leopold's second daughter Stephanie married Crown Prince Rudolf of Austria, but lost him to Baroness Vetsera, with whom he committed suicide in the hunting lodge at Meyerling. Leopold kept his youngest daughter, Clementine, by his side for many years, forbidding her to marry. When he eventually died, she promptly married Prince Victor Napoleon, head of the Napoleon family. Perhaps she had a little happiness in later life. It is ironic that the son of the great schemer, organizer and expositor of kingship should have brought such misery on his own family, though perhaps by his own standards Leopold II regarded himself as a success.

As we noted at the beginning of this book the lives of royalty often prove to be of compelling interest. Monarchs wield great influence, as did Victoria, her grandson the kaiser and her granddaughter Tsarina Alexandra. The circumstances of their childhood often leave them less disciplined or inhibited in their behaviour so that they may show extremes of human behaviour, ranging from the altruistic Pedro of Brazil to the monstrous Leopold II of Belgium.

If Queen Victoria was not the daughter of the Duke of Kent then the British throne should have passed to Ernest Augustus, the Duke of Cumberland. When Victoria ascended the British throne the throne of Hanover passed to Ernest Augustus (or Ernst August as he was known in Hanover), as the Hanoverian throne could only be passed to males. His son, blind George V of Hanover, unwisely sided with the Austrians in the war of 1866 and was deposed by the victorious Prussians, who annexed his kingdom. George's grandson, another Ernst August, Prince of Hanover, married Louise, a daughter of the last kaiser, in 1913. This was the last of the great royal family gatherings before the First World War destroyed their world, and the wedding ceremonies ended with the legendary Fackeltanz, or torch dance, in which only those of the rank of 'Royal Highness' or above, could take part. Their son, also Ernst August, fought on the Russian front and was wounded at Kharkov, but was imprisoned by Hitler after the July plot of 1944. After the war he fought a successful legal battle to establish his claim to be a British subject, as a descendant of the Hanoverians.[7] His eldest son, yet another Ernst August, born in 1954, is the present head of the Welf (Guelf) family and is a prince of both Britain and Hanover. His younger brother, Prince Ludwig Rudolf, married Countess Isabelle Thurn Valsassina but committed suicide after his young wife died of a drug overdose. Inherited wealth, and the boredom that it may cause, can be as dangerous as haemophilia.

Our early human and pre-human ancestors no doubt lived in hierarchical structured societies and for many people a king or queen still forms the natural centre and representation of a state. At the end of the twentieth century the wheel of history is turning full circle. In Britain the sexual behaviour of some of the younger members of the royal family, widely advertised by foreign-owned newspapers of republican sympathies, are discrediting the royal family as much as the family of George III did two hundred years ago, but the end of the Cold War and the collapse of Communism in Eastern Europe and Russia have produced some most unexpected results. Descendants of the monarchs who were disposed of in 1918 have suddenly become popular. Ex-King Michael of Romania, exiled by the Communists in 1947, made a surprise visit to Bucharest in 1990 where he was welcomed by a group of monarchists in the Central University Square. One nineteen-year-old product of the Communist system said: 'We are very happy. The King represents stability and peace.' The Romanian government, formed of ex-Communists, fearing Michael Hohenzollern's popularity, prevented the royal family from visiting their ancestors' tombs, the ostensible purpose of the visit, and hastily deported them.

Further south the Bulgarian monarchy was abolished as the result of a plebiscite held under Communist auspices in 1946, but when Princess Maria-Luisa, sister of the last King Simeon, visited Bulgaria, over 50,000 people thronged the streets of Sofia chanting, 'We want Simeon, we want our king'. A poll showed that 41.2 per cent of Bulgarians wanted the return of the monarchy. Simeon is a Coburg by descent in the male line. The ruling ex-Communists hastily passed a law requiring presidential candidates to have been resident in Bulgaria for at least five years, in order to exclude his candidature.

In 1991 Grand Duke Vladimir Kirillovich Romanov, son of a first cousin of the last tsar, visited St Petersburg, the first Romanov to see the city for over seventy years. The reception was friendly and small groups of monarchists, some wearing tsarist uniforms and others clutching portraits of the last tsar, followed him around. A service was held at St Isaac's Cathedral in his honour, by Patriarch Aleksy II. When Vladimir died he was interred with his ancestors in the fortress of Sts Peter and Paul. Monarchist feeling is not strong but viewed across the seventy years of Communist terror, mismanagement and corruption, the tsarist era appears more attractive than in 1917 and if conditions in Russia do not improve the current regime may become discredited as well.

When Alexander Karadjordjevic, the Crown Prince of Yugoslavia, descended through his grandmother Marie, the daughter of Ferdinand I of Romania, from Prince Alfred, a son of Queen Victoria, visited Belgrade, over 70,000 people gave him a triumphant welcome. The break up of Yugoslavia and the subsequent war between Serbia, Croatia and Bosnia make it impossible to imagine the resurrection of the Yugoslavian throne, but many Serbs still have some loyalty to their old monarchy. His father King Peter was driven into exile in 1941 when Yugoslavia bravely resisted Hitler's demands and was betrayed when the West backed Tito instead of the legitimate government.

In July 1994 the Estonian Royalist Party, representing one-tenth of the Estonian electorate, invited Prince Edward to become King of Estonia. This is the more remarkable because Estonia has never had a king before, previously being ruled by the Teutonic Knights, the Swedes or the Russians. The proposers felt that a constitutional monarchy would best combine 'ancient culture with modern political reality'.

The closely related dynasties of Europe were rightly damned by their failure to prevent the First World War but the horrors of the Communist governments in Russia and Eastern Europe and of the Second World War have, at least in the eyes of many, rehabilitated them.

CHAPTER ELEVEN

A Breed Apart

History may be studied in order to understand how we arrived at our present state or because it is often more intriguing than fiction. Is it a random, totally chaotic series of events? How many foresaw in 1988 that the Soviet empire was about to collapse, or even that there was a small but significant probability that one or more monarchs, all inevitably descended from Queen Victoria, might be invited back to thrones in Eastern Europe. How decisive is the influence of the individual? Were only the trumpets of Gorbachov capable of bringing down the Berlin Wall or might others have done the same? Prince Albert, on his deathbed, probably averted war with the Northern States; could the tsar, perhaps with Rasputin at his shoulder, have averted the First World War? Efforts to construct predictive theories based on history have been peculiarly unsuccessful but historical experience can be used in order to avoid repeating the more obvious mistakes of the past. While the history of mankind may have been 'little more than the register of the crimes, failings and misfortune of mankind' (Gibbon), lessons may still be learned.

The story of Queen Victoria's gene contains both sober warnings and tentative grounds for hope. It is a story of power: of what kings offer their subjects and what commoners expect of their monarchs. Do the trivial sexual peccadillos of minor royalty matter or does the peculiar interest they excite reflect the link between power and sex? Biologically sex and power are related. The Coburgs were the ultimate dynasts, losing every battle on the ground and making all their conquests in the marriage bed (Duke Francis's son Ernst backed the Prussians against Napoleon in the 1790s while his brother Leopold fought for Napoleon against the Russians in 1812). Leopold and his relatives and descendants were ruthlessly ambitious and sexually aggressive, twice marrying the Crown Princess of Britain (Charlotte and Victoria), together with those of Portugal and Brazil. The creativity of the family of the Dukes of Coburg must be admired. For five generations Duke Francis's opportunistic and promiscuous descendants expanded their control over nations great and small. By any criterion of territorial acquisition they had become the most successful family in human history: quite probably, their record will never be challenged. But then nature (or a misjudged liaison) injected a single defective gene into the family which within fifty years contributed to two of the bloodiest wars in history.

Leopold, the younger son of a minor duke, pursued his dynastic ambitions with a unique pertinacity. It is clear from the letter to his elder brother that he had determined to marry Charlotte, the heir to the British throne, before he had even visited Britain. In spite of her untimely death, by the time Leopold died his family was firmly established in Britain, Germany and Portugal. It is difficult to understand what had inspired these imperial ambitions. His sister Juliana's brief marriage to Constantine, the tsar's younger brother, was not an auspicious beginning, and although Juliana would have become tsarina if the marriage had endured, this was not apparent when Leopold courted Charlotte.

The part played by Stockmar in the dynastic ambitions deserves examination. One of our strengths as a species is to make alliances, usually between males and sometimes between those who are not our genetic relations. Stockmar, three years Leopold's senior, was first appointed as Leopold's physician but rapidly became private secretary and comptroller to the household. He later became mentor and private secretary to the much younger Albert. He was highly intelligent and diplomatic and gained widespread respect. On many occasions he played a key role. He tried to negotiate Leopold's acquisition of the throne of Greece and when that failed, successfully negotiated his selection as King of the Belgians. He then retired to Coburg as it was felt he might overshadow the new king, but in 1836 he negotiated the marriage of Leopold's nephew to the widowed Queen of Portugal. As soon as Victoria came to the throne he came to Britain as her adviser and persuaded Melbourne, the prime minister, to block Conroy's design to make Victoire regent and himself Victoria's secretary on the death of William IV. A year later he accompanied Albert on the grand tour, coaching him for the position of Prince Consort to Victoria. His influence was clearly decisive in the ascent of the Coburgs and he was evidently a brilliant negotiator and manipulator with a profound grasp of European politics and human nature. Although born in Coburg he was of Swedish descent. His loyalty to Leopold was remarkable; did he have any Coburg blood in his veins?

Among animals the drive for leadership is sexual. It is the top baboon and the dominant chimpanzee that mate most frequently. Evolution has tailored behaviour so as to secure the greatest probability of passing an individual's genes to the next generation. Among mammals, such as ourselves, the female makes a disproportionately greater investment in reproduction than the male – she must carry the progeny and then suckle the baby – and hence can only have relatively few offspring in a lifetime. The male, however, in the time it takes one female to deliver and breast-feed a child, has the potential to father many children. Hence nearly all mammals are polygamous and, although the female has the physical burden of pregnancy, it is the males who are larger because they must compete and in the last resort fight, to gain access to the females.

Men, on average, are 10 to 15 per cent larger than women and there is no doubt that biologically we are a polygamous species, as are our nearest relatives, the chimpanzees. At the same time adults in all societies are capable of establishing passionate, sexually exclusive relationships, and fathers usually contribute to the upbringing of their children. In short, human beings are balanced on a knife-edge between monogamy and polygamy.

In some respects human systems of government have declined from the level of the early primates because their dominant males have to be in fine physical condition and are frequently challenged by aspiring rivals. A great danger in modern societies of both east and west is that leaders frequently continue in power, even when they are sick or senile. It is noteworthy that the European Union, which rotates its leader every six months, does not meet the instinctive human need for an identifiable leader. Whatever the other faults of the Community this is an excellent thing and will temper the tendency of the EU, now the greatest economic power in the world, to dominate its neighbours and abuse its strength. However, it is likely that the European Union will in due course condense into a superstate superseding the national loyalties of its citizens. An essential stage in the process will be the enhancement of the powers and period of office of the President.

Modern societies are structured so that most senior positions are held by the elderly. Democratic societies usually elect their leaders for periods of four or five years. Even if fit when elected, a man or woman in their late sixties or seventies has a fair probability of a major debilitating illness within their period of office, a probability increased by the stress of that office, yet they and their society are strangely reluctant to replace them when they do fall ill. Dictators such as Franco and Brezhnev clung to office as long as possible, retarding and paralysing their societies as they did so. In constitutional monarchies incapacity or senility in the monarch is no disadvantage, providing the ministers are young and capable; indeed the extent to which the growth of constitutional monarchy was facilitated by monarchical age and incapacity is worthy of study. The power of British prime ministers grew considerably during the long reigns of George III and Victoria.

The dangers of ill-health among those in power are most strikingly displayed in the Russian royal family. The tsarevitch's illness during the last fatal days of July 1914, coinciding with Rasputin's absence in Siberia, may have distracted the tsar from the international crisis which led to the First World War. By providing Rasputin with a power-base the tsarevitch's condition totally ruined the reputation of the Russian royal family and even when the tsar abdicated, it prevented an orthodox succession, which might have saved the dynasty. Apart from the haemophilia the outbreak of measles which affected the Russian royal children just as the Petrograd riots began in 1917 distanced the tsarina even further than usual from reality.

Illness has played direct roles at many critical times in history and it is interesting to observe how often national leaders have been discovered to be ill when they fell from power. Napoleon was a sick man at Waterloo, Sir Anthony Eden was ill during the Suez crisis, Herr Honnecker was suffering from cancer when he was swept from power in East Germany, Roosevelt was dying when he ceded Eastern Europe to Stalin at Yalta. Churchill had at least one cerebral stroke while in power which impaired his judgement.

The contemporary state often gives even more power, in absolute terms, to its leaders than any nineteenth-century monarch held. Giant wealth, sophisticated technologies and, above all, control of nuclear weapons, are concentrated in the hands of very few, often old, people. The tsar and his generals, over many months, could send six million to war on the eastern front in 1914 but they were never in a position where they might have only fifteen minutes to think about pressing the trigger of the ultimate weapons of human destruction. Would Khruschev or Kennedy have reacted less prudently at the time of the Cuban Missile Crisis if, like the tsar when abdicating at Pskov, they had been obsessed with illness in themselves or their family? Nation states will always be run by human beings open to physical and psychological disease, possibly with dire consequences: we should therefore be aware that neither hereditary kings nor elected presidents will ever be free from the risk of illness. The more power vested in our leaders and the more complex and rapid the reaction time of our technology, the more likely that their illnesses may one day affect the body politic of a nation – or of the whole globe. Monarchs and other national leaders often fail to make effective use of the available scientific and medical knowledge in ordering national affairs. Ill-health among the leadership is an ever-present danger and open government is essential to ensure that unfit leaders are rapidly and smoothly replaced.

During the nineteenth century the highest levels of European society were almost totally divorced from contemporary scientific and medical knowledge. Until the use of chloroform by Victoria to reduce the pains of Leopold's birth, the medical assistance and advice the British royal family received did at least as much harm as good, and until the Romanian royal family declined a Russian bride no European royalty, or their advisors, seems to have had an accurate knowledge of the laws of genetics, although the inheritance of haemophilia had been understood empirically for at least two generations. Today, the whole population in the west has access to medical assistance and genetic counselling vastly superior to that available to royalty only a century ago.

The mismatch in western civilization between the structure of our scientific and industrial establishments and that of our political establishments continues. In the former power is disseminated and the abilities of a whole population are utilized while in the latter power is concentrated in a hierarchical fashion, in a manner which goes back at least to the Neolithic and even beyond to our sub-human ancestors. Most primate societies are dominated by a mature male who has first choice of food and females but is required to defend his group against rivals. Even today human societies, particularly when in danger, prefer an identifiable leader rather than government by committee or by plebiscite. When rapid decisions are required the system has its advantages but in peacetime power is unreasonably concentrated in individuals, whether presidents, prime ministers or Communist Party secretaries. The British are unusual in that they are more willing than most people to accept a woman as leader, for example Boudicca, Elizabeth I or Mrs Thatcher, but male or female, president or party secretary, the leader, once established, is surrounded in all countries by a mystique which dulls criticism and may confuse it with treason. The British system, which concentrates the mystique around a constitutional monarch and the power in the prime minister, reduces but does not eliminate this danger. The obsession of the British establishment with secrecy and its draconian libel laws and security legislation offsets any advantage this division of labour might give.

The desire for a single recognizable leader is so ingrained in our natures that an identifiable leader will be a feature of our society in some form or other for the foreseeable future, in spite of the rational side of our nature which pleads for a society with a more egalitarian or democratic system of direction. In future, we might moderate the system by demanding more medical information on a leader, both when standing for office and while holding it. A free press might be expected to perform this function but in Britain it is largely prevented by the secrecy which is cultivated as part of the mystique, while in the USA the efforts of the press to date have been clumsy and trivial. An enlightened society should not be expected to elect presidents or prime ministers in their late sixties or early seventies, as the probability of significant deterioration during their time in office is too great.

Monarchs and aristocrats, through wealth and power, are often less constrained in their sexual behaviour than their subjects. Victoria's family shows clearly, and on numerous occasions, the fine balance between male fidelity and infidelity. The Duke of Kent was reluctant to desert Madam de St Laurent, although his numerous brothers had little reluctance in changing partners and his brother-in-law Leopold is said to have raped his own brother's mistress. Albert and Victoria's passion seems to have lasted twenty-one years of marriage, while Albert's brother Ernest was a rake who, according to Albert, required treatment for his venereal disease. Albert's own death may have been hastened by the discovery of his eldest son's first sexual adventures, but Edward VII more than made up for his parents' chastity. He had several deep emotional relationships with married women such as Lillie Langtry, Alice Keppel[1] and Daisy Warwick, as well as having numerous one-night stands. He would eye the audience from his box in the theatre and send an equerry to invite the most attractive woman to join him. It was an offer that was rarely refused, although one night in Paris the subject of his interest proved to be Prince Yussopov, later to be Rasputin's assassin, who was in the habit of dressing in women's clothes.

The futile bloodshed of the First World War could so obviously have been avoided and most of the responsibility clearly lay with the closely related monarchs of Europe. When the war ended, monarchy as an institution had been widely discredited and Germany, Austria-Hungary and Russia became republics. By 1945 Yugoslavia, Romania, Spain, Italy, Bulgaria and Albania had joined them but the dictatorships which replaced them usually proved to be worse, and many now look back to the monarchist years as a golden age.

As long as they retained any real power monarchs and aristocrats created history by virtue of the authority and trust placed in them. The kings and queens of Europe all claimed their thrones by right of descent. When new nations like Romania or Bulgaria appeared they had to be ruled by scions of other European royal houses.

Leadership, by definition, turns on a single individual, and as long as Victoria's gene manifested its painful effects on the collaterals it made little difference to European and world history. But when the heirs to the Russian and Spanish thrones developed haemophilia then the disease helped to trigger two of the bloodiest civil wars of the twentieth century. Victoria's pathological gene was an exceptionally rare one, and history will probably never determine whether Victoire slept with some haemophiliac in a desperate attempt to conceive the child she needed to win the war of the hymen, or whether the egg or sperm that became Victoria had suffered a 1 in 25 to 50,000 mutation. Whatever its origin, haemophilia in Victoria's son Leopold influenced her life and in turn, to a slight extent, the life of the country. In the family of her grandchild Alexandra, it had a dramatic effect in clearing the path for Rasputin's rise to influence and power and distracting both tsar and tsarina from affairs of state. At one level, the possible sexual adventures of Queen Victoria's mother or whether Anastasia was who she claimed to be, may be seen to be as personal trivia beside the history of nations. But the personal stories of royalty continue to fascinate, because in a very real way they are the very stuff of history, as well as the triumphs and tragedies of real people.

An aristocracy often displays more extremes of human behaviour, perhaps because it is subject to fewer economic and social constraints than the rest of society. The childhood of royal children was not always confined by normal restraints. George III's children were whipped regularly, but many royal children were little constrained by authority or education. The Portuguese royal family were the last in Europe to bring up their children without any discipline whatsoever. King Miguel, a contemporary of Leopold I, was a monster, while his brother Pedro, the last Emperor of Brazil, is still fondly remembered as a humane patron of the arts and sciences. The antics of some of the Hanoverians are scarcely credible today, but the last Hanoverian, Queen Victoria, was held up as an exemplar to the whole nation. Leopold I of the Belgians, Victoria's 'dearest uncle', fathered a pitiless brute who was responsible for the deaths of millions in the Congo and imprisoned his own daughter for most of her life.

The effects of natural selection have eliminated Victoria's gene from most of her descendants and the decline in the number of kingdoms and the growth of constitutional monarchy has eliminated the gene from all positions of influence, but as it can remain hidden in a female line it could still be carried by some of Victoria's female descendants. There is a slight chance that it still survives among the descendants of Prince Leopold and a much greater chance that it survives among the descendants of the Spanish royal house, but it is unlikely that the gene will ever again have detectable effects on world history.

Notes

1. Officers of state continued to attend royal deliveries until the birth of Prince Charles to Queen Elizabeth in 1948, although only the Home Secretary was required to be present and then in a room adjoining the delivery room.

2. Culpeper wrote in a 1651 *Dictionary for Midwives*, 'Unless you draw back the blood you can never stop it; as you must pump out the Water of a Ship before you can stop the leak.'

3. Forceps of this type had been invented by the Chamberlens, a Huguenot family who came to England in 1569. Their forceps were a giant leap forward on the hooks and violent, painful and destructive methods employed previously. However, the family deliberately kept their invention a secret for many decades, literally blindfolding the women in labour so they wouldn't see how the operation was done. 'He who keeps secret so beneficial an instrument as the harmless obstetrical forceps', wrote one contemporary, 'deserves to have a worm devour his vitals for all eternity.' However, infection and other complications were common and the great eighteenth-century obstetrician and teacher, William Hunter, used to produce a rusty pair of forceps and tell his students 'where they save one they murder twenty'.

4. There was a teratoma, a benign tumour of the right ovary, which was unusual but could not have been associated with her death. The possibility of pulmonary emboli was not recognized in 1817 and could have been missed at the post-mortem.

5. Blood transfusions, directly from a donor, were first used for post-partum haemorrhage much later in the nineteenth century. Caesarian operation was known in 1817 but was invariably reserved for cases where a mother died in labour and a valiant attempt was made to save the child, if still alive.

CHAPTER TWO

1. The confusing variety of titles requires some explanation. The family surname was Wettin. In the Middle Ages they ruled all Saxony but as the territory was repeatedly divided among the multiplying heirs the various fragments continued to be distinguished by the prefix Saxe-, as in Saxe-Coburg and Saxe-Meiningen. To further complicate the situation Coburg lay in two separate parts, one centred on Coburg, the other on the even smaller Gotha, hence the full title Saxe-Coburg-Gotha. When marriage with heiress cousins reunited sections, titles such as Saxe-Coburg-Gotha-Saalfeld, Saxe-Coburg-Saalfeld for short, were created.

CHAPTER THREE

1. Christened Elizabeth.
2. Roger Fulford, *The Royal Dukes*, Duckworth, 1933.
3. M. Gillen, *The Prince and His Lady*, St Martin's Press, New York, 1971, p. 130.
4. Leopold to Victoria, 21 May 1845.
5. Duke of Kent to Wetherall, 14 November 1818.
6. Madame Siebold was one of the first women to qualify as a physician and she also called herself Dr Heidenreich. She had attended the University of Gottingen 'like a man'.

CHAPTER FOUR

1. I. MacAlpine and R. Hunter, *George III and the Mad Business*, Allen Lane, 1969.
2. On one such trip in 1825 Victoria almost died of dysentery.
3. Ashdown, p.86.
4. C.C.F. Greville, 21 September 1836.
5. 8 September 1831.
6. Victoria was about 5 ft tall and puberty tends to be later in individuals whom childhood nutrition leaves this short.
7. The emphases are Victoria's.
8. The lad was sentenced to death but later reprieved and confined to a mental asylum for life.
9. Dr John Snow is also remembered as the brilliant physician who traced a cholera epidemic to one water pump in Soho. When the authorities refused to believe that dirty water was the cause, he went at night and unscrewed the handle from the pump – the epidemic stopped. Until then it had been assumed that it was an airborne disease.
10. *Unberufen* – a superstitious remark to ward off evil, roughly equivalent to 'touch wood'.
11. Victoria to Vicky, 10 April 1858.
12. 2 March 1859.
13. 2 May 1859.
14. 2 September 1859.
15. 16 November 1861.
16. 'It is your little wife.'
17. It was without doubt a common disease. The Prince of Wales (in 1871), the queen's second son Alfred (in 1863) and her grandson George (in 1890) all nearly died of typhoid. Two of Victoria's second cousins – King Pedro of Portugal and his brother – had died from the disease earlier in the year of Albert's death.
18. Elizabeth Longford, *Darling Loosey*, Weidenfeld & Nicolson, 1991, p. 125.
19. Lillie was famous for her conversation as well as her good looks. On one occasion in her long friendship with Edward, he remarked, 'I have spent enough on you to buy a battleship.' Lillie replied, 'You have spent enough in me, Sir, to float a battleship!'
20. Journal, 14 January 1875.

21. Letter to Gladstone, 31 January 1875.

22. Memorandum, 23 April 1880.

23. 1 September 1882.

24. The Countess of Warwick was also noted for her repartee and at one official function a guest, warning of Edward's approach, said, 'Hush, the King is coming.' In a stage whisper the Countess remarked, 'That is the first time for a long time.'

CHAPTER FIVE

1. E. Radzinsky, *The Last Tsar*, Doubleday, New York, 1992, p. 264.

CHAPTER SIX

1. W. Bullock and Sir P. Fildes, *Haemophilia*, A Treasury of Human Inheritance, Vol. I, Eugenics Society, 1911.

2. M. Gillen, *The Duke and his Lady*, Sidgwick & Jackson, 1970.

3. 16 January 1790.

4. 28 July 1837.

5. 22 March 1829.

6. Greville, 25 February 1822.

7. Greville, 8 August 1829.

8. Greville, 8 August 1829.

9. Greville, 21 July 1830.

10. Greville, 29 February 1840.

11. Greville, 5 December 1841.

12. 15 February 1864.

13. 29 February 1840.

14. MacAlpine and Hunter, *George III and the Mad Business*.

15. *Daily Telegraph*, 21 March 1995.

CHAPTER SEVEN

1. Edward VIII abdicated in 1936 to marry a commoner, Mrs Simpson.

2. Von Schlieffen took as his military model the attack by Hannibal on the Roman flank at the battle of Cannae in 216 BC.

3. The father of the Chancellor of the Exchequer in the Attlee Government.

4. M. Harrison, 1972, *Clarence*.

5. K. Rose, *George V*, Weidenfeld & Nicolson, 1987.

6. S. Knight, *Jack the Ripper, the Final Solution*, Granada, 1977.

7. Ferdinand's mother was herself a granddaughter of Queen Victoria.

8. Elizabeth's husband, Grand Duke Sergei, was murdered by anarchists in 1905, when she retired from public life and founded a religious order devoted to the relief of the poor and sick. She was thrown to her death, down a mineshaft, by

the Communists in 1918, but has recently been canonized by the Russian Orthodox Church.

9. Churchill, Stalin and Roosevelt met in Nicholas's palace for the Yalta Conference in 1945.

10. Rasputin in Russian sounds uncannily similar to rasputstvo, the word for debauchery.

11. 7 September 1916. My own Sweetheart, . . . Gregory begs you earnestly to name Protopopov (Minister of the Interior) . . . he likes our Friend since at least 4 years and that says much for a man.

12. Felix's father was said to have a portrait gallery with paintings of his three hundred mistresses.

13. 12 March on our calendar – at this time Russia still adhered to the old calendar which was 13 days out of step with our present calendar. The modern calendar was adopted shortly after the tsar's abdication.

14. The kaiser died in 1941 after the beginning of the Second World War: by helping to start the First he had helped create the situation that led to the Second.

CHAPTER EIGHT

1. In 1960 the American U2 spy plane was shot down by the Soviets over the city.

2. The house was demolished twenty years ago by Boris Yeltsin, later President of Russia, but then acting under orders. The site is now a car park.

3. Sverdlov was head of the Central Executive Committee in Moscow, an old friend of Goloschchekin, and Ekaterinburg would be renamed in his honour until the end of Communism when it reverted to Ekaterinburg.

4. Eighteen pounds of small, /2 carat, diamonds would be worth over £60 million at 1992 prices. If larger gem stones were included, which is likely, the value might well be over £100 million at today's prices. (Pers. comm. Banks Lyon, Jewellers, Lancaster.)

5. *Sunday Times*, 11 December 1994.

6. *Daily Telegraph*, 12 September 1992.

7. *The Times*, 10 July 1993, and *Nature Genetics* 6, 130–5.

8. The hammer toe and oddities of the fingers were known features of the royal children.

9. J.B. Lowell, *Anastasia, the Lost Princess*, Robson Books, 1992, pp. 282–3.

10. To this day Queen Elizabeth II sometimes still wears the tsar's mother's diamond tiara.

11. *The Times*, 6 October 1994.

12. *Daily Telegraph*, 11 September 1992.

13. M. Occleshaw, *The Romanov Conspiracies*.

14. *Daily Telegraph*, 7 May 1994.

15. Lowell, *Anastasia the Lost Princess*, p. 443.

16. Lowell, *Anastasia the Lost Princess*.

17. Prince Frederick of Saxe-Altenburg befriended Anna Anderson and

supported her for many years. His sister had married Prince Sigismund of Prussia who was a son of Anastasia's Aunt Irene.

CHAPTER NINE

1. Sir Charles Petrie, *King Alfonso XIII*, Billing & Sons, Guildford and London, 1963.
2. *Geoffrey Madan's Notebooks*, ed. Gere and Sparrow, Oxford University Press, 1981, p. 120.
3. *The Times*, 3 January 1940.
4. V.A. McKusik, 'The Royal Haemophilia', *Scientific American*, 213, 2, 1965, pp. 88–95.

CHAPTER TEN

1. V.A. McKusick, 'The Royal Haemophilia', *Scientific American*, 213, 2 (1965), 88–95.
2. *The Times*, 8 March 1954.
3. R.F. Hamilton, *Who Voted for Hitler?* Princeton University Press, 1982.
4. J. Costello, *Ten Days that Saved the West*, Bantam Press, 1990, esp. pp 201, 321 and Appendix 8.
5. 10 October 1988.
6. J. Costello, *The Mask of Treachery*, W. Morrow, New York, 1988.
7. It is partly thanks to Prince Ernst August that the British royal house has retained the family name of Windsor. 'Queen Mary sent for me on February 18 to say that Prince Ernst August of Hanover had come back from Broadlands and informed her that Lord Mountbatten had said to an assembled house party of royal guests that the House of Mountbatten now reigned. The poor old lady, who had spent a sleepless night, was relieved when I said that I doubted if the Cabinet would contemplate such a change. Indeed when I told the PM he had at once consulted the Cabinet who said unanimously that they would tolerate no such thing.' From *The Fringes of Power. Downing Street Diaries 1939–1955*, by John Colville, Hodder and Stoughton, 1985.

CHAPTER ELEVEN

1. Camilla Parker Bowles is the great-granddaughter of Alice Keppel.

Bibliography

Place of publication given only if outside London.

Andrews, A. *The Follies of King Edward VII*. Lexington Press, 1975.

Aronson, T. *The King in Love: Edward VII's Mistresses: Lillie Langtry, Daisy Warwick, Alice Keppel and others*. John Murray, 1988.

Ashdown, D.M. *Queen Victoria's Mother*. Robert Hale, 1974.

Ashdown, D.M. *Royal Paramours*. Robert Hale, 1979.

Aspinall, A. *Letters of the Princess Charlotte, 1811–1817*. Home & van Thal, 1949.

Benson, E.F. *Queen Victoria*. Barnes & Noble, New York, 1992.

Buckle, G.F. *The Letters of Queen Victoria*. John Murray, 1928.

Bullock, W. and Fildes, P. *Haemophilia*. Eugenics Society, 1911.

Charlot, M. *Victoria: the Young Queen*. Blackwell, 1991.

Colville, J. *The Fringes of Power. Downing Street Diaries 1939–1955*. Hodder & Stoughton, 1985.

Cooper, P.M. *The Story of Claremont*. Nelson & E. Saunders Ltd, 1956.

Corbett, V. *A Royal Catastrophe, the Death in Childbirth of the Princess Charlotte of Wales*. L.P. Lowe, Worcestershire, 1985.

Costello, J. *The Mask of Treachery*. W. Morrow, New York, 1988.

Costello, J. *Ten Days that Saved the West*. Bantam Press, 1990.

Cowles, V. *Gay Monarch: The Life and Pleasures of Edward VII*. Harper & Brothers, New York, 1956.

Duff, D. *Albert and Victoria*. Published by Frederick Muller, republished by Readers Union Ltd, Newton Abbot, Devon, 1973.

Finestone, J. *The Last Courts of Europe: A Royal Family Album 1860–1914*. Dent & Sons, 1981.

Fulford, R. *The Wicked Uncles, the Father of Queen Victoria and His Brothers*. Loring & Mussey, New York, 1933.

Fulford, R. *Royal Dukes, the Father and Uncles of Queen Victoria*. Duckworth, 1933.

Fulford, R. *Dearest Child. Letters between Queen Victoria and the Princess Royal*. Evans Bros, 1966.

Gillen, M. *The Prince and His Lady*. Sidgwick & Jackson, 1970.

Greece, Prince Michael of. *Nicholas and Alexandra: The Family Albums*. Tauris Parke Books, 1992.

Greville, C.C.F. *The Greville Memoirs, a Journal of the Reign of King George IV and King William IV*. Longman, 1874.

Hall, U. *The Private Lives of Britain's Royal Women: Their Passions and Power*. Contemporary Books, Chicago, 1990.

Hamilton, R.F. *Who Voted for Hitler?* Princeton University Press, 1982.

Hardy, A. *Queen Victoria Was Amused*. John Murray, 1976.

Harrison, M. *Clarence: Was he Jack the Ripper?* Drake Publishing Inc., New York, 1972.

Hibbert, C. *The Royal Victorians: King Edward VII, His Family and Friends.* J.B. Lippincott Co., Philadelphia & New York, 1976.

Hindley, G. *The Royal Families of Europe.* Lyric Books, 1979.

Hitler, A. *Mein Kampf.* Translated by R. Manheim. Hutchinson, 1976.

De Jonge, A. *The Life and Times of Grigorii Rasputin.* Dorset Press, 1982.

Knight, S. *Jack the Ripper, the Final Solution.* Granada, 1977.

Lowell, J.B. *Anastasia, the Lost Princess.* Robson Books, 1992.

MacAlpine, I. and Hunter, R. *George III and the Mad Business.* Penguin, Allen Lane, 1969.

McKusik, V.A. 'The Royal Haemophilia'. *Scientific American,* 213, 2, 88–95, 1965.

Madan, G. *Geoffrey Madan's Notebooks.* Ed. Gene & Sparrow, Oxford University Press, 1981.

Massie, R.K. *Nicholas and Alexandra.* World Books, 1968.

Oakley, J. *Rasputin: Rascal Master.* St Martin's Press, 1989.

Occleshaw, M. *The Romanov Conspiracies.* Orion Press, 1994.

Petrie, C. *King Alphonso XIII.* Billing & Sons, Guildford, 1963.

Pipes, R. *Russia under the Old Regime.* Charles Scribner's Sons, New York, 1974.

Plowden, A. *The Young Victoria.* Weidenfeld & Nicolson, 1981.

Radzinsky, E. *The Last Tsar.* Doubleday, New York, 1992.

Rose, K. *George V.* Weidenfeld & Nicolson, 1987.

Smith, E.A. *A Queen on Trial: The Affair of Queen Caroline.* Alan Sutton, Stroud, 1993.

Woodham-Smith, C. *Queen Victoria: From her Birth to the Death of the Prince Consort.* Alfred A. Knopf, New York, 1972.

Sokolov, N. *Judicial Enquiry into the Assassination of the Russian Imperial Family.*

Stone, N. *The Eastern Front 1914–1917.* Charles Scribner's Sons, New York, 1975.

Strachey, L. *Queen Victoria.* Harcourt Brace Jovanovich, New York, 1921.

Summers, A. and Mangold, T. *The File on the Tsar.* Gollancz, 1976.

Taylor, E. *The Fall of the Dynasties: The Collapse of the Old Order 1905–1922.* Dorset Press, New York, 1963.

Van der Kiste, J. *Queen Victoria's Children.* Alan Sutton, Stroud, 1986.

Weintraub, S. *Victoria: An Intimate Biography.* E.P. Dutton, New York, 1988.

Whittle, T. *The Last Kaiser: A Biography of Wilhelm II, German Emperor and King of Prussia.* Times Books, New York, 1977.

Index

Bold type denotes plate numbers.

Exclamation marks

An exclamation mark is used at the end of a sentence or phrase to emphasize some special meaning within it.

It can mark surprise, humour or joy.

I don't believe it!

Silly me!

What a beautiful day!

It can show fear, anger, pain and danger.

Don't shoot!

How dare you!

Ouch!

When someone is giving an order or shouting, an exclamation mark is used.

Stand up straight!	Halt!

Attention!	Call the police!

An exclamation mark can sometimes appear in the middle of a sentence.

Good gracious! what has happened?

Don't use one to make your own comment on something.

The fat lady ate fifty(!) cream buns.

Don't

1. Don't use more than one exclamation mark at a time.

Wow!!!	What!!

2. Don't use them too often or they will lose their effect and make what you write boring to read.

Too many here.

Dear Polly
How are you? I'm fine!
I went to Jill's party
last night! It was
fantastic!! Didn't get
home until 4am!!!
Mum was furious — I
can't go out for the
rest of the week!
Can you imagine!!!
Oh well! See you.
love Sue.

Commas

We ate chocolate, jelly and cake.

This makes it sound as though the jelly was made of chocolate.

We ate chocolate jelly and cake.

A comma is used to to mark a brief pause, much shorter than a pause made by a full stop. It can be used to separate two words, or groups of words, in a sentence, in order to make the meaning clear.

Commas are the most common punctuation mark, but you have to be careful how you use them. You can easily change the meaning of a sentence by moving a comma to a different place or taking it away altogether.

Lists

When there is a list of words in a sentence, each word in the list is separated from the next by a comma.

They may be nouns,

We will need hammers, nails and a saw.

The last word in the list is usually joined to the the list by "and", instead of a comma.

or adjectives,

Mr Cherry was a warm, hospitable man.

or verbs.

She stopped, stared and ran.

The list may consist of groups of words divided by commas, instead of single words.

Sam frightens the cat, teases the dog, bullies his brother and annoys the neighbours.

There is no comma before the first word in the list, or after the last.

Try these

Can you see where the commas should be?

1. The monster was huge fat and spiky.
2. Everyone threw spears stones swords and boiling oil at the creature.
3. It roared growled spat and groaned but still it did not die.
4. A knight appeared wearing bright shining armour and pierced the beast with his special magic sword.
5. The huge beast screamed fell to the ground rolled over and died.
6. The king rewarded the knight with gold silver diamonds rubies and other precious things.

All these sentences need commas to help clarify their meaning. Can you see where they should be?